SPEAKING OF ABORTION

MORALITY AND SOCIETY

A Series Edited by Alan Wolfe

SPEAKING

OF

ABORTION

TELEVISION AND AUTHORITY

IN THE LIVES OF WOMEN

ANDREA L. PRESS & ELIZABETH R. COLE

The University of Chicago Press   Chicago & London

Andrea L. Press is associate professor of media studies at the University of Illinois, Urbana-Champaign, and the author of *Women Watching Television: Gender, Class, and Generation in the American Television Experience.* Elizabeth R. Cole is assistant professor of psychology and African American studies at Northeastern University.

The University of Chicago Press, Chicago 60637
The University of Chicago Press, Ltd., London
© 1999 by The University of Chicago
All rights reserved. Published 1999
08 07 06 05 04 03 02 01 00 99   1 2 3 4 5

ISBN: 0-226-68031-2 (cloth)

Library of Congress Cataloging-in-Publication Data

Press, Andrea Lee.
    Speaking of abortion : television and authority in the lives of women /
Andrea L. Press and Elizabeth R. Cole.
        p.   cm. — (Morality and society)
    Includes bibliographical references and index.
    ISBN 0-226-68031-2   (alk. paper)
    1. Abortion—United States—Public opinion. 2. Women—United States—
Attitudes. 3. Television and women—United States.
    I. Cole, Elizabeth R. II. Title. III. Series.
    HQ767.5.U5P73   1999
    363.46'0973—dc21   98-19443
                                                                            CIP

TO BRUCE, FOR HIS GENEROSITY, ENDLESS ENTHUSIASM,
COMPANIONSHIP, AND LOVE AS HE READ, COMMENTED,
DEMANDED, AND REREAD

AND IN LOVING MEMORY OF MY GRANDMOTHER,
EVELYN SCHUCKMAN, 1907–1995

כי אל-אשר תלכי אלך

A. L. P.

TO MY MOTHER, JANET BROWN,
FOR ALL SHE TAUGHT ME ABOUT CHOICE

E. R. C.

CONTENTS

PREFACE

Each individual feminist knower is also multiple in a way that mirrors the situation of women as a class. It is the thinker whose consciousness is bifurcated, the outsider within, the marginal person now also located at the center, the person committed to two agendas that are themselves at least partially in conflict (socialist feminist, black feminist, Jewish feminist, woman scientist), who has generated feminist sciences and new knowledges.

SANDRA HARDING, *Whose Science? Whose Knowledge?*

When we began our study of conversations about abortion by pro-life and pro-choice women, we borrowed our methods from market researchers. Through newspaper advertisements and Parent-Teacher Association meetings, we recruited contacts who were willing to invite a group of their like-minded friends to discuss these issues with us. Because these women usually had children and often had jobs, we offered to conduct the interviews in their homes, a natural setting for discussion. Leaving the university and traveling to our informants' neighborhoods fundamentally changed the nature of our relationship to our informants, to our topic, and in some ways to each other as collaborators.

On their territory, in their homes, we were stripped of the authority and the illusion of objectivity that students grant to faculty in the classroom. As we studied our informants, we ourselves became objects of study. Our respondents were curious about our own marital status, our reproductive histories, our views on abortion. As we sat in their living rooms, often eating snacks they had prepared, they were the hostesses and we were their guests. In this turnabout of roles it became obvious that we too were women, subject to all the constraints and contradictions of postmodern, post-sexual-revolution America. Our subjects had in effect restored our subjectivity, thereby complicating the whole practice and meaning of research.

As our respondents drew us personally into the stories of their lives— the challenges they had faced and the choices they had made—we became more and more self-conscious about our own unvoiced experiences in relation to theirs. Such reflection has increasingly become a natural part of the ethnographic process, which over the past two decades has been sharply questioned within the social sciences (Clifford 1988; Clifford and Marcus 1986; Clough 1992; Cole and Phillips 1995; Collins 1997; Denzin 1997; Ellis and Flaherty 1992; Frankenberg 1993; Harding 1997; Hartsock 1997; Hekman 1997; Smith 1997; Wyche and Crosby 1996). As we struggled to interpret these conversations, to distill some larger meaning out of this collection of mainly autobiographical narratives, we feared we might never be able to understand our respondents; everything we could know about them seemed hopelessly refracted through the prism of our own lives as middle-class women, educated in the social sciences and committed to feminist principles.

This struggle is familiar to many feminist researchers. Critical social scientists and feminist scholars have increasingly come to question the ideal of the objective scientist, what Sandra Harding calls the "view from nowhere." In its place, feminist philosophers of science have developed an epistemological approach referred to as standpoint theory (Harding 1991). The basic premise of standpoint theory is that knowledge necessarily is socially situated because every knower is grounded in his or her own particular identities, including gender, class, and race. The ideal of "objective" or "neutral" knowledge is at best a myth and at worst a tool of oppression, invalidating any viewpoints other than those held by the powerful.

Standpoint theorists argue that "better knowledge" is generated when researchers begin by attempting to understand their own subjective position in relation to their "subjects." Of course, like trying to discover what one's own face looks like without a mirror, this self-examination is difficult; to varying extents, we are all used to considering our own standpoints as "the view from nowhere." For those of us who identify as members of groups that are traditionally situated outside the academy, such as women and people of color, it may be easier to recognize our own subjectivity with respect to dominant paradigms of knowledge (Collins 1990). Struggling to integrate disparate views as individuals who are simultaneously within and outside the mainstream, we are habitually self-conscious about our own standpoints. Yet this problematizing of one's own epistemological perspective is accessible to anyone and is perhaps most readily begun by examining our own multiple and contradictory identities. In the areas of our experience where our identities are potentially at odds with each other, we see the relation between our various standpoints more clearly.

In the abortion study, both of us began to understand our contradictory roles as committed pro-choice feminists who were endeavoring to make a systematic inquiry into the lives of women who were often very different from us. In the course of our fieldwork, as we became more aware of our multiple standpoints, we sometimes feared that our ability to know anything was so limited by its socially situated nature that no valid analysis would be possible. Eventually we came to see that although recognizing our own perspectives and assumptions was the key to helping us understand those whose experiences were very different from ours, it was even more vital in our research on women whose views were very similar to our own. Only by interrogating our own worldview could we hear what was unspoken in the discourse of the women who were most like us.

Both of us approached the work feeling in some ways like "outsiders" in relation to the women we were studying. Some of these outsider statuses we shared: as university-affiliated women, we were officially "sanctioned" as observers in a way our informants were not. This set up a distance between us and those we studied, and we struggled to assess its impact. Also, we are both decidedly pro-choice in our views, a perspective that created a chasm, in our own minds at least, between us and our pro-life informants. In addition, we shared a generally leftist political orientation, which made our interviews with more politically conservative groups something of a bonding experience for the two of us as we discussed our personal reactions to group members' comments on the way home from the interviews.

But in other areas we differed in our identity as outsiders. For Andrea this distancing occurred primarily on the dimension of religion, and for Liz, on the dimension of race. Because the topic of religion often came up, particularly in discussions with pro-life women, Andrea felt her identity as a Jew acutely throughout the project. She was continually conscious of trying to "pass" as Christian, which she felt was the "normative" identity in our society. Indeed, there were several times when she felt that it might have upset informants were she to reveal her Jewish identity (or that it might have invited conversion attempts).

It was interesting to reflect on how this outsider status with respect to what Andrea considers our society's dominant religion affected her general demeanor during interviews. Our postinterview conversations made her aware that she categorized most people in our society under the general rubric "Christian" and therefore as different from her. This tendency had become so ingrained in her approach to others that it was largely unconscious yet ever present, particularly salient in the context of a project like ours that often foregrounded religious identity. Yet it took Liz's comments to make Andrea conscious of the ubiquitousness of this approach. Liz's continuing awareness of Andrea's own outsider feelings highlighted for Andrea what had become her general way-of-being as a Jew living in an almost totally Christian society.

In Liz's case, consciousness of her "otherness" was also integral to her interview experiences. Liz, who is of mixed racial ancestry, identifies as African American. However, because of her hair, her features, and her very light complexion, others often do not recognize her as Black. This, together with her "silent partner" role as note taker in the focus group interviews, seemed to make her virtually invisible to many of the groups. Because the discourse of abortion in the United States is associated with larger questions of economic and racial inequality, we were often privy to respondents' uncensored opinion that the behavior of members of minority groups made abortion desirable or even necessary. One woman asserted in a joking tone that the pregnant Latina character in the television episode we showed her should "go back to Mexico and have [her] baby there; they all have it real easy, all they do is squat and have it. . . . I'm just teasing. I hope nobody here is Mexican."

Another group, which considered itself pro-life, clucked sympathetically as a White respondent argued that perhaps her sister should have aborted the children she had conceived by her Black boyfriend. Photos of the mixed-race nieces she felt should never have been born smiled down at us as Liz cringed over her notepad. At these moments Liz wanted to declare her identity openly, to announce her objection to the respondents' characterizations of people of color; but she was acutely conscious that the research was being made possible only by her willingness to pass for White. To remain silent, Liz had to convince herself that she was not being victimized by her invisibility; instead, she was choosing to make use of her ability to slip unnoticed into other camps. However, this necessary psychological distance made it hard for her to approach these transcripts with an attitude of suspended judgment. In such cases she looked to Andrea to begin to make sense of the sessions.

We also differed in our emotional orientation toward our interviews. This was perhaps the least obvious difference in our experiences, because the emotional dimension of social science work is so seldom discussed or consciously analyzed (Hochschild 1983). Andrea enjoyed entering what she considered to be a new identity during many interviews, one that allowed her to feel she "related" to her subjects. In an extreme example, when interviewing a group of pro-life women organized by a minister's wife, she got quite chummy with the hostess and chatted for another hour after the discussion ended, learning more personal information about the woman (with whom she had little in common except middle-class status), her friends, and their neighborhood. The minister's wife, extremely committed to and emotional about her firmly pro-life perspective, seemed never to realize that Andrea was pro-choice.

Liz, on the other hand, was not so comfortable with "passing," perhaps because she was more accustomed to doing so racially. In her personal life Liz is all too familiar with the awkward moments when acquaintances realize she is not a member of the group to which they assumed she belonged. She felt it was almost dishonest to engage this respondent in what appeared to be friendly conversation when the real motive was data collection. In retrospect, a large part of Liz's discomfort is probably disciplinary in origin: as a psychologist, she has been trained to keep a distance from subjects (and patients) and to scrupulously police the boundaries between the roles of observer and observed. In contrast, Andrea's training in anthropology and sociology, and feminist research in these fields, endorsed methods involving participant observation in nearly every sense of the term.

These emotional differences were underscored in a private discussion we had on how to answer questions about our own perspectives on abortion should they come up (in fact, they almost never did). Although Liz tended to think we should answer all questions honestly, revealing our pro-choice leanings, Andrea believed quite firmly that we should describe ourselves as "open to all perspectives," since openness seemed a necessary component of successfully listening to others' views, which the project required. And in fact, although Andrea is probably even more extreme in her pro-choice views than Liz, during interviews she found herself repeatedly identifying with the perspectives of those with quite different opinions, as a part of the general project of participating in the cultures she was observing. In a sense, then, given this fluid identity, describing herself as "open to other perspectives" was not entirely misleading in Andrea's case, though perhaps it would have been for Liz. Because Andrea was the senior researcher when the project began, this was the course we followed, though in the end not a single pro-life group directly asked our views on abortion (pro-choice groups sometimes did, and in these cases we revealed our agreement with them).

Although literary critics have recently explored the meaning and significance of "passing" in popular culture (Collins 1990), little has been written on this topic by social scientists, although the practice is in some ways integral to our methods of data collection. Even the silent, anonymous experimenter is in some ways passing; inscrutability invites subjects to interpret the researcher's thoughts, feelings, and motives in any way they choose, and it is based on this projection that participants decide whether to continue with the data collection. In our project we attempted to cultivate an air of approachability and openness. This stance included trying to appear relatively neutral on any dimension on which we were conscious of differing from our respondents. For both of us, this consciousness of our differences sometimes made it difficult to see our respondents clearly; their lives at times invoked sensitive issues in our own lives. Thus collaboration was essential to the research. We each relied on the other's views to balance our own, and in the course of the work we grew to know each other well enough that we could confront the issue when we believed our own experiences were obscuring our view of the respondents' reality. In this way we believe we have arrived at an analysis that is not "objective" but is in stereo; that is, it has developed through the merging of two separate viewpoints.

Our differences from our respondents also sometimes clarified our own experience. Perhaps less dramatically than on the issues discussed above, we differed in social class background as well. Although Andrea is from a solidly middle-class family (her parents, the children of immigrants, were upwardly mobile and college educated), Liz's class background is somewhat mixed. Though her father was college educated, her family had always struggled financially, first as her father worked his way through graduate school and later because of a failed business and her parents' divorce. Thus, although her family had the expectation of higher education, Liz does not consider her background middle class in an economic sense.

The class difference surfaced often in our working-class interviews, sometimes in minor reminders of our difference from our informants, sometimes precipitating major epiphanies concerning what separated us. One painful blunder testified to the care necessary to engage research subjects from different class backgrounds. Quite often our informants served refreshments during our interviews, ranging from a glass of water to a full meal. On one occasion a particularly friendly working-class woman offered us margaritas out of a large pitcher she had mixed for the group. We discovered later that this group spent a lot of time socializing together in bars. Not much of a drinker, Andrea immediately declined, and following her example, Liz declined as well. Andrea quickly realized her mistake as the embarrassed hostess apologized profusely for having prepared alcoholic drinks, taking our refusal to mean that alcohol was inappropriate to a "professional" interview setting, with which she was not at all familiar. Clearly the incident had increased her nervousness about entertaining university professionals in her modest home. Try as Andrea would to laugh off the incident by referring to her own "allergy" to alcohol, sleepiness, and so on, it was too late. The damage had been done, exacerbating awkwardness and undermining rapport. Only too late did we realize that in this context alcohol had functioned as a class signifier. Our hostess's own consciousness that her class position was different from ours was clearly revealed in one of her parting comments. Inquiring into our choice of informants for the study in general (we never explicitly explained that we were comparing social class groups and never used the word "class" in our discussions), she rephrased our euphemistic explanation of our questionnaire items on socioeconomic status by joking that our informants could be categorized into "high class, low class, and no class, like us." This comment poignantly reflected our hostess's attitude about her position in society generally; more specifically, it alluded to her own construction of her difference from us.

At other times the experience of class difference in our interviews raised our consciousness about how our own social class backgrounds helped establish particular identities for us in the world and in relation to others. One incident in this vein occurred after a particularly affecting group discussion. During an interview with working-class pro-life women, we heard stories of privation that made us realize these women were much poorer than we had thought. On the way home from the interview, we discussed what we came to refer to as the "potato chip" story. A woman in the group whose husband had left her with two small children and almost no money told how, as a special treat, she would buy her children one bag of potato chips each week, which had to be carefully rationed to last. They played a game they called "hide the potato chips," in which she hid the bag in a new place every afternoon and the children had to find it before they could eat any. Through fun she attempted to soften their poverty. In our private discussion, we marveled at how strong this woman must have been to come through her deprivation so seemingly upbeat; we also were appalled at the need to ration something as commonplace as potato chips as if they were an extravagant luxury.

Andrea's response was primarily shame at her own worries about budgeting, because this story highlighted how affluent she was compared with this woman (the interview occurred at a time when she was feeling rather poor and was frustrated by her repeated failure to budget her money successfully).

Liz responded differently to this story. Although she could recall her own mother's creative efforts to cope with economic hardship, she suddenly recognized the disparity between her own family's economic hardships and the deprivation the respondent endured. In Liz's family there was an implicit belief that financial difficulties were temporary and could be surmounted through an individual's efforts at work and education. During this session Liz experienced the revelation that her personal concept of "choice" was fundamentally different than it was for these women. Her pro-choice attitudes were rooted in her belief in her own agency. This belief was probably a function both of her family's access to education and of the traditional African American conviction that through patient struggle one can overcome all kinds of adversity. In contrast, for the women in this group, personal agency was expressed in the immediate ways each one dealt with the lot she had been given. They perceived the "choices" in their lives as limited to how they would cope with their husbands, their children, and their economic circumstances. Liz's own ambitions, held since childhood, of being a writer, of working in the world of ideas, appeared to be completely outside these women's experience. And in that session Liz came to understand the distinction between her own worldview and theirs in a fundamentally new way. In moments like these, listening carefully to our respondents' stories clarified not only their experience but also our own; listening to difference became a way to understand more deeply, not a barrier dividing us from our respondents.

Finally, this work has taught us much about how difficult it is to address the "view from nowhere," that is, the danger of believing that one's own standpoint is neutral or objective. Our final task in writing the book was to analyze our own conversations with pro-choice middle-class women—the informant groups most like ourselves (see chapter 5). We left writing this chapter until last because we found deconstructing the thoughts of those most like us to be the most difficult analytic work of the book. For months we found it simply impossible to put enough distance between us and these women to reach any sort of theoretical conclusions about their words, unlike those of working-class and pro-life women. The middle-class pro-choice chapter held up completion of the book for a year. This most challenging aspect of our writing became a key that enabled us to create the theoretical frame of the book—the recognition of women's common focus on the discourses of authority in their speaking about abortion. Initially cognizant of how our own views differed from those of others, we came also to see the visions we shared, the structuring effect of each group of women's responses to particular sets of authorities. In this way were we able to make sense of the disparate voices that constitute the text that follows.

ACKNOWLEDGMENTS

In writing this book we received much institutional and personal assistance, and we are grateful for the opportunity to acknowledge it here. First, we owe an enormous intellectual debt to Bruce A. Williams and Michael Delli Carpini, who originated many aspects of the research design we later adapted and who allowed us the privilege of working with them on several papers and grant proposals. We are deeply indebted to their fine analytic minds and their knowledge of political science, which complemented our own disciplinary backgrounds. Second, we could not have carried out the research without several grants from the University of Michigan made available to Andrea Press, including awards from the Office of the Vice President for Research and from the Rackham Graduate School. These grants made it possible for Elizabeth Cole to begin working on the project as a research assistant. This relationship was cemented when we jointly won the Research Partnership Award from the Rackham Graduate School of the University of Michigan to finance our continuing work. This funding helped our partnership evolve from professor-assistant into one of true coauthors. The Communication Department and the Women's Studies Program at the University of Michigan and the Institute for Communication Research at the University of Illinois also helped greatly by supporting the project in innumerable ways, and by granting release time to Andrea. We are extremely indebted to Cliff Christians, Frank Beaver, Neal Malamuth, and Abigail Stewart for this help.

We were very fortunate to have the aid of gifted colleagues and friends as our work progressed. Julia Adams, Elizabeth S. Anderson, Linda Blum, Jon Cruz, and Bruce A. Williams read and commented on many drafts and outlines of emerging chapters and helped with countless points of information and references. We owe a special thank-you to Abby Stewart for her ongoing encouragement and comments. Celeste Condit and Faye

Ginsburg generously lent us the videotapes of television abortion shows that made this research possible. Celeste Condit, Sharon Hayes, Michele Lamont, Justin Lewis, Ellen Seiter, and several anonymous reviewers provided extremely useful reviews of the manuscript at various stages. At the University of Chicago Press, Alan Wolfe proved an inspiring series editor, providing vital intellectual support and commentary throughout the project, and Douglas Mitchell was an exemplary editor, both challenging and encouraging as needed.

Our work was greatly enhanced by the research assistance provided by Tondra Bowman, Sara Connell, John Conte, and Gretchen Soderlund. Judith Drummond's amazingly prompt and accurate transcribing made this project workable. We are also grateful for the administrative backing of the staff at the Institute of Communication Research, Diane Tipps and Anita Specht, who made Liz's many visits to Champaign easier and helped in myriad ways both large and small.

We presented this project to many groups of students and colleagues and benefited enormously from their responses. For providing valuable feedback on our work, we thank Wendy Griswold at the University of Chicago and the members of the Culture and Society Workshop, the Department of Sociology at the University of Michigan, the Institute of Communication Research, the Department of Speech Communication, and the Unit for Criticism and Interpretive Theory at the University of Illinois at Urbana-Champaign, the Communication Department at Cornell University, the Department of Sociology at Tufts University, the Communication Department at the University of Massachusetts at Amherst, the Department of Sociology at Northwestern University, the Women's Studies Program and the Department of Communication at the University of Missouri, and the Sociology Department at the University of Wisconsin at Madison.

Finally, we thank all the women who generously shared with us their homes and their lives. Without their inspiration this book could never have been written. Andrea includes a special thanks to Jessie for her cheerful and inspiring presence. And for his help in the ongoing struggle, especially in the final stretch, we thank Bruce A. Williams for his patience, generosity, and analytic insight. This book has benefited enormously from his repeated readings and careful comments.

*   *   *

Portions of chapter 2 originally appeared as Andrea L. Press and Elizabeth R. Cole, "Reconciling Faith and Fact: Pro-Life Women Discuss Media, Science, and the Abortion Debate," *Critical Studies in Mass Communi-*

cation 12, no. 4 (1995): 280–342 (used by permission of the National Communication Association). Portions of chapter 3 originally appeared as Andrea L. Press and Elizabeth R. Cole, "Women Like Us: Working-Class Women Respond to Television Representations of Abortion," in *Reading, Viewing, Listening: Audiences and Cultural Reception,* edited by Jon Cruz and Justin Lewis, 55–80 (Boulder: Westview Press, 1994).

INTRODUCTION
Speaking of Abortion

From 1989 through 1993, we watched television with other women in their homes. Several times a week, we loaded up the car with videotapes, tape recorders, and sometimes a videotape recorder and located the homes of our informants on the map of southeastern Michigan. We traveled to houses in town and to suburban subdivisions, to modern condominium parks and to public housing projects. And women—strangers—invited their friends over for the afternoon or the evening and opened their homes for us to meet them. We introduced ourselves by our first names and sat on their couches. We ate their snacks, and we spent a few hours talking about things that women often talk about: their lives, their friends, their children, and what they'd seen on television. As women participating in these discussions, we know these are not separate threads of conversation: each of these topics flows easily into the others and exists in dialogue with them. But as social scientists we were trying to mine these conversations to understand how women connect the private data of personal experience to larger public issues, especially as they are depicted on television. So we focused these discussions on one of the most contested social issues of our time, one firmly straddling the problematic intersection of public policy and private life: abortion.

The abortion debate is most often characterized as a dichotomous conflict between two parallel camps, a "clash of the absolutes" (Tribe 1990). As the evening news regularly makes us witness to the physical contests of the two groups, movement activists on both sides of the debate have come to personify the two ideological positions, and the abortion clinic and the women it serves have become the terrain of struggle. The issue of abortion and the controversy it engenders have become, via the media, a symbol for myriad contested values in twentieth-century America: the role of legal authorities in regulating the lives of individuals; the power of technology and those who control it to redefine ideas about life, death, and health; the relevance of the ideal of individual liberty in a society increasingly splintered along the lines of race, class, and often gender privilege; and finally, the status and importance of religious beliefs in a secular society. Abortion, ostensibly the struggle over who will control and protect the bodies of women and children, is better understood as a dispute over the control of the body politic in an age when ideological struggle assumes a literal, organic location.

We soon found that the labels pro-choice and pro-life as defined by activists were inadequate to capture the subtleties of the positions expressed by many of the nonactivist women we talked with. As noted by political theorist Mary Ann Glendon, public "political rhetoric has grown increasingly out of touch with the more complex ways of speaking that Americans employ around the kitchen table, in their schools, workplaces, and in their various communities of memory and mutual aid" (1991, xii). Our close attention to the views of nonactivist women led us to challenge the accuracy of the pro-choice and pro-life labels that currently organize our culture's commonsense views of the topic, as well as much of the academic literature. Many women who would conventionally be identified as members of either camp are ambivalent about abortion in ways that are not captured by these conventional labels. Although most of our informants were readily able (and willing) to place themselves in one position or the other, when they spoke of the issue it was clear that the legality of the procedure was of only secondary concern to them; this was true whether they were speaking of the issue in the abstract, in relation to particular reproductive experiences that they and their friends had encountered, or in response to television representations. Instead, the suitability of particular abortion decisions was primary in their thinking. All groups had views about how such decisions should be made, who should take part in them, and the appropriateness of different choices given the situational context of the pregnancy. The labels pro-choice and pro-life do not fully describe the complex and internally differentiated perspectives of these two positions; however, in the following chapters we use the labels because these are the terms with which most women identified themselves.

ABORTION, TELEVISION, AND THE CULTURAL CONVERSATION

When women talk about abortion, we contend, they participate in a cultural conversation in which the media are ongoing participants as well. Not only do we derive ideas, opinions, and values in part from media representations, but at times we engage in dialogue with these representations, not unlike the conversations we have with each other. This is particularly true of television (Fiske 1987; Gitlin 1980, 1983).[1]

Entertainment television, the form most widely viewed (Lichter, Lichter, and Rothman 1991), is arguably the most pervasive medium in our current cultural experience. But its influence on, and engagement with, American public opinion has received little attention.[2] In the course of our interviews, we asked women to view one of three television shows we had chosen as emblematic of the representation of the abortion issue in prime-time television dramas (see chapter 2 for a fuller discussion of these shows).

MASS MEDIA AND POLITICAL OPINION

Although analyzing representations themselves is certainly important, their actual force in our society cannot be discerned in isolation from the social context in which they are received. Rather, representations can be truly understood only when considered as active forces that interact with the thoughts and actions of particular persons, sometimes contradicting and sometimes supporting their beliefs and experiences. Through this process, these depictions become ideas (or, in other terms, ideologies) that are *lived*.

Few researchers have examined women's responses to television's discourse, their challenges to it, and their opinions about it. We treat the issue of abortion as a case study in order to tease out some of the strands of the interaction between women's thoughts, values, and beliefs, the way they understand their personal experiences, and the complex ways these factors interact with their response to entertainment television. This work is grounded in two traditions of media research. The first is the important and growing literature about the relation between mass media and politics in contemporary society (Cruz and Lewis 1994; Delli Carpini and

Williams 1994, 1996; Gamson 1992; Gitlin 1983, 1986; Iyengar and Kinder 1987; Jhally and Lewis 1992; Just et al. 1996; Lewis 1991; Liebes and Katz 1990). This scholarship stresses the importance of understanding our collective discourse as structured and influenced by the prevalence of the mass media with which citizens constantly interact. Television in particular has been the focus of much of this literature on mass media and politics. Although some important works have analyzed media texts about abortion (see especially Condit 1990), none have looked specifically at citizens' interactions with these texts.

Most relevant to our work in this tradition is William Gamson's *Talking Politics* (1992). Gamson challenged models of audience response to media that portray ordinary people as passive and nonevaluative consumers of media accounts of social and political issues. He argued that people form their views and their conversational approach to social issues through several levels of analysis, weaving media discourse together with experiential knowledge and "popular wisdom" (117). Moreover, people navigate these three sources of knowledge in part through what Gamson calls "cultural resonances": symbols that draw on larger cultural themes that are particularly powerful in conversational discourse (135). However, some themes hold more currency than others within particular subgroups. For example, for both historical and contemporary reasons, the theme of harmony with nature is particularly potent for those holding pro-life sentiments.

Another important influence on our work is the cultural studies school of media research, grounded in the work of the Centre for Contemporary Cultural Studies at the University of Birmingham. Often called the "Birmingham school," these researchers (Brunsdon and Morley 1978; Hall 1973, 1980a,b, 1982; Hobson 1982; McRobbie 1978, 1984; Morley 1980, 1981, 1986, 1992; Willis 1977, 1978), using primarily qualitative and ethnographic methods, transformed our conventional notions of what media "reception" studies are really about. David Morley, for example, studied response to a television news show using focus group interviews (1980) and studied television watching in families by using interviews and ethnographic observations (1986). Dorothy Hobson (1982) interviewed housewives about their reactions to a popular soap opera, observing them as they watched. Each of these studies, like most of the work produced by Birmingham school researchers, emphasized the importance of social class identity in understanding reception.

The most detailed study in this regard was Morley's (1980) work that explored how a television news show, *Nationwide,* was received by members of twenty-eight occupational groups, each described and placed in relation to its social class position. In this work Morley draws on the work of sociologist Frank Parkin (1971) and Stuart Hall (1973) in dividing responses into three categories, each related in a general way to social class position: dominant, negotiated, and oppositional readings (1980, 134–36). Dominant readings are defined as those "fully within the interpretative framework which the message itself proposes and prefers." Negotiated readings are those that agree in major respects with the dominant or preferred reading but are modified or inflected somewhat given the reader's particular position or interests. Oppositional readings are those that interpret the dominant meanings in a directly oppositional way, perhaps best understood as "a running critique" of the preferred reading (Morley 1992, 89). As we listened to women's discussions of abortion and their responses to the televised treatments of abortion we showed them, we found the readings reflected their perceptions of their own locations in relation to social authorities. We discuss these readings further in the chapters that follow.

METHODOLOGY

From 1989 through 1993 we collected data on women's attitudes toward abortion by conducting focus group interviews with small groups of friends that met in respondents' homes. The focus group method,[3] based on semistructured interviews with small groups of respondents, simulates the casual and intimate settings in which television is most often watched and discussed. We developed this method in order to elicit responses that might approximate women's reactions when viewing television in their everyday lives, outside the research context. Using small groups of people who knew each other also provided a supportive and nonconfrontational atmosphere in which respondents could discuss the personal, potentially emotional, and possibly controversial issue of abortion.

We solicited respondents through newspaper advertisements and announcements at Parent-Teacher Association meetings in Ann Arbor, Michigan, and surrounding towns. Women recruited in this way agreed to host a group meeting in their homes, inviting female friends or relatives they felt held similar attitudes toward abortion. Before beginning the interview, respondents completed a brief questionnaire that asked about their views on abortion, use of the mass media, and demographic information (used to assess social class). The interview itself began with a general discussion of abortion, after which we showed each group one of three prime-time entertainment shows dealing with abortion (these shows are described in chapter 2). After the viewing, the interview resumed with a discussion of the show. Interviews lasted approximately three hours, and all women were paid for participating.

ABORTION AND SOCIAL CLASS

The relation between cultural thinking about abortion and social class issues has long been a theme in feminist defenses of the pro-choice position (Ginsburg 1989; Luker 1984),[4] but it has never explicitly entered more popularly accessible discussions of abortion from either the pro-choice or the pro-life side of the debate. Others have analyzed in great depth the conventions marking abortion rhetoric in our culture's literature and mass media (Condit 1990). On prime-time television, for example, the medium we examine in this project, images of economically needy women seeking abortions predominate over images of middle-class women in similar circumstances, even though large numbers of middle-class women seek abortions as well (Condit 1990; Luker 1984; Petchesky 1990). The abortion-seeking subject, on television, is working-class or poor, articulated by a series of signifiers typical of television's portrayal of working-class or poor women (we discuss this in detail in chapter 2). Nevertheless, the implicit social class issues that riddle the representations of abortion dominant in our mass media have been virtually ignored, as has the effect this feature may have on both pro-life and pro-choice constituencies.

Gender and race have been broadly discussed in the academic literature; class, by contrast, has been relatively overlooked. Although at one time Americans thought the meaning of the categories "gender" and "race" was self-evident, in the wake of current academic work, particularly postmodernist and deconstructionist theory, we no longer take such an innocent perspective on these terms. One result of academic attention to these issues is that their apparent unity as concepts has been deconstructed. Our discussions with women of different social classes serve to deconstruct the meaning of "class" as well, particularly as a category for making sense of women's experiences. We find that women differ importantly in their readings of the classed subtext of television's treatment of abortion, both as a function of their own social class and by virtue of the way they understand their own class position (their class consciousness).

Scholars have long noted the difficulty of categorizing women by social class as traditionally conceived, and indeed class categories themselves have become increasingly problematic as work in capitalist societies becomes more and more specialized and diversified.[5] Similarly, scholars differ in their conceptualization of class consciousness. Social scientists working in the Marxist tradition (e.g., Lockwood 1966; Wright 1985) assume that it refers to how fully members of a class apprehend the material reality of their structural class position (Gurin, Miller, and Gurin 1980; Heaton 1987).[6] Other scholars of social class have rejected these assumptions, construing social class as a category of lived experience, one that is continually constructed and reconstructed as individuals conceive and reproduce their own identities and the parameters of their worlds. By this definition, class is understood more as a subjective than an objective category, as it has traditionally been conceived in sociological works and other academic literature.[7] These theorists attempt instead to articulate the subjectivities of social class.

For example, in her scholarly memoir, British historian Carolyn Steedman (1986) uses stories drawn from her own childhood and the life of her mother to illustrate how a lifetime of experiences colored by the material reality of working-class life gives rise to a particular kind of working-class subjectivity, or even selfhood. For those whose lives are shaped by an unquenched desire for material things, the autobiographical story contains a kind of implicit political analysis. She argues that the "stories" that encapsulate such experience are not so much reflections of objective reality as accounts that people fashion to make sense of their lives; these stories come to constitute, in a sense, individuals' unique personal identities.

> The story of two lives that follows points finally to a consideration of what people—particularly working-class children of the recent past—come to understand of themselves when all they possess is their labour, and what becomes of the notion of class consciousness when it is seen as a structure of feeling that can be learned in childhood, with one of its components a proper envy, the desire of people for things of the earth. Class and gender, and their articulations, are the bits and pieces from which psychological selfhood is made. (1986, 7)

Steedman observes that class consciousness has traditionally been understood as "a possible set of reactions that people might have to discovering the implications of the position they occupy within the realm of production" (1986, 13). She argues that the concept is better understood as a kind of "psychological consciousness," the thoughts, emotions and desires through which individuals see themselves in the context of a classed society.

Class is similarly viewed as a subjective and discursive construct by

Gareth Stedman Jones. In his series of historical studies of the British working class (1983), for example, "class is treated as a discursive rather than as an ontological reality" (8), and the language used to describe class necessarily structures experience itself. Concepts such as "interest, identification, grievance, and aspiration" (22), the nuts and bolts of class consciousness, are not merely reflected by but actually produced through political languages.

Our attempt to understand the discussion of television and abortion among the women we interviewed is closer to the approach taken by Steedman and Jones than to the traditional Marxist approach. As in Press's earlier work (1991b), our project here is in part concerned with addressing how social class may shape the ways women understand abortion as a personal experience, as it is depicted on television, and as a political and moral issue. However, Ien Ang has criticized Press (1991b) and others (Seiter et al. 1989) for the way in which their projects have dealt with the subjectivity of women as television viewers. Ang warns against the "creeping essentialism that lurks behind the classificatory move in interpreting certain types of response as originating from either working-class or middle-class experience" (1996, 116). She argues that such classifications not only threaten to reify the differences between the two class groups but also represent the classes as artificially homogeneous. Class is not a totalizing identity: as Michael Emmison and Mark Western (1990) remind us, respondents' identities encompass a wide range of factors other than class, including gender, racial and ethnic groups, religious preferences, and sexual orientation, any of which may be more salient in a given context. To escape the danger posed by reification of class categories, Ang urges researchers to recognize the "multiplicity and transgression in the way women belonging to both [working-class and middle-class] groups can make sense of the media" (1996, 117).[8]

Yet this argument, taken to its logical extreme, may be equally perilous: if we shatter the class categories into an infinite number of shards defined by these other identities, we may overlook the ways the material circumstances of working-class lives may lead to the "development of class consciousness . . . through the exigencies of difficult and lonely lives" (Steedman 1986, 13). It is possible to recognize the commonalties shared by women in similar social class positions without insisting that class is a unified and undifferentiated category that determines people's consciousness and behavior in isolation from other identities. In this book we aim to navigate between the two opposing problems of reification and fragmentation. Although we do look for, and often find, similarities in the discourses of women within class groupings, we also discern differences within classes (see our discussion of working-class women in chapter 4) as well as similarities across classes (as in our discussion of pro-life women in chapter 3) that are key to our understanding of the relation between women's social identities and their discourses on abortion.

In the literature on social class and American culture and values, there has been much discussion of the relation between gender and class (Gans 1967; Halle 1984; Ortner 1992; Sennett and Cobb 1972).[9] Sherry Ortner (1992) argues that working-class people regard upward mobility with intense ambivalence. Moving upward presents dilemmas as well as opportunities because it requires leaving old cultural forms behind and embracing new ones. Class members tend to view themselves as divided between those who see upward mobility as possible and strive for it and those who embrace the working-class identity and lifestyle.[10] Because working-class women may work in offices or other "clean" work sites, they may take on the symbolic association of a higher class. Women therefore become agents of upward mobility. In contrast, middle-class people focus their class concerns on the possibility of downward mobility, and this anxiety is often played out in conflicts between parents and children. Sexuality in general becomes identified with the "outside," or with the working class in general; sexual relations therefore are more easily imagined as taking place with members of the lower class. In the chapters that follow, these themes are audible in women's conversations about abortion. Particularly among the pro-choice, who view abortion as an acceptable resolution to conflicts between women's desire for upward mobility and the outcomes of sexuality, women's classed identities—both implicitly and explicitly articulated—are engaged by the abortion issue and its treatment in entertainment television.

MAPPING THE PRO-CHOICE AND PRO-LIFE POSITIONS

Although abortion itself has been much discussed in the feminist literature, existing research addresses a limited number of themes. Most research has focused on the experiences and attitudes of abortion activists, as do Kristin Luker's *Abortion and the Politics of Motherhood* (1984) and Faye Ginsburg's *Contested Lives: The Abortion Debate in an American Community* (1989). Both of these studies provide valuable information on the meaning of pro-choice and pro-life positions in the lives of those who become active in the debate on abortion. Each traces the impact of the feminist movement on pro-life and pro-choice women activists, showing how women's perspectives on abortion, and on their own identities, are in part a reaction to, and exist in dialogue with, this broader cultural move-ment that at many levels has become a part of our common sense. It is useful to discuss the contributions of each in some depth, because they demonstrate the need for the approach we offer here.

Luker argues that pro-life and pro-choice activists inhabit different social realities and possess different worldviews. The abortion debate merely reflects these differences; the issue is so hotly contested precisely because it crystallizes fundamentally disparate understandings of sex roles and sexuality, parenthood, and human nature (Luker 1984). The conflict over the legality of abortion actually represents a struggle be-tween groups subscribing to two philosophies that not only contradict each other but threaten each other's existence.

The linchpin of the pro-life worldview, in Luker's scheme, is the idea that men and women have different gender roles (occupy different spheres), and that this is desirable. Mothering is the work of women and is a valuable, full-time job; it is the ability to create and nurture life that gives women their social standing and makes them special. Pro-life women believe that married people ought to welcome the children they conceive; to put off childbearing in order to pursue financial or career goals is to grossly undervalue life. Thus pro-life activists argue that abor-tion undermines motherhood and, by extension, the natural role of women.

Luker paints the pro-choice worldview as similarly coherent. In con-trast to the pro-life activists, pro-choice activists believe the sexes are equal and therefore similar. Consequently they believe that unless women are able to control their fertility they will be denied equal oppor-tunity to achieve their own fulfillment. Contrary to the pro-life activists, those who subscribe to the pro-choice position argue that is precisely the compulsory nature of motherhood that causes the devaluation of the role. They believe that the quality of parenting is enhanced when it is freely chosen by women who feel prepared (emotionally, financially, and otherwise) to take on its demands.

Not surprisingly, Luker finds that the women who hold these incon-gruous worldviews inhabit similarly disparate worlds. The pro-life activists generally have more children, less education, and lower personal and family incomes than their pro-choice counterparts (that is, there are so-cial class differences, though Luker does not use this label). In addition, the pro-life activists are much more likely to attend church and to say that religion is important to them. Thus Luker prefaces her study by stat-ing that her book "is a sociology of knowledge. It argues that how people align themselves in the abortion debate depends in part upon the social worlds in which they live" (1984, 8). In our reading, social class characteristics constitute a large part of these differences.

In contrast to Luker, Ginsburg (1989) focuses more on the qualities the two groups of abortion activists share than on those that divide them. Although Luker sees the activists as inhabiting different social worlds, Ginsburg views the participants in the abortion debate primarily with respect to their specific role as political activists, and thus as agents of social change. Ginsburg's study is grounded in a historical overview of women's grassroots activism. She argues that through their efforts to generate change, individuals are themselves transformed. She views such political activism as an important way to participate in the type of group activities that are necessary to establish a social identity, because it is through such socially derived identities that individuals understand and define themselves.

Perhaps as a consequence of her approach, Ginsburg finds the activists driven by a common concern: "Whether prolife or prochoice, activists express their motivation for social action as a desire to alter the meaning and circumstance of procreation in order to make conditions better for the next generation. In other words, they are concerned, as female activists, with their role in reproducing the culture, but in terms different from the present" (Ginsburg 1989, 144). Pro-life and pro-choice activists were alike in that they both structured the narrative of their life stories to represent reproductive events as critical points at which they were compelled to reassess their place in the social hierarchy of gender. In spite of differences among the activists' narratives, Ginsburg found that every story emphasized the friction between the demands of the home and the workplace. Thus Ginsburg concluded that at root the abortion debate is actually about women's struggle to understand what their gendered social role will become as they are increasingly expected to be both homemakers and breadwinners. Activists in both groups were trying to ensure that women would preserve some form of emotional and economic security in the face of rising divorce rates and women's continuing economic devaluation as workers. Pro-choice activists wanted to guarantee women's ability to compete in a social structure predicated on the "male model"; their pro-life counterparts believed they must assert and protect the primacy of women's roles as nurturers or this value would be lost to society (Ginsburg 1989).

Although the study of activists is important, these groups are not typical of American women, most of whom do not pursue any form of direct, issue-oriented political activism. Though both Luker and Ginsburg see abortion as an issue that relates to women's vision of their broader social roles in both family and work, their focus on activists limits their ability to connect abortion to the broader social, political, and philosophical themes governing ordinary women's (as well as men's) consciousness, identity, and political culture. This is our focus in this book.

There has been little research in this area. An exception is the work by James Hunter (1994). He interviewed a small sample of nonactivist men and women about their abortion opinions in an attempt to understand what he terms America's "culture wars." He used abortion as a case study representing a broad spectrum of hotly contested issues that he feared threatened to divide contemporary American society. Hunter set out to answer the question of how we can debate such divisive issues in a democratic society. However, he found little common ground from which citizens constructively discuss this issue.

Hunter characterized the responses of the individuals he interviewed as "ambivalent." He found that they cited their personal experience above all other types of reasoning when attempting to justify their abortion opinions. In his view their arguments were more emotional than principled, which worked to relativize and privatize their reasoning. Hunter argued that in his sample this ambivalent, emotional response was characteristic of those endorsing both the pro-life and pro-choice positions. However, because he argued that the culture wars are fought primarily within the White middle class, his sample was confined almost entirely to that group.

Like Hunter, we found that the nonactivist women we interviewed held a more heterogeneous, and sometimes more ambivalent, set of attitudes than did the activists in the Luker and Ginsburg studies. Unlike Hunter, we assert that the culture wars are fought at every social class level; indeed, they must be understood as essentially clashes between those in differential positions of power and authority.[11] Consequently we sample a broader range of social class groups than he includes in his study. In addition, we probe more deeply into women's abortion opinions, arguing not only that women are ambivalent, but also that their opinions are grounded in their more basic convictions about issues of power and justice in our social fabric.

The opinion categories used to characterize the position camps on abortion—the pro-choice and pro-life labels—have primarily been developed by activists and do not describe the more varied and nuanced opinions many women hold toward such a complex issue. Yet these labels are nonetheless meaningful; women who share a self-identification as pro-life or pro-choice do share many opinions, concerns, and reservations. We argue that our understanding of the meaning of these terms must be broadened to encompass more than respondents' attitudes toward the appropriate legal status of abortion; they reveal women's fundamental concerns about their relation to institutions of power and authority. This approach, which interrogates the pro-life and pro-choice labels without rejecting them, promises to illuminate what is at stake in the abortion debate and the reasons this issue continues to be so fiercely contested.

This ambivalence was illustrated by the discrepancies that sometimes occurred between the elaborated thoughts about abortion we heard in the group interviews and the women's responses to a survey research type of questionnaire item that asked them to endorse a position on abortion. The demographic questionnaire our respondents completed included an item adapted from the National Election Study (Miller, Kinder, and Rosenstone 1993)[12] that gauged their opinion on the appropriate legal status of abortion. Although we used this questionnaire primarily to gather background information about our informants, it also let us compare responses to a conventional survey research question on abortion with open-ended responses from the focus group interviews.[13] We found this closed-ended survey item of limited use in assessing women's attitudes about abortion. The four themes explicated below are examples of the way the categories of pro-life and pro-choice, as assessed by survey items tapping abortion opinion, may not fully represent the complexity of women's views on this subject.

First, we found that respondents who endorsed the same opinion category on the questionnaire sometimes used very different rationales to explain their positions in the interview. Thus the pro-choice and pro-life labels suggest a homogeneity within abortion opinion groups that may be misleading. This homogenizing effect was particularly marked for those who described themselves as pro-choice (Press and Cole 1992), because we found that women gave many different rationales to justify and explicate pro-choice positions. Particularly, we noted differences between pro-choice women of different social classes.

Many of the middle-class women we spoke with justified their pro-choice position by arguing, in a personal vein, that only an individual woman's feeling—indeed, her own anguish—can determine whether abortion would be right or wrong in her case. This is an extremely subjective logic that does not seek absolute principles by which to judge the morality of a particular abortion. Rather, it argues that the decision in each case must depend on factors that those not directly involved have no means to assess. For example, for some women these involve the affective state of the woman concerned. An abortion that may be justified in a woman who was very upset over her decision might be unjustifiable for a woman whose emotional reaction was less extreme.

Often women explained that they were pro-choice because no one has the right to make a decision for another and because no one can fully duplicate another's experience—emotional, financial, and so forth—in facing an unwanted pregnancy. One middle-class woman articulated this position especially clearly. She participated in a group composed of White, well-educated members of a liberal Presbyterian church; all the women in this group worked or attended school, mainly in the fields of health care and human services.[14] This respondent endorsed the most liberal position on the abortion item on the questionnaire, but in the interview she explicitly juxtaposed the nuances of her pro-choice stance on abortion with the wording of the item from the questionnaire:

> [On] the question on the questionnaire that states several possible stances and [asks] whether you agree, I checked that the laws should allow abortion for any reason. While I feel very strongly about my own situation, and my own desire never to have an abortion, and the effort that I went to to make sure that I didn't ever have to, I don't think there ought to be any restriction on anybody else's decision making. And part of that comes out of the . . . [Presbyterian] General Assembly discussions when these women, these clergy, were talking about the interviews that they had done with women around the country who had had abortions and the anguish that so many of them go through before they [decide]—I mean, maybe it's not totally anguish with everybody, but certainly the thought that goes into deciding that that has to be done. . . . So if someone comes to that decision, regardless of whether or not I agree with it, I can't argue with their right to do that. [Presbyterians]

In contrast, many of the working-class women justified their positions by drawing on concepts from their own experience of group membership, as women and as people who are economically disadvantaged. Unlike the middle-class women, working-class women felt they were in a subordinate relationship to those in authority, such as doctors and judges. This led them, at times, to subordinate their feelings about what is right and wrong with respect to abortion to the ultimately more pressing concern with navigating an often unfair, unjust legal system in which they are "one down" before they begin. These women described themselves as adopting a pro-choice position as a survival strategy rather than as a matter of principle. Their strategic thinking about the legality of abortion was rooted in their own experience. For them, pro-choice is a tactical stance, necessary to strengthen their position in the continuing negotiation with authority that characterizes their lives. One woman from a working-class group who, like the woman quoted above, also endorsed the most liberal position on the abortion item on the questionnaire illustrated this stance well. The woman who organized her group invited a longtime friend, a cousin, and a coworker from the large discount chain store where she was employed. All were White, one had some college education, and the others had graduated from high school. Notwithstanding their pro-choice views, three of the four were Catholic. This respondent phrased her pro-choice position as follows:

> I remember something on TV not too long ago about this retarded girl, she was Black . . . and the state was trying to make her have a hysterectomy so she wouldn't have retarded children and such, knowing the state would have to pay for them and take care of them and all this, you know. I think she won her case where they could not force her into having a hysterectomy. I think sometimes when the state tries to step in and have a little more authority than what they should have and therefore, it goes right back to the same point— Who are they to tell women that abortions are legal or illegal? You know, we're not communist here and I agreed with that girl [in the lawsuit]. I don't care if she is retarded, I don't think the state has any right to tell her she could not ever have children. And I think it's the same way with abortion, they should have no right to tell us whether they can or cannot [have an abortion]. . . . They're not in your home, they don't know what your status is, they don't know what your financial [situation] is, so how can they possibly say it's illegal or legal? [Chain Store Workers]

In sum, we found that the pro-choice label, conventionally used to characterize a particular position on the laws concerning abortion in our society, is better described as an umbrella term encompassing a range of beliefs about the morality of abortion and the desirability of laws to govern it. In fact, the pro-choice label masks a wide range of opinions that spring from radically dissimilar value positions, experiences, and fears— differences engendered by women's embeddedness within different social classes and other positions in our society.

Our second objection to surveys as the measure of abortion opinion is that we found the response categories participants choose may bear little resemblance to their opinions as they describe them at length. Particularly on the topic of abortion, endorsing opinion categories of "pro-life" and "pro-choice" may signify respondents' identification with religious or political institutions as much as their specific attitudes. This was well illustrated by one group we interviewed, composed of two friends who took turns baby-sitting with each other's children. Both were White married women in their late thirties. Both had worked in the medical field and had some college. Deeply religious, they had chosen options b and c on the questionnaire's abortion item, corresponding to a somewhat moderated pro-life position (see note 12 for the text of the items). As they described their personal experiences, however, their rhetoric had a decidedly pro-choice flavor. One woman, a Catholic, movingly described the way her own experience of a defective pregnancy tempered her pro-life position:

> But we went [for an ultrasound] to go check the sex of my baby, and my baby had no brain or no skull. So, right then, it was like, "I want this baby out of me right now." I could not have that abortion fast enough. . . . I never want to make that decision again. However, I sure feel a lot more humble and a lot more compassion for women that do have abortions. I mean, even if they do it for a reason I don't agree with it, you know, there's still a lot more compassion in me. . . . Like no, I don't agree that abortion should be birth-control . . . you know . . . I really don't agree with that at all. But I'm not going to judge it now. [Baby-Sitters]

Which best represents this woman's opinion on abortion? Her repeated self-identification throughout the interview as pro-life? The negative comments she made elsewhere in the interview about women who choose abortion? Or her explicit endorsement of individual choice? "We're all human beings and we're not here to judge each other. That's for God . . . So . . . I am pro-life, but you know, it is up to God and the person." Indeed, her choice of the rather vague response option, "The law should permit abortion for reasons other than rape, incest, or danger to the woman's life, but only after the need for the abortion has been clearly established," perhaps indicates her ambivalence, but it also reflects the original *Roe vs. Wade* ruling.

Her friend, who endorsed the response option permitting abortion in cases of rape, incest, or danger to the mother's life, described a similar experience when doctors told her there was a problem with her fetus, yet she opted to continue with the pregnancy anyway and eventually bore a healthy child. Using her own case as an example, she too arrived at a seemingly pro-choice argument:

> And I would find it violently abhorrent if they had told me, "You have to abort this baby because it's deformed," and that's a choice that some . . . like in China, that's not a choice. You know, you have your one baby and so our government could make those choices for us, and I don't think they should. I think I have the right to have that baby. But if there were something really wrong and I wanted to say I can't handle having a baby with a major deformity and I don't believe this is the right thing to bring this child into the world, I

believe a private physician should have been able, legally allowed to perform an abortion.

Third, survey questions ask respondents to make judgments about issues in the abstract, which may differ dramatically from their views about a particular case. By tapping into our respondents' more detailed discussions of the issue, however, we were able to see their reactions to actual situations that were raised both in group conversations and in the televised abortion scenarios we showed them.

One woman in a strongly pro-life group illustrated this clearly. The woman who organized this group held a graduate degree, worked in education, and was married to a minister. However, her friends differed from her in social class: none had as much as a bachelor's degree, nor did any of them hold professional jobs. All were White and married, and all but one were mothers; the one woman who did not have children complained bitterly about the difficulties of adoption, which she blamed in part on the availability of abortion. The group viewed an excerpt from a made-for-television movie in which the heroine, Ellen, seeks an abortion because she is single and financially unstable. Her daughter from an earlier abusive marriage now lives with Ellen's mother, and the pain Ellen feels at that separation is vividly depicted in the clip. One respondent in the pro-life group responded strongly to Ellen's plight:

ANDREA PRESS: So, would you have advised her to have the baby, maybe live with her father?

FIRST WOMAN: I think I wouldn't have. Not since she's gone through it [an unwanted pregnancy] once.

SECOND WOMAN: What do you think you would have recommended?

FIRST WOMAN: I'm not really for abortion, but. . . .

THIRD WOMAN: You can say it honestly . . . no one's going to jump down your back.

FIRST WOMAN: In this case, she suffered that loss, I would advise her for an abortion.

ANDREA PRESS: Really? What did you check on this form?

FIRST WOMAN: Only for rape and incest. [Suburban Group]

Although this respondent, like her friends in the group, characterized herself as pro-life, Ellen's grim life circumstances warranted an exception to her views. As she acknowleged, "You feel compassion for people and the trials in their lives."

The final, and perhaps the most striking, theme we identified was that, given free response options, some women endorsed more than one re-

sponse category. Large-scale surveys conducted by professional survey organizations are generally administered by trained interviewers either over
the telephone or face-to-face. In this case respondents are constrained
from choosing more than one response option. In our study, however,
a substantial minority (13 percent) endorsed more than one option on
the abortion item. Notably, all but one of these were working-class
women.

Sometimes the options endorsed were from both pro-life and pro-
choice opinions as conventionally defined. More often several of the pro-
choice positions were endorsed, although sometimes the options chosen
seemed incompatible. Our method benefited greatly from combining
this survey dimension with extended face-to-face interaction. It allowed
us to collect survey answers that reflected women's ambivalence better
than a conventional survey could have and to shed light on this ambivalence in particular cases by drawing from the transcripts of our extended
discussions. In sum, our interviews suggest to us that women's ambivalence about abortion is belied by their readiness to take on the labels
pro-choice and pro-life.

SITUATING THE SELF IN RELATION TO SOCIAL AUTHORITY

In the minds of most Americans, abortion is sharply distinguished from
other minor medical procedures. One pro-choice informant called on
a popular comparison to express this essential difference: "It's not a decision that's easily made—you just don't say, 'I'm going to go have an abortion,' like you're going to go have a tooth extracted or something like
that" [Presbyterians]. There are many reasons abortion has this unique
status, including those associated with the social and political meaning
of women's bodies, the historical and contemporary legal regulation of
the procedure itself and communication related to it, and prevailing
moral and emotional mores concerning the circumstances, both external
and internal to the individual, in which abortion is considered a legitimate choice. Because of abortion's intimate ties to each of these long-
contested social issues, it is rarely viewed simply as a straightforward medical procedure. Instead, it has become transformed into a social issue that
opens out on larger questions of the appropriate role of medical, legal
and social authorities in the lives of individuals. These broader questions
are the fuel of the long-burning debate over abortion. Abortion as an
issue highlights women's awareness of their relation to structures of

power, and this is true even for women who are not otherwise politically interested or active.

Although the abortion issue is manifestly about women's reproductive experiences and the right to choose, our conversations showed us that in fact the issue is a prism through which general discussions of power and authority in our society—in particular, medical, legal, and therapeutic authority—are refracted both in media representations and among those who receive them. We argue that when women talk about abortion, either as a personal experience or as a public issue, they acknowledge sources of power and social control and locate themselves in relation to power in different ways, colored by both their social class position and their particular ideological perspective.

Theoretical literature about how mechanisms and structures of power penetrate our everyday lives and practices has mushroomed since the popularization of Foucault's ideas over the past two decades. Examining the social history of Western culture reveals entire discourses about madness or criminality, sexuality, and the family that Foucault and others (Butler 1990, 1993, 1997; Donzelot 1979; Scott 1988, 1996) argue are expressions of the structures of power in our societies. Specifically, some poststructuralist and postmodernist theorists characterize regulation of abortion in general as evidence of a more far-reaching historical tendency to regulate all sexual and reproductive behavior (Chauncey 1994; Foucault 1985; Weeks 1985, 1989, 1995). Much of this literature discusses the unconscious influences of these structures on our choices and beliefs.

Although postmodernist and poststructuralist scholars have for the most part neither integrated ethnographic insights nor used ethnographic or interviewing data to illuminate them, in our work we draw on a small but growing body of ethnographic and sociological research that is influenced by this body of theory (DeVault 1991; Ellis and Flaherty 1992).[15] By virtue of their different social locations, we argue, women may be able to perceive these structures through their gaps and fissures, places where these structures might be amenable to change. This argument is important because one charge often leveled against Foucault and his followers is that their work cannot account for political critique or conscious attempts at social change.

Notions of individual autonomy versus the relative power of communal norms in influencing the moral and political views of individuals are central to our discussion of women, power, and social class. In the chapters that follow we draw heavily on the debate between liberals and communitarians in social theory, particularly when interpreting the sources and dynamics of the convictions of women in different cultural and social class locations. For some women, we argue, the strength of their belief in the autonomous individual, and the primacy of emotion in defining their concept of the individual, is central for understanding their opinions about abortion. For others the power of their belief in the authority of their own particular religious communities is central as they formulate their stance on the abortion debate. Women's attitudes toward the locus of legitimate authority differ according to the importance they assign to the individual and the community. The forms these differing logics take are well explicated in the liberal/communitarian debate (Reynolds and Norman 1988; Sandel 1982, 1984).

These structures of authority are personified by the professionals women come in contact with during the course of their daily lives. As sources of authority, these professionals are charged with safeguarding collectively held values and consequently come to be identified with those values. Officers of the criminal justice system protect law and order; medical professionals are thought to secure our health using procedures grounded in scientific truth; and a newer type of authority, the "helping" or therapeutic professionals, aim to defend a set of long-standing values concerned with containing deviant behavior and the promotion of self-actualization. Abortion is a nexus where these three types of authority regularly come into play, influencing not only women's decision making but their concrete access to abortion and other resources relevant to their reproductive roles. Among the women we interviewed, different groups were preoccupied with different aspects of authority, related in part to their underlying concern with the values each type of authority represents. We consider each type in turn.

Notions about the legitimacy of the medical profession and the status of scientific "facts" are central to the rhetoric of abortion in political struggles around the issue. This is evident, for example, in former president Ronald Reagan's comment that "someday science will discover the point at which life begins." In fact, the conflation of scientific fact with moral and political issues and the idea that science can give us the "true" and correct answers to questions of policy have long been evident in American political rhetoric, despite having been widely criticized in recent literature about science. Bruce Williams and Albert Matheny (1995) trace the origins of these ideas to the American Progressive Era, which witnessed the emergence of a class of professionals who gained power because of their privileged access to scientific training and expertise.[16] At this time it was widely believed that scientific knowledge would resolve conflicts of interest and confusion in various areas of public policy. These convictions have been challenged in the academy of late, particularly in the discourses of postmodernism; however, they have persisted in many realms of political and social debate, particularly surrounding the abortion controversy.

Ordinary women invoke the authority of medical and scientific fact in their discourse about abortion. This is particularly true of pro-life women, who believe that science will validate their biblically derived morality and worldview. Because their communities live voluntarily and self-consciously outside the norms and practices of the wider society, however, they must seek their own specialized sources of scientific information and medical expertise to support their beliefs and practices. We discuss this more fully in chapter 3.

The abortion debate also raises wide-ranging, historically contested questions about the role of justice and legal authority in private life. This is evident in much of the rhetoric of the pro-choice movement, which has invoked the language of rights, individual autonomy, and freedom in order to frame the issue as centered on a woman's right to self-determination (Eisenstein 1981; Petchesky 1990; Rudy 1996). But for some women who describe themselves as pro-choice, this individualistic rationale is an inadequate justification. In particular, some pro-choice working-class women see themselves not as bearers of protected individual rights, but as members of a group that is continually threatened by the state's efforts to protect the rights of others who are not like them. This tension evokes long-standing conflicts in social theory concerning the appropriate bases of social control, with some nostalgically invoking a community that enforces traditionally shared standards and others advocating a more abstract set of principles enforced by bureaucracies and their technological apparatus. Currently these two positions are represented in the writings of communitarian and liberal social theorists, who disagree about what behaviors should be regulated and, more important, about what sources of authority institutions should draw on to legitimate this control (Bellah et al. 1985, 1991; Rawls 1971; Reynolds and Norman 1988; Rosenblum 1989; Sandel 1982, 1984, 1996; Yack 1988). But the position expressed by these pro-choice working-class women challenges this dichotomy between the authority of the traditional community and the liberal bureaucratic state. Situated within their own community, the women offer a critique of both liberal and communitarian logics. We discuss this more fully in chapter 4.

Many commentators have described the ominous growth of surveillance in modern societies, made possible by technological developments and their institutional incarnations (Donzelot 1979; Foucault 1965, 1977, 1985). Conscious that resources are inequitably distributed—including individual freedoms as well as material assets—some working-class women who endorse pro-choice positions are nevertheless well aware that in practice "choice" applies selectively. Consequently they suspect that their class location sets them up as the front-line targets of the new surveillance technology and fear that attempts to safeguard choice will actually give the state the ability to regulate their reproduction. However, it must be emphasized that this critical stance springs not from their class position per se, but rather from their analysis situating them as subject to authority. Other groups of pro-choice working-class women we talked with identified with these sources of authority; for them these surveillance technologies offered the opportunity to safeguard their identity as upwardly mobile members of the working class. We also discuss these perspectives in chapter 4.

Surveillance practices are not limited to the legal, bureaucratic level. Arguably, they are internalized through individual development and socialization so that in a sense individuals come to police themselves. To deal with individuals who prove incapable of self-regulation, there has grown up a class of professionals who diagnose and treat this dysfunction. Therapeutic activity seeks, through contact with professional authority figures, to "strengthen" the autonomous individual by molding him or her according to a middle-class ideal (Rieff 1966; Bellah et al. 1985).[17] This therapeutic approach to social control characterizes discussions of abortion both on entertainment television and among the middle-class pro-choice women with whom we spoke. The rise of the therapeutic professions over the course of the twentieth century promoted a concept of the perfectible personality. What were once considered character flaws were now seen as personality disorders that should be diagnosed and treated rather than judged and condemned (Herman 1995). Therapeutic ideology constructs a particular type of individual, one who can "need help" in various ways, primarily psychological and material. Although liberal society depends on the efforts of individuals and on competition between them, certain individuals can be unlucky or disadvantaged, and in need of help at different levels. Through therapy, they can be strengthened, "shored up" according to a model of society based on the combined efforts of many strong, autonomous individuals. In this discourse a decision about an unplanned pregnancy becomes not a moral dilemma but a psychological trauma to be resolved. For the middle-class pro-choice women we spoke with, decisions about abortion were not so much judged right or wrong as considered evidence of psychological health or disturbance. We discuss this further in chapter 5.

In our conversations we found that women's incorporation of these themes of internal and external authority varied along lines of social class and abortion opinion. Our groups disagreed on whether they thought abortion could legitimately be regulated, and by whom, and on whether they perceived such regulation as potentially injurious to women. Although some believed that according to the dictates of the Bible or other traditions abortion should always be prohibited, others felt that such limitations on the freedom of individuals unfairly affected and oppressed those with fewer resources, who might be situated in less powerful, and less recognized, traditions. Others simply ignored tradition and focused on individual-centered qualities in judging whether abortion decisions were right or wrong. Considerations such as the suffering individual women experienced in making their decisions or the relative carelessness of the sexual behavior leading to their pregnancies became central in their evaluations.

We began this study thinking the abortion issue would serve as a window onto women's moral thinking. As we started interviewing, however, we soon realized that although women expressed moral ideas in their discussions about abortion, these ideas were couched in an explicitly political language. The political dimension of their speech did not focus on the explicitly political question of whether abortion should be legal. Instead, it communicated more implicitly some of the social and political assumptions underlying their moral beliefs. Our discussions convinced us that abortion was interesting precisely because it reflected differences in women's political perspectives.

Our interviews illustrate the conflicting yet complementary strains of thought characterizing American political discourse and practice. In both settings, a focus on community exists alongside more individualistic logics, though the particular combinations of these types of thinking vary, as do the communities invoked as justifying particular modes of action. The different arguments women employ may be better understood in terms of the debate between communitarianism and liberalism. The subject of much literature in social and political theory over the past three decades, this debate crystallizes sometimes conflicting emphases on community and individualism that underlie the "habits of the heart" in American life.[18] Communitarian theorists (MacIntyre 1984; Sandel 1982, 1984; Unger 1975) argue that individuals and their values are inextricably embedded in a specific historical and social context. According to this perspective, social values are derived from particular traditions that arise within concrete communities, and therefore these values cannot be understood abstractly or in isolation from these traditions. In contrast, liberalism argues that values are universal and abstract; its basic unit of analysis is the individual (Kohlberg 1969, 1973, 1976, 1981; Rawls 1971). Liberal theorists have argued that a communitarian logic makes it impossible to assess the tradition from which values are drawn, and that only the values liberalism identifies provide a basis from which traditions may be critiqued.[19]

The debate between liberals and communitarians is particularly relevant to the discussion of women's views about abortion. Framing these conversations in terms of this debate makes it clear that when women discuss abortion, their concerns are not limited to the private sphere of individual life choices, morality,[20] and the role of women in the workplace and the home. Rather, as women express their concerns about abortion they take part in a larger political conversation that taps into broader questions of how the good society might best be organized. We discuss this more fully in chapter 6.

In the following chapter we explore more fully the media dimension of the study and explain how we used television to spark discussion of particular dimensions of the abortion issue in our focus group interviews.

ABORTION ON PRIME-TIME TELEVISION

The study of the mass media in general, and television in particular, has long been recognized as important to those interested in culture and in feminist issues (Mellencamp 1990; Taylor 1989; Tedesco 1974; Weibel 1977; Zoonen 1994). Recent works equate the rise of modern notions of domesticity with the growth of television as the primary medium of the domestic world and the most ubiquitous medium generally (Haralovich 1992; Leibman 1995; Spigel 1992). They note the parallel development of the family in American society over the past three decades, the proliferation of images of the family on prime-time television, and the increasing ubiquity of television in our domestic spaces. Some argue (Coontz 1992; Leibman 1995) that television images not only have strongly encouraged popular misconceptions about the family but have changed the shape of the family itself. All contend that it is impossible to study the development of the American family over the past few decades without discussing the rise and impact of the mass media that represent it. The evolution of television images of abortion reflects television's changing imagery of families, and of women's role within them, complementing the trend toward incorporating feminist discourse into the language of entertainment television (Dow 1996). A version of liberal feminism, in which the autonomy of the individual is highlighted as the key feminist goal, serves as the general frame through which abortion is most often depicted (Jaggar 1983).

At first entirely absent from television, depictions of abortion have been introduced slowly, most likely in response to the controversy engendered by an episode of the television show *Maude* broadcast by CBS in 1972.[1] In this show the lead character opted for an abortion primarily because she felt she was too old to raise another child. The network was flooded with angry calls and letters from viewers objecting to this rationale for abortion (Montgomery 1989). In their minds such representations were tantamount to giving moral sanction to the pro-choice position. Future network programming responded by aiming for explicitly "balanced" representations of the issue.

In a careful review of prime-time entertainment television episodes dealing with abortion in the "post-*Maude*" period from 1973 to 1985, Celeste Condit (1987, 1990) concludes that these representations may be categorized into three types. In "regulatory" programs, professionals such as physicians and police officers are called on to defend the rights of individual women seeking abortion against the (sometimes illegal) activities of pro-life demonstrators. Even though some of these professional characters may themselves find abortion morally troubling, the shows ultimately affirm their responsibility to uphold women's rights to abortion under the law.

In contrast, the shows in the "miscarriage/false pregnancy" category present female characters who consider abortion, most often because of career or family issues but occasionally because of the health of the fetus. After a period of painful reflection and deliberation, these characters invariably decide to carry the pregnancy to term. In this, characters who were previously depicted as career oriented are shown to make the "pro-family" choice. However, they are customarily spared the consequences of their decisions by acts of fortune or nature; generally they realize they were not pregnant at all, or they suffer a miscarriage. In "pro-abortion" shows, the third type of representation, characters both contemplate abortion and ultimately undergo the procedure. However, as in the "miscarriage/false pregnancy" shows, this choice is depicted as both problematic and painful; characters often are shown experiencing guilt or regret. This mitigates somewhat the otherwise pro-choice tenor of these shows.

Taken together, these three types define the norm of generally acceptable abortion themes that has developed on prime-time television since the *Maude* episodes first aired. Essentially, women can decide to abort, but they are always depicted as experiencing serious emotional conflict over the decision, and the choice is legitimated by some compelling circumstance external to the character. Both Condit (1987, 1990) and Lynne Joyrich (1996) observe that no leading character of a prime-time series has been shown to choose an abortion since *Maude;* even peripheral characters will reliably decide against abortion as long as they are married to men who can provide a middle-class living and the fetus is healthy (Condit 1990).

We argue that this norm is implicitly coded by social class. On television, middle-class or upper-class women seek abortion only in the most extreme cases: rape, incest, to save the mother's life, or if genetic testing reveals a severely deformed fetus. Network television representations do not show women who choose abortion to further their careers or to maintain middle-class comfort for their families; the absence of these images suggests that television does not condone these choices (Condit 1990, 123-46). Indeed, the *Murphy Brown* incident,[2] made famous by former vice president Dan Quayle, in which the single Murphy becomes pregnant and after much reflection decides to carry the pregnancy and raise the child, is a striking illustration of prime-time television's tendency to depict abortion as taking place only among poor or working-class women. Murphy is portrayed as an outspoken feminist, the type of woman who might be open to this choice. Yet in the episodes in which she discovers her pregnancy and makes her decision, the word "abortion" is never uttered. The case of *Beverly Hills 90210*'s Andrea, who, faced with an unplanned pregnancy, chooses marriage and motherhood despite her ambitions for a career in medicine,[3] similarly supports this argument. When single middle-class women are occasionally shown seeking (or contemplating) abortion, the choice is presented as a questionable and selfish solution to a problem with other possible resolutions. Because financial hardship is, by this unstated standard, a "legitimate" circumstance for choosing abortion, in general it is only poor or working-class women who actually obtain abortions. Consequently, on prime-time television abortion has become a "classed" issue, in which women's social class almost wholly determines whether abortion is shown as a viable choice.[4]

In general these prime-time treatments depoliticize abortion, depicting it as an issue that revolves around the life conditions and choices of individual women. This reframing is consistent with Americans' attitudes toward social class. Americans usually overlook factors affecting the social mobility of individuals as group members, that is, by virtue of gender, race, or class membership; instead they explain mobility or the lack of it by pointing to the qualities of individuals, such as character, talent, or the willingness to work diligently. For example, Americans (and their popular narratives) rarely criticize the labor markets and business practices that make it difficult for single or impoverished women to care for their children (Hochschild 1997; Sidel 1996). Rather, attention is focused on whether they attempt to better their own situation, something the narrative assumes is possible. Narratives focus on individuals' heroic efforts to conquer their material handicaps.

Because we could show only a few programs to our focus group participants, we were faced with deciding how to select them. We chose three shows—*Cagney and Lacey, Dallas,* and excerpts from the made-for-television movie titled *Roe vs. Wade*—to represent a diverse sampling of television's treatment of the abortion issue. We were confident that most participants in our groups would be familiar with the shows' premises and characters, because both *Cagney and Lacey* (D'Acci 1994) and *Dallas* (Ang 1985; Liebes and Katz 1990) were popular and long running, widely shown in syndication.

These shows are diverse in three ways. First, taken together, they are representative of all the types of television depictions of abortion as defined by Condit's (1990) taxonomy: both *Roe vs. Wade* and *Cagney and Lacey* represent the "regulatory" type of show, and a subplot within the *Cagney and Lacey* episode can be categorized as "pro-abortion" (Condit 1990); the *Dallas* episode is an example of the "miscarriage/false pregnancy" genre. Second, we selected shows in which the women seeking abortion occupied a wide range of social class positions: both Mrs. Herrera, the heroine of the subplot of *Cagney and Lacey,* and Ellen, the protagonist in *Roe vs. Wade,* are working class, though the former has aspirations of upward mobility whereas the latter has little hope for or interest in such advancement; Donna of *Dallas* is comfortably upper middle class. Third, although we limited our selection to dramas, we attempted to include a variety of television treatments (e.g., police shows, prime-time "soaps," and made-for-television movies). In selecting these programs and showing them to our participants, we did not aim to "isolate" these factors in order to make "controlled" comparisons (we did not attempt to compare women's responses to working-class characters in regulatory shows versus pro-abortion shows). Rather, our goal was to identify several shows that, taken together, touched on many of the salient themes in prime-time television's treatment of abortion.

TELEVISION NARRATIVES

Here we briefly summarize the narratives of the three television shows we played for our respondents. The *Cagney and Lacey* episode we chose is titled "The Clinic" (first aired 11 November 1985). This was a controversial episode, not shown by every affiliate. We edited out a secondary subplot (which did not deal with abortion) and used a forty-minute version focusing on the story lines most relevant to the abortion and clinic plots, summarized here. Mrs. Herrera, a Latina, comes to the police precinct for help in crossing a picket line of antiabortion protesters at a women's clinic where she seeks an abortion. She tells officers Cagney and Lacey that she wants to finish business school, where she is studying to become a court stenographer: the alternative (in her view), staying home with a baby and going on welfare, is unattractive to her. She explains that her husband is on disability. In the course of the episode the clinic is firebombed, killing a homeless person who took shelter there. Cagney and Lacey are called on to investigate the bombing, and they interview pro-life protest leader Arlene Crenshaw, who argues the case for anti-abortion protest, likening the struggle to resistance to the Holocaust. They also meet with the clinic doctor, who expresses his outrage that the bomber does not appreciate that women seek abortion because they face desperate circumstances (he offers the example of pregnant twelve-year-olds). When abortion was illegal, he observes, women would mutilate themselves out of desperation. Lacey, who is visibly pregnant in the episode, later tearfully recounts to her husband her experience as an unmarried pregnant teenager, when she made the difficult decision to spend her college money to travel to Puerto Rico for an abortion rather than risking an illegal one in the United States.

At several points in the episode, Cagney expresses doubts about the morality of abortion, linking them to her Catholic upbringing. Her father is shocked that "someone who once wanted to be a nun" would consider supporting abortion rights. During a confrontation in the police locker room Lacey accuses Cagney of "walking the fence" on abortion: she argues that Cagney would herself choose abortion if faced with an unplanned pregnancy as a single, thirty-eight-year-old woman. Cagney acknowledges that this is true, but she protests that nevertheless "it feels wrong." At the end of the episode we learn that the clinic was bombed by one of the pro-life protesters, a woman with an antiwar protest record (Cagney and Lacey trace her through her government file). When they confront the suspect, she threatens to blow up Cagney, Lacey, and herself with another home-made bomb; she relents only when Lacey points out that because she is pregnant, the act would constitute "baby killing."

The clip from *Dallas* was a composite of two consecutive episodes titled "Quandary" and "Close Encounters," first aired on 8 November and 15 November 1985. We edited these episodes down to the scenes where Donna and Ray must decide whether to abort a fetus they learn carries the genetic marker for Down's syndrome. The clip begins with Ray and Donna discussing Down's syndrome. Donna says she wants to have the baby whatever the problems, but Ray has doubts. Donna asks him to come with her to a doctor's office to learn more. The female doctor tells them some of the medical problems the syndrome entails. Part of this discussion takes place on a park bench in a green, shaded area. At the doctor's suggestion, they later visit a school where they watch children with Down's syndrome playing soccer. They discuss how "normal" the children seem and how loving they are toward one of the attendants. A stray ball rolls to Donna, who picks it up and hands it to Ray. He throws it back and one of the children catches it. They exchange glances in what appears to be a moment of bonding. We then infer that Ray is softening toward their own pregnancy. In the next scene, however, he and Donna attend a rodeo with others of the Ewing clan. She gets too close to a fenced-in bull and is kicked in the abdomen through the fence. Badly injured, she is rushed to the hospital. Family members sit in the waiting room as she is wheeled through into surgery. At this point Ray tells the doctor how much Donna wants her baby and asks him to save it if possible. The doctor asks whom he should save if he has to make a choice, and Ray says he should save Donna. After a time of tense waiting, the doctor emerges and says that Donna will recover but that she has lost the baby boy.

We also used the first forty minutes of the made-for-television movie *Roe vs. Wade,* first aired in 1989. This film starred Holly Hunter as "Jane Roe," plaintiff of the famous abortion rights case tried before the Supreme Court in 1972 (she is called Ellen Russell in the film; the real plaintiff's name was Norma McCorvey). In the clip we used, we are introduced to Ellen as she resigns from her job as a carnival barker. She phones to tell her mother she has just discovered she is pregnant, and we learn that the mother is raising Ellen's daughter Cheryl, born several years ago (on learning she was pregnant Ellen had briefly married Cheryl's father, but they divorced soon afterward). Her mother reacts with unsupportive criticism of Ellen's lifestyle and her morals and makes it clear that she is not willing to raise another child for her. Ellen then visits her father, who reacts more sympathetically and offers her a place to stay.

Apparently this offer does not make Ellen any more eager to carry the pregnancy. She goes to a doctor, claiming the pregnancy is the result of a rape. When Ellen asks for help, meaning an abortion or abortion referral, the doctor refuses, offering only a referral to an adoption lawyer. In the doctor's waiting room she learns from other patients about a place nearby that offers illegal abortions. She goes to this address but is so horrified by the unsanitary and unprofessional conditions that she immediately leaves. Visiting the adoption lawyer, she again asks for a referral to a doctor willing to perform an abortion, saying that her life is too unstable, and her continual search for work too unsuccessful, for her to keep the baby. She emphatically states that she is not willing to go on welfare: "I'm not trash." She also describes the immense pain of giving up her first child. The attorney tells her he knows of no doctors willing to perform abortions; he suggests she either travel to a state where abortion is legal or try to change the laws in Texas. She scoffs, saying she does not have the resources to do either. He then tells her that two women lawyers need a plaintiff so they can bring a case challenging the abortion laws in the state of Texas and asks if she will meet them. Ellen meets Sarah Weddington and her associate Linda Coffee and agrees to be their plaintiff. The women are shown bonding (Ellen calls them the "Three Musketeers" and says she trusts them implicitly). In the forty-minute clip our respondents viewed, we see several male lawyers take issue with Sarah Weddington on the abortion case. We also see Ellen drinking beer and playing pool in a bar with her friends, telling them the story of her first marriage (she left because of her husband's abuse, selling his clothes as she went) and saying how much she misses her daughter. Ellen's colorful language, her interest in astrology, her beer drinking, and her informal dress all effectively establish her as decidedly "lower class."

When the clip was over the interviewer told each group that viewed it the rest of the story, using almost identical words each time (they were invariably curious about the outcome). The case, though successful, takes months to try. In the meantime Ellen has the baby and gives it up for adoption. She is shown in the hospital, not allowed even to hold it for a minute. She then becomes extremely depressed and attempts suicide. Eventually she gets a more stable job and is shown living with a friend. When she reads about the court's decision in her favor in *Roe vs. Wade,* she proudly shows the article to her friend, revealing that she is the plaintiff Jane Roe and clearly reveling in her accomplishment.

PREFERRED READINGS

As we read these depictions, abortion is portrayed as a sometimes necessary evil, a part of these women's struggles. The shows do not question the imperative of upward mobility for members of the working class,
even when an act as morally problematic as abortion is presented as necessary to achieve it. The ambivalence with which working-class people
actually regard upward mobility (Halle 1984; Ortner 1991) is entirely
absent from these classed treatments of abortion. In this sense, then,
television assumes a middle-class perspective on the morality of the abortion issue. Yet by reproducing the split between conformist, upwardly
mobile members of the working class, like Mrs. Herrera, and those less
so, like Ellen, television also cleverly captures the internal splits characterizing working-class people's views of themselves.[5] Thus television embodies some aspects of the working class's cosmology as well, enough so
that its worldview is not perceived as particularly foreign by many of its
members.

The episode of *Dallas* confirms that for the well-off, aborting even a
deformed fetus is taboo on television. In contrast to the shows featuring
working-class heroines, issues of socioeconomic mobility are absent from
this narrative, whose characters are depicted as being able to offer a child
all the advantages. The abortion decision becomes loosely equated with
the stability of the couple, with the strength of their love. Donna cannot
imagine aborting a child "conceived in love," whatever its problems
("there are always problems"). For those who are affluent, choosing abortion would challenge their stability, their legitimacy: it is wrong in almost
every case.

Television's abortion language makes the broader society's perspectives more concrete, viewing them in terms of the liberal/communitarian
debate. With its image of the generally acceptable abortion, prime-time
television leans toward a liberal perspective. Privileging the actions of
individual women over a description of their social context, prime-time
abortions are paradoxically depicted as occurring only within particular
social class groups. Yet the identities and parameters of these groups are
never articulated. Group identity is implicit but never becomes part of
the stories' explicit language. Women's differential abilities to see
through this logic, to question the relationships suggested between legitimate choices and social class membership, reflect their different relation
to the general sets of beliefs often taken for consensus in our society.
The heroines were seen to draw strength from within themselves at times,
but they also rely on others in their families and communities. Pro-choice

working-class women drew from the vocabulary both of self and of community to express their resistance to the classed dimensions of television's abortion portrayals. Pro-life women rejected the terms of these portrayals almost entirely, substituting a strengthened notion of community that would have shifted the possible, and rational, choices.

More ambiguous in the scenarios we used was the positioning of authorities with respect to the abortion heroines. At times the shows—again, in our preferred reading of them—took a noncommittal perspective toward these authorities. The *Roe vs. Wade* movie, for example, shows us middle-class women lawyers who try to help the working-class protagonist but who act in some ways that can be construed as exploitative. The doctor Ellen consults tries to help her, but his limited efforts can also be seen as self-interested. What is clear is that the authority structures that prime-time abortion scenarios rest on do have fault lines, which can be interpreted in many ways. The internal complexities and divisions of television's perspectives are clearly visible in how different groups perceived the protagonists in our excerpts from entertainment television. Therefore, despite our attempts to summarize the narratives of the shows we used, we do not view their meanings as fixed but see them as open to interpretation and as continually negotiated by viewers in the context of their complex thoughts and beliefs on the abortion issue and on any other issues the shows might raise. In the rest of this chapter, we illustrate the widely discrepant ways different groups of women interpreted the characters and events in the television shows they viewed during our interviews.

WOMEN'S RESPONSES TO TELEVISION'S CULTURAL DIALOGUE

In the *Cagney and Lacey* episode, Mrs. Herrera seeks an abortion because she wants to finish business school and become a court stenographer. She believes that having the child would dash her hopes of upward mobility, making her drop out of school and perhaps even go on welfare. But she is Catholic, and having an abortion contradicts, in her words, "everything I was brought up to believe." She has not told her husband she is pregnant because he is on disability and she doesn't want to worry him. Distressed and desperate, she confides in the two women police officers who have been assigned to escort her through the crowd of pro-life picketers to reach the women's clinic. "All my friends have *babies*," she laments in a vaguely Spanish accent, "and they don't do anything."

A pair of White, Catholic, middle-class sisters, both in their thirties, who described themselves as pro-choice empathized with Mrs. Herrera's plight. The first, who was single and worked in research, said, "Probably a lot of women make that decision in those circumstances. You know that maybe one of the reasons why they move toward abortion is because of economic circumstances. I wouldn't be surprised if that drives a lot of the decisions behind getting an abortion."

Her sister, a new mother whose husband worked in the computer industry, agreed, offering a social analysis in which Mrs. Herrera would face insurmountable barriers to upward mobility if she carried her pregnancy to term.

> I think she was a pretty rare individual to break away from her religious and her family convictions to even go to the clinic in the first place. As she was saying, all of her friends were pregnant at her age, and then they never went anywhere from that point because they were always home with the kids. And that is true, once you are home with a child, you can't afford to pay the money to even get you started with a child going to day care. And most of them, the kind of jobs they can get, they are such low-paying jobs, that they can't afford day care in the first place. So it's pretty much of a trap for a lot of people. [Sisters]

They concurred with Mrs. Herrera's own assessment that, as a woman facing an unwanted pregnancy, abortion was perhaps her best alternative.

In contrast, a second pair of pro-choice friends minimized the television character's financial concerns. Both were White and in their thirties and had finished high school. These women were themselves single mothers: one supported her three children on Aid to Families with Dependent Children, and the other worked as a waitress. "Well, she said she didn't want to go on welfare," one observed.

"Yeah, like that's some big major sin," shot back her friend derisively. "I [myself] wasn't too big about the idea."

The interviewer interrupted: "She knows how hard it would be to bring up kids on welfare." But the first respondent quickly rejected financial justifications for decisions about being a parent.

"It's hard bringing up kids with or without money. . . . If you're doing a good parenting job. . . . You can't just throw your kid in the room full of toys and go off to work and expect to have a wonderful child. It's not money that makes a good parent." These women scornfully rejected Mrs. Herrera's perspective that without stable employment she could not be a parent. [Single Mothers]

In one pro-choice reading, Mrs. Herrera's choice to have an abortion is legitimated by her respectable desire for self-improvement, as well as by the circumstances of her pregnancy within marriage. She is the classic working-class woman; stabilizing her unemployed husband, she is the family's hope for upward mobility. Yet clearly this heroine's circumstances, her available options, and her choice are also amenable to a variety of other interpretations: that she is self-pitying, that she places too high a value on financial success, that she is antichild. Through their readings of Mrs. Herrera, our respondents revealed their responses to the class-based morality play latent in most of entertainment television's treatments of abortion. In the chapters that follow, we argue that these responses varied with the respondents' sense of their own position in the socioeconomic structure of our society and with their objective class position understood in a sociological sense.

Two friends who endorsed pro-life positions also rejected Mrs. Herrera's rationale, but in a very different way. They received this scene skeptically, their comments dripping with sarcasm. "Well, of course she can't go to school and have this baby. Now, one of my best friends got pregnant; three months later, she was accepted to medical school. She had the baby in the first week of August, and she went to the medical school in September, and she just finished her first semester. So you give me this crap about, 'Oh, if I have this baby I can't go to school. . . .' Even the way she says 'baby.' You know, 'I have to stay home with this *baby*.' What could be worse! God, send me to Siberia!"

Her friend responded in kind. "Oh, what about that poor little Spanish girl!" she exclaimed in mock horror. "If you make her have that baby she won't ever finish her school and she'll be doomed to a life of sitting in front of the TV eating bonbons!" Even more scornfully than the pro-choice welfare mother, these women rejected both of Mrs. Herrera's claims: that she cannot mother effectively without money, and that she cannot go to school and get a good job if she becomes a mother. [Baby-Sitters]

In contrast to Mrs. Herrera's ambition and stability, we are introduced to Ellen Russell as she picks up her last week's wages and ambles away from her job as a barker at a carnival in the made-for-television movie *Roe vs. Wade.* Soon afterward she finds herself pregnant. Having left her husband and allowed her mother to adopt her daughter Cheryl, Ellen is preoccupied with the pain of separation from her daughter and is adamant that she will not give away another child. For this reason she is desperate to obtain an abortion, although she cannot do so under current state laws in Texas. She gives up the idea of obtaining an illegal abortion after she visits an abortionist and witnesses the horrible conditions there. She is eventually referred to a well-meaning lawyer who suggests she travel to New York, where abortion is legal. Characteristically irreverent, Ellen snorts, "On what, my good looks?"

Asked to assess Ellen's real options, a group of middle-class pro-choice women shared her horror at illegal abortion and interpreted her cheekiness as spunk and determination. The woman who organized this group invited two women she and her husband had known in college and graduate school and a third she had met through work. All were White, in their mid-thirties, and married with small children. Three of them ran small businesses out of their homes. Their husbands had professional jobs in the auto industry and as college faculty. "Well, she also obviously checked out the illegal abortion, and that didn't appeal to her at all, because just one look around the room. . . ."

Her friend concurred. "Those cans hanging by ropes from the ceiling! Got to make you have a couple thoughts about the whole idea. I thought that she was portrayed as an incredibly resourceful person. Or maybe not resourceful is the right word, but tenacious—that for a young woman of that kind of socioeconomic background and the kind of resources that she had had at her disposal, she was really able to hold it together."

Another in the group admired Ellen's character, saying, "I thought it was interesting that they definitely portrayed the socioeconomic class she was in. I mean, it was very strong . . . walking across the railroad tracks . . . the other side of the tracks. I think that was very strong." [Entrepreneurs] This group read the show as definitely specifying Ellen's social class and saw her as a strong character in the context of this clearly lower-class identity.

Another group, whose less affluent members described themselves as pro-life, offered an evaluation of Ellen's character and opportunities that was diametrically opposed to this portrait of courage and determination. The woman who organized this group invited her neighbor and her young adult daughter. One of the respondents worked in a fast-food restaurant, another worked at a gas station, and the third was a homemaker. The older women were both married to men with blue-collar jobs, and all were White. "If she had wanted that abortion, if she had truly strived to do it and thought about it, I mean, wouldn't it cost less money to travel up there [to New York]? She hitchhiked on the way home. She could hitchhike to another state."

"Yeah, if she wanted it that bad."

"She could have found the means. It's almost like she didn't really want it. I mean, she wanted it to be easy. She didn't want to have to go out and find different ways to get it. She wanted people to hand her the answer on a silver platter. She wanted that lawyer to give her the right decision." This group of women found that Ellen's behavior offered abundant evidence of her lack of strength and general weakness of character. [Service Workers]

An affluent woman in another group of pro-life women interpreted the same show very differently, rejecting the depiction of Ellen's character as a piece of manipulative pro-choice propaganda. "I feel that they really dramatized to the public how hurting she was, how down and out she was, how irresponsible she was. I think they really played up the fact that she was an extremely irresponsible person. . . ." "Well, she was," seconded her friend. She continued,

> I think they really highlighted that, and it makes you want to have compassion on all these people that just have nothing going for them: have no money, have no intelligence to make right decisions for themselves and all of a sudden, we're supposed to have pity on her because she's basically on the street. Maybe that was really how it really was, OK. And so, I can't judge, but it makes you say, "Well, maybe there really is a place for abortion for those type of people." I think they want us to feel that way seeing her hanging out in the bar, playing pool with that man. They're making us say, "Those poor irresponsible people, you know, of course they should have an abortion. They're not fit to be parents." That's what I feel it wanted me to feel. [Suburban Group]

This last group's remarks reveal a hidden similarity between the interpretations of the first two. The first two groups both accepted television's emphasis on the narrative tale of the individual, interpreting Ellen's dilemma and her available choices in terms of her individual personality and disposition. Either Ellen is tenacious and resourceful or she is uncommitted and looking for an easy handout, but in either case the show tells a story about a woman who has a personal problem and is looking for her own particular solution. This was true even for the middle-class pro-choice women who made a point of mentioning Ellen's socioeconomic status. In contrast, the speaker in the last group refused to accept Ellen as an individual, insisting that she was a representation, constructed to convey a specific message about abortion. The groups we interviewed varied widely in their ability and willingness to adopt such a critical and distanced stance toward the television programs we showed them. We suggest that this critical distance was in many cases created and maintained by individuals' sense of belonging to communities that defined themselves as outside the mainstream, by virtue of either their class position or their religious views.

Despite Ellen's and Mrs. Herrera's discrepant personalities and approaches to life, their common plight of facing an unwanted pregnancy in dire financial circumstances led them to act in similar ways. Because their lack of resources made them relatively helpless to handle their situations themselves, they sought help from sources of power and authority, primarily medical personnel and representatives of law such as lawyers and police officers. The women we interviewed offered a wide spectrum of opinions about the appropriate role of these authorities and their intentions toward the women who sought their help.

In a third scenario, an episode of *Dallas,* Ray and Donna, an upper-middle-class couple, are devastated to discover that their unborn child carries the genetic marker for Down's syndrome. They agonize over whether to abort the child whose birth they hoped would save their ailing marriage. Searching for answers, they consult a woman doctor, who takes them to the idyllic calm of a tree-lined park and gently suggests they visit a school for children with this disability, as the best way to make an informed decision.

One group that viewed the *Dallas* clip was composed of women living in the university family housing complex. All were married to men with academic careers; one was working on her own doctorate, another was a professional in a health field, and the third was a homemaker. All three were White and were immigrants to the United States. One woman in the group received the doctor's parkside consultation with some skepticism, noting, "I found myself wondering if that's what real doctors do, if they wander out in the park with the trees . . . you know, [sit on the] park bench while having a consultation about aborting your Down's syndrome fetus while the passers-by go around with their shopping trolleys or whatever." But the same woman praised other aspects of the doctor's approach, commenting, "I did like the way she was offering them more information and they had to go and get it. Not giving facts over the counter; they had to want to go and see the children. And I think that was obviously very important. The husband needed to want to go, and not sit down and see a movie or something. He had to get himself there and see. And I liked that." These women praised the doctor's therapeutic attitude toward the troubled couple, which softened her discussion of the relevant facts. [Campus Family Housing]

Others took a different attitude in general toward the depiction of professionals gathering and disseminating information in the television shows we viewed. This was particularly true of the women in the Chain Store Managers group, who viewed the clip from *Roe vs. Wade.* Three of these women worked in management at the same discount chain store, and the fourth was a secretary. One had completed high school, two had community college degrees, and the fourth had a master's degree. All were White and in their forties, and three of the four were single. Thus, though by virtue of their jobs and their education they would be classified as working class, they were slightly better off than some of the other working-class women we interviewed. Women in this group felt that, rather than empathizing with abortion decisions and thereby lessening the pain, professionals ought to promote a centralized data bank to track women who repeatedly seek abortion and stop their abuse of the health care system:

> There has to be some kind of control. We need a national computerized system here. Get an abortion in Boone, Kentucky, . . . and then if they move to Ypsilanti, Michigan, to get another abortion, that's it, chick! Twice and you're out. I'm serious. OK. We are the government, we have a responsibility to stop all this endless waste. It's a waste of money, it's a waste of good professional time. Why should some doctor spend all the time aborting some woman? I know one [woman] who has had seven abortions. I'm ahead of you. Why should some doctor spend good medical time and taxpayers' money, or anybody's money, to keep aborting the same person over and over again? [Chain Store Managers]

Rather than viewing the appropriate role of professionals as compassionate caretakers of those in need, this group expressed an authoritarian vision in which authorities, with whom they identify, practice surveillance techniques to guard against the abuse of freedom, which the group feels is inevitable.

The variations and nuances in the ways women discuss abortion reveal the complexity and fluidity of their discourses. At times these discussions resonated with the classed nature of television's portrayal of abortion, and at other times women objected to these depictions. The ways women weave the interpretations of gender, class, and power present in television representations of abortion into their own discussions make visible the cultural background against which they conceive and express their ideas about abortion in particular and gender and class more generally. Women form their ideas about abortion, the family, and their own identity as individuals in dialogue with these television images; it is this conversation that we seek to understand through analysis of these group discussions. Following Just et al. (1996), we found that in our interviews, television served different functions for different groups.[6] Some groups adhered to television's perspectives on particular issues related to abortion depictions, accepting, for example, the classed dimension of its abortion portrayals. Others resisted these perspectives, using television scenarios as a jumping-off point for expressing their own divergent views. Still others spoke relatively little about television, even after viewing an abortion show, ignoring media perspectives to go on expressing their own experiences or opinions.

In the following chapters we dissect and explain women's varying responses to television, which we present in the context of discussing their broader opinions on abortion, and at times on related social and political issues as well. We use the media as one voice in the ongoing conversations through which people construct their ideas about their personal and group identities, and through which they formulate and reformulate their political and moral values. In the rest of this book we analyze some aspects of the conversations that members of various groups had in the course of our discussions about abortion and issues that proved related to it, and in expressing their reactions to the shows. We hope to illustrate that responses to television are complicated and multilayered and should be conceived not as a discrete occurrence but rather as one step in the ongoing set of dialogues through which people construct their beliefs, opinions, and identities.

RECONCILING FAITH AND FACT

The Pro-Life Perspective

Julianne's[1] comfortable suburban home was about half an hour outside Ann Arbor, Michigan. Her furnishings had a country theme, with many family photographs on the mantel and samplers embroidered with Bible verses in her immaculate bathroom. Julianne herself was similarly well kept—petite, attractive, and dressed in carefully coordinated casual clothes. In conversation she revealed a well-read, practical intelligence, combined with a gracious and nurturing personal style that made us think she was well suited to teaching, the career she had left to stay home with her young children. On the topic of abortion, her views were at once strongly emotional and clearly articulated.

"I think the thing that bothers me," she said, "is why can't there be truth in the matter? If people are to know the truth, then they need to be told the truth. Have you heard of Dr. Wilke?"[2]

"No," Andrea confessed.

Julianne warmed to the task of educating us. "He's one of the leading doctors in this nation that is in the pro-life movement. He spoke at a big thing here about a year and a half ago. He flies all over the country. And he was just telling about the misrepresentation in the newspapers, in all forms of media, and until it becomes truthful and accurate, this country's never going to know. I guess what I'm saying is, like, I think that if the media says that 30,000 people attended the pro-life march in Washington, D.C., [in reality] it will be like 150,000. And on the other side, there might be 15,000 at the pro-choice march in Washington and it will be in big headlines across the front of the newspaper." [Suburban Group]

Despite her supremely mainstream, middle-American appearance, Julianne's remarks betrayed an extreme suspicion about the motives of those who produce mass media and the accuracy of the information they disseminate. Like most of the pro-life women we interviewed, she blamed these media for keeping the "truth" from the American public. If this truth were known, it not only would reveal the strength of the pro-life movement but, even more important, would also expose the danger that abortion poses to women's spiritual, psychological, and physical well-being. Julianne, and others like her, believed their position on abortion was supported not only by biblical authority, but also by scientific and medical knowledge.

For pro-life women, as for most laypeople in United States culture generally, science approximates a general "voice of authority," or the authoritative description of fact.[3] This depiction may bear little resemblance to the construction of the "scientific" by practitioners of biomedical technology.[4] In the struggle over the legal status of abortion in the United States, the pro-life movement has conspicuously rallied around images generated through scientific technology. Pro-life literature and placards often include photographs of the fetus, suspended still and solitary within the uterus. Pro-life activists readily juxtapose these images—made possible through the contemporary technology of laparoscopic photography—with ancient biblical condemnations of abortion. As they have framed the issue, science and Scripture do not represent competing logics; within the pro-life discourse, technology and theology are harmonious and mutually confirming. Pro-life women seek to prove this rhetorically through the careful construction of a particular version of scientific logic that supports their religious beliefs.

Most laypeople receive their information about science through modern communication technologies; it has already been screened, processed, and interpreted in the mass media. But different people and groups bring varying degrees and types of skepticism to their reception of media products. Religious people in general, and pro-life women in particular, self-consciously see themselves as outsiders to mainstream culture (Lawless 1988; Neitz 1987) and therefore, we argue, constitute a particularly critical culture when viewing mainstream media products.[5] Because laypeople's understanding of science and technical issues is so bound up with their presentation in the media, we discuss here not only the pro-life position on the technology of birth and abortion, but also pro-life women's attitudes toward the media.

Recent theorizing suggests that audiences are not passive and nonevaluative consumers of mass media depictions of social and political issues (Morley 1986; Seiter et al. 1989). William Gamson argues that people form their views and their conversational approach to social issues through several levels of analysis, weaving media discourse together with experiential knowledge and "popular wisdom" (1992, 117). Moreover, people navigate these three sources of knowledge in part through what Gamson calls "cultural resonances": symbols that draw on larger cultural themes and that are particularly powerful in conversational discourse (1992, 135). However, some themes hold more currency than others within particular subgroups. Noticing the absence from mainstream media of many themes that predominate in their lives, pro-life women develop a critical attitude toward conventional media culture. They constitute an unusually resistant viewing culture, an extreme not often discussed in the literature about the media audience. We argue that their responses can be characterized as both alternative and oppositional. In some respects pro-life women entirely reject the terms of the dominant culture in their viewing, constructing an alternative culture relying on media products espousing values not readily found in mainstream culture. In other respects their readings are oppositional as well, in that they are specifically critical of many of the values predominating in our mainstream secular culture and in the media that reflect it.[6]

Pro-life beliefs are rooted in several religious traditions, including fundamentalist and evangelical groups.[7] Popular interpretations of the debate about Darwinism have overstated the bifurcation between scientific and religious discourse in these communities; many fundamentalist and evangelical Christians make no such distinction (Marsden 1991; Nelkin 1982; Wuthnow 1989). George Marsden (1991) argues that the modern understanding of evangelical religion's break with science exaggerates its rejection of Darwinism in the early twentieth century. Meanwhile, it underemphasizes the degree to which scientific theories were thought to illustrate, and glorify, God's handiwork in creating nature as described in the Bible. We argue that the way many pro-life women used their own image of science to justify their views on abortion reflects their more general attitudes toward the relation between science and religion as they have evolved in a variety of religious groups.[8]

Other feminist scholars have deconstructed the scientific rhetoric employed by those espousing the pro-life position (Condit 1990; Petchesky 1987). Our aim is different. Here we explore the ways pro-life women understand the relation between their concept of science and technology and what they believe are the divine intentions of God.[9]

In this chapter we examine how pro-life women construct and argue their position on abortion. In particular, we focus on the way they interpret the teachings of religious and scientific authorities to support their arguments. We contend that pro-life women—although resisting mainstream secular and rationalistic values through their religious convictions—simultaneously draw on at least some of those values as they invoke a specific construction of scientific rationalism. This approach is particularly salient in their response to, and reactions against, popular media treatments of abortion. We conclude that although in some respects they constitute a culture oppositional to dominant secular and rationalistic values, in others they are forced to confront those values and incorporate them into their own thought and argument. In doing so they create a culture in some respects alternative to the mainstream, in Raymond Williams's (1978) terms.

Although in later chapters we will discuss the ways women endorse the pro-choice position along lines differentiated by social class, we found no such division among the pro-life groups we spoke with. There are two possible reasons for this discrepancy. First, as we describe more fully in the rest of this chapter, pro-life women appeared to be relatively homogeneous in their self-conscious outsider stance: even as they rejected the values, the social authorities, and the cultural products of the mainstream, they simultaneously turned to their own sources for entertainment, medical and scientific information, and spiritual guidance. In this way they created an enclave of shared values and beliefs that appeared to be fairly undifferentiated by social class. Second, this alternative community is defined, in part, by its rejection of secular values that pro-life women view as not only amoral but excessively materialistic. Indeed, Faye Ginsburg (1989) argues pro-life women activists implicitly criticize the materialism of mainstream culture through their constructions of their own life stories, which emphasize their roles as caregivers rather than as wage earners. In our interviews, across class lines pro-life women described their deliberate efforts to distance themselves from a mainstream culture that they regarded as dominated by consumerism. In our concluding chapter we contrast pro-life women's views on social class itself with those of pro-choice women.

INVOKING FACT AND SCIENTIFIC AUTHORITY

The pro-life women we interviewed employed discourses of science, truth, and fact in supporting their position on abortion. But their version of science bears little resemblance to the construction of the "scientific" made by practitioners of biomedical technology, which is rooted in the principles of hypothesis testing, objectivity, and control. Indeed, pro-life women invoked the discourse of science as an authoritative description of fact; in this they are no different from other laypeople. However, their heavy use of scientific discourse and their interweaving of such discourse with religious themes are distinctive. We found this juxtaposition of scientific claims with pro-life beliefs noteworthy because it reflects pro-life women's particular relation to mainstream cultural values more generally and sets the stage for their response to mainstream sources of authority and information, including the media.

Almost without exception, the pro-life women we interviewed stated their positions on abortion by appealing to arguments grounded in what they believed to be scientific fact. The notion that their arguments were scientifically "documented" was extremely prominent in their discourse. A woman from a group of White, Catholic, college-educated homemakers in their forties, who met through a Christian community organization, succinctly summed up this basic perspective on the issue: "I just wish, you know, that the whole thing could be presented with the minimum amount of the emotional clouds around it and that more of the facts of what's going on could get laid out there." The issue, the same woman continued, is "giving women correct information; . . . telling it like it is." [Christian Community Group]

The interpenetration of scientific and theological modes of reasoning predominated in the language of the pro-life women we interviewed. The general position they articulated is that the scientific facts about abortion speak for themselves. They believed that if most women had access to accurate information, they would cease to condone or choose abortion. As one woman from a group of White working-class members of a Pentecostal church put it, "I don't condemn the woman [who chooses abortion], I don't. And I think she needs all the support she can get, I think she needs *literature*. I think she needs to be told before she gets it done, the *truth*. The *truth* though, not a bunch of lies like they normally do" (italics added). [Pentecostals] According to this analysis, abortion is legally available because the real facts about abortion—in her words, the *truth*—are not widely available. From this perspective truth itself, defined at least in part as scientific truth, would have the power to halt abortions were it widely known.

But what are the "true facts" (as one of pro-life informant put it) about abortion that are so difficult for the average woman to obtain? At the most basic level, many of the pro-life women we interviewed believed that the physical facts about abortion, such as what the fetus looks like at the time most abortions are performed, are hidden from common knowledge. One of a group of mothers sharing membership in a cooperative nursery school decried pregnant women's general lack of knowledge. All the women in this group were White, in their thirties, and married to men with professional jobs; all three had at least some college, but none were working outside the home at the time of the interview. This respondent described her own experience with educating women about fetal development in her role as a volunteer at a pregnancy counseling center: "Probably one of the biggest things is just giving them information, because so many women just don't realize the truth . . . whatever terms they may have heard. . . . Just giving them that information is really helpful. I've shown pictures of what the baby looks like at whatever weeks, whatever [stage] they're at." [Nursery School Group] She went on to discuss how the experience of becoming pregnant changed her own perspective on abortion, not because of her new maternal feelings, but because pregnancy piqued her interest in fetal development: "I mean, I never knew before I was pregnant that a baby had a heartbeat at eight weeks or what was formed at ten weeks. Why should I have? I had no interest in that before I was pregnant."

Pro-life women also argued that the harmful physical consequences of abortion are often withheld. As a woman in a group of Catholic pro-life women argued, "[Abortion] poses a potential danger to the mother because it's so easy, that area is so intricate, it's so difficult to get at. . . . They could slice through something that, you know, could cause a lot of problems for the mother." [Catholics] This woman betrays her own belief that the female body is dauntingly complex, a mysterious, delicate organ, essentially unknowable from the perspective of science. A woman in another group made a similar argument: "Abortion has been legal long enough that they've been able to find that there are complications. Women are not told that. They're not told that they may never be able to bear children afterward because of the scar tissue built up or because they needed a hysterectomy because they ruptured their uteruses during the procedure. Women have come back and said, I wish I would have at least known ahead of time." [Pentecostals] Another woman demanded to know, if abortion is "so safe," as so-called experts claim, then "why do

they give every woman who has had an abortion . . . antibiotics? . . . It's
to kill the infection that they just caused." [Suburban Group]

Each of these women argued against abortion by challenging the safety
of the procedure and invoking the inevitable dangers of a medical procedure that tampers with nature. According to their logic, abortion can
harm women physically in ways that the scientific, medical, media, and
pro-choice establishments consistently keep out of the domain of common knowledge. Their arguments are also tinged with an almost feminist
sentiment about the perils the technocratic establishment holds for
women. At the same time, these comments highlight the unknowable
and mysterious qualities of nature and biology, and in doing so they studi-
ously avoid feminist rhetoric stressing the need for women to seize control of their own bodies.

Pro-life women argued that women are also unaware that abortion
often results in emotional distress that can persist indefinitely. Many of
the pro-life women recounted examples to document that abortion
causes severe and continuing mental anguish. Comments made in a
group whose members belonged to a Quaker[10] church illustrate this perspective well. Two women in this group worked as secretaries, another
was a teacher, and the fourth was a homemaker; all were mothers and
were married to men with blue-collar jobs. Two of the women argued:

FIRST WOMAN: There's . . . tons of documented cases where women have gone
back after they've had an abortion and shown how it has traumatically changed
their lives and they're regretful that they made that decision. And those kinds
of things need to be shown to that person [considering abortion].

SECOND WOMAN: All pregnancy clinics ought to stress the emotional and psychological effects of the abortion because the young girls don't realize until after
the fact.

Several women expressed the main point of these arguments about abortion's psychological danger by saying that abortion is not the "answer"
to problems, because in fact it often causes even greater physical and
mental problems than pregnancy and childbirth would entail. One
woman summed up the argument about abortion's physical and mental
danger in describing a friend's experience of abortion and its aftermath:
"It messed up her life to have the abortion, both physically and emotionally." [Catholics]

Whatever the state of theological doctrine in the various churches our
informants belonged to, the popular perspectives they held on the issues
explored here corroborate the thesis (Marsden 1991; Nelkin 1982) that
many American religions interpret scientific fact as supporting, and in-

deed glorifying, biblical accounts of God's relation to nature. In fact, the reason pro-life informants so often looked to science to justify their moral perspectives on abortion is that they expected facts to corroborate their biblically derived morality.[11] Even when their interpretations of science challenged their view of morality, the pro-life women we interviewed were capable of reinterpreting scientific information—or their accounts of it—to be more in accord with their beliefs. Although the solutions to some problems may be unclear—such as the question of fertility drugs and multiple fetuses—our informants nonetheless expressed the hope that with further research, science would dictate a conclusion consonant with the biblical proscription on abortion.

ACCOMMODATING PUBLIC DISCOURSE TO PRIVATE THINKING

The views of pro-life women were distinguished by the conviction that all natural events have a purpose originating with God. This includes the belief that pregnancy occurs for a reason. As one pro-life woman argued, "No matter how it comes about, if life results, he has purposed it to happen and has a purpose for your life." [Suburban Group] From this perspective, they interpreted abortion as inherently wrong, because it interferes with God's will. As one woman from the same group argued, "If you're focusing in on what is right morally, who decides? For me it's God." Another from the group insisted, "If he didn't want you to have a baby, he wouldn't have given it to you." Similarly, a woman from a different group argued, "God is the one who is responsible for making the baby, for making the connections, so if he didn't want it to happen, it wouldn't happen." [Quakers]

These explanations extend to pro-life women's interpretations of their own experiences as well. This was clear in the comments made in a group of young mothers. The woman who organized this group invited a friend from church and a woman she had worked with at a pregnancy counseling center. All were in their mid-thirties, married to men with professional jobs, and were themselves homemakers. A pregnant woman in this group eloquently expressed the way she believed God operates in the lives of individuals as she described being, in effect, "second-guessed" by God:

> I was lonely and bored and didn't know what to do with myself, and I said [to my husband] Charlie, "Let's have another baby," and he said, "OK, let's try." And I said, "OK, let's try," and afterward, we said, "What did we do! We'll

never do that again, we don't really want more kids. What, are we crazy?" So, that's why I say this [pregnancy] was sort of a surprise. You know, we tried it, but then in retrospect we really weren't quite so sure. But God had other plans in mind, so. . . . [Stay-at-Home Mothers]

In these arguments, women interpreted pregnancy as evidence of God's plans; the women felt that pregnancy was a signal about how one should live one's life, and as such its message should not be ignored. This contrasts sharply with the belief that pregnancy ought to be the direct result of individual choice and agency, the most common interpretation among pro-choice respondents.

More broadly, these notions of purpose pervaded the pro-life women's entire understanding of science. Rather than viewing the natural world as constituted by a random series of events, pro-life women saw a divine plan inscribed into nature. For them the natural world was not an entity to be studied in abstraction from themselves and their lives. Rather, because they understood both as products of God's will, nature and personal experience were interconnected by this divine presence.

For example, some pro-life women argued that the deleterious physical, mental, and situational results of abortion as compared with childbirth are evidence that abortion is wrong, even when pregnancy is unplanned or unwanted. Women frequently described the unfortunate consequences of abortion, often intimating that God purposely caused the tragic events that could follow. This was well illustrated in remarks made by a woman in a group of friends and neighbors who, though of diverse backgrounds, all described themselves as pro-life: three of the women were White, Catholic, and single; a fourth, who was African American, listed her religion as Apostolic and was married. One woman in this group described in great detail how a friend's abortion had a series of consequences that virtually ruined her life:

> She had several miscarriages [after her abortion], which . . . has to screw up your system, getting pregnant and miscarrying, and her hormones were [all messed up]. She had a child two years later, and the miscarriage occurred during those two years after the abortion. And the one she finally ended up being able to carry full term was a troubled pregnancy and through four months of her pregnancy she had to lie in bed so that she would not lose that one. But she does see a counselor for having had the abortion. She lost self respect, she lost a lot of her feelings. . . . She couldn't get happy. [Catholics]

Pro-life women in our sample believed that interfering with the natural process of pregnancy—in effect, refusing to live one's life according to God's wishes—has negative repercussions.[12] These can be direct and concrete, as in the thinking of the women cited above, or can be conceived of much more vaguely and indirectly—as a general period of bad luck, for example. Women we interviewed recounted similar stories they had read, often in abortion literature published by religious organizations. In fact, pro-life women used these stories—which often took the form of scientific case studies—as parables, much as stories from the Bible are used as evidence in sermons and other religious discourse.

For example, one woman documented the harmful consequences of abortion by describing an inspirational story she had read. In this case, after the abortion procedure the woman was left alone in the hospital to expel the fetus. To her horror, the fetus was developed enough for her to tell that it was "a little girl." Her connection to the daughter she aborted haunted her the rest of her life:

> And after a few years, she got married and she had like three boys or something, and her husband really wanted a girl and she had the three boys. And then after a while, something happened, I don't remember what, but she couldn't have kids anymore. She had written a note, a letter to her daughter, she had named her daughter and everything and then her and her husband wound up adopting a little girl. [Quakers]

Some pro-life women described opposing narratives of the miraculous outcome of pregnancy and childbirth as a counterfoil to what they viewed as the nearly inevitable negative effects of abortion. Another woman offered this example, again derived from inspirational literature she had read:

> I read a story about a woman that she had a hole in her lung, she was very sick. And she was in the hospital for a long time. They told her that she wasn't going to get any better or anything and that she was dying. She wanted to go home for Christmas. At this point she was very weak and they said yes, go ahead, because this might be the last Christmas that you spend with your family. And so she went home for Christmas, came home, and about a month or so later, she started vomiting. And lo and behold, she was pregnant and as that baby developed it pushed her lung up and it closed the hole and she was perfectly well. And she had a normal baby. That was life threatening, she was dying, and because she unintentionally got pregnant . . . that baby saved her life. So, is it right to have an abortion when it's life threatening? [Quakers]

In these arguments, although abortion may have deleterious, unintended consequences, choosing to carry an unplanned pregnancy to term can lead to almost miraculous positive results, mentally as well as physically. In both instances narratives are used as factual case history evidence supporting the evils of abortion and the therapeutic value of giving birth even under seemingly dangerous conditions.

PRESENTING AN OPPOSITIONAL READING OF THE MAINSTREAM

How do these accounts come to be taken as authoritative while the same women often reject more generally accepted scientific data? For the women in our sample, the quest for the "true facts"—for the evidence of God's ways, meanings, and purposes—was both important and difficult. It required wading through much of the information that mainstream society presents as "objective." It also necessitated an active search for truly legitimate authorities who are not corrupted by what they consider the biases of secular society. Pro-life women's critical stance toward authorities extended both to the mass media and to medical authorities as well.

Suspicion of Generally Disseminated Information. Many of the pro-life women we interviewed believed the medical community was generally biased against the pro-life position. In effect, because many women felt their own pro-life position was derived from facts, they thought this bias amounted to a prejudice against the truth. Many spoke about the need to be on guard against such bias and to seek out their own experts and their own information to counter it. Their chosen authorities legitimated a perspective that was oppositional to those of the mainstream.

For example, one woman revealed that she had suffered a miscarriage while on vacation, forcing her to consult an unfamiliar doctor:

> I remember him looking at me and just sitting there and saying, Well, your baby is dead, you've had a missed abortion [miscarriage]. I sat there having no idea what that meant at all, and I remember being numb when he told me that and crying; I just remember feeling tears. I don't really remember crying and he took out a box of Kleenexes and threw them across the desk at me and said, "It's not worth crying about. You have two babies now," he said. "Why don't you just go ahead and enjoy your vacation?" So that's the value that he put on that life that I had been feeling. [Nursery School Group]

Later, when she found out this doctor performed abortions, she interpreted his treatment of her as part of a pattern of ignorance about the facts of pregnancy and devaluation of human life: "I probably would have never gone to him if I had known that." Implicit in her story was the

assumption that she could have avoided this upsetting interaction if she
had first determined the doctor's position on abortion.

Many women attributed avarice as well as bias to most doctors. Several
claimed that many doctors are interested primarily in money and therefore practice abortion because, in the words of one informant, "abortion
is a very profitable business." One informant (in a group that viewed the
Cagney and Lacey episode) criticized doctors for "raking it in" at abortion
clinics,

> I don't believe in abortion clinics. Because I think they are run . . . like mills.
> I mean they're like animals' mills. Oh, this doctor [on television] is so compas-
> sionate about this and a lot of them aren't. The doctors really want to make
> some quick bucks. You know, they can spend a day at the clinic and rake it
> in. [Baby-Sitters]

Other women expressed similar sentiments:

FIRST WOMAN: A lot of them will do it [perform abortions] for money. For a
price they'll do it.

SECOND WOMAN: But even in their [Hippocratic] oath, they state in their oath
that they take, that they will do nothing to bring about the disruption of life.
That they will do nothing to cause potential danger to a human being, and
abortion does both of those. . . . [But] it's very hard to find one that isn't in
it for the money. [Catholics]

Similarly, many women discussed the pro-choice slant of the mass media on political events related to abortion. Women in pro-life groups
repeatedly confirmed each other's shared perceptions of the overt pro-
choice bias of the major media in American society. One woman—speaking in particular of television news—summed up her perspective by saying, "I feel like that . . . what I've seen and what I've heard . . . out in
the world is not what I see on TV a lot of the times." This perspective
was reiterated by another woman, who mentioned a recent newspaper
article she felt had misrepresented the size of the fetus at ten weeks of
pregnancy: "Completely inaccurate. . . . At ten weeks, the feet are completely formed. You have [in the newspaper account] still like a little
thing, like a seminothingness. It wasn't true at all. When I read that kind
of stuff it provokes me." [Suburban Group]

Other women talked more generally about media attempts to hide or
distort facts. Members of one group, composed of women who worked
as volunteers at a pro-life pregnancy counseling center, discussed media

reporting of RU-486—a drug used to induce abortions—which at the time was unavailable in the United States. Women in this group were well educated, with most having at least a bachelor's degree, and all were married to men with professional occupations. One woman criticized the media for obscuring the real reasons for the government's reluctance to approve the drug: the health risks it poses to women. Instead she argued that news reports have focused on the political struggles surrounding the drug, which "make it sound like it's a big political thing." She argued that drug approval is a set of orderly procedures, which the media have distorted by "mak[ing] it into an event instead of a process." In her terms, the media have effectively hidden the truth about abortion in this instance, transforming what is at stake into a "big political" issue rather than a simple matter of medical fact. [Volunteers]

Our informants offered complex explanations for media distortion of the facts. Women in several groups claimed that the vast majority—some said over 90 percent—of media personnel were pro-choice (they offered no sources for this information). This assumption seemed to guide their feelings about the media and their mode of reporting abortion-related news. Another explanation, mentioned earlier in the context of RU-486, was that the media customarily turn factual events into political ones, distorting the true nature of these news stories. When asked why they felt this happened so often, one woman mentioned the media's need to capitalize on such issues as abortion and RU-486, "moral issues that are hot politically" and therefore sensational news. [Volunteers] Another in the same group blamed the media's tendency to follow a "politically correct" line on potentially controversial issues. Her friend mentioned that for financial reasons media are afraid to be on the "wrong side" of particular issues, because they might be boycotted or might upset a strong lobby.

Suspicion of Television. Pro-life women's distance from traditional societal authority, and their suspicion of what passes for "fact" in mainstream society, shaped their oppositional responses to television and to television images of medical authority. Several times, for example, women in pro-life groups greeted our announcement that we would break to show a tape with the comment, "We have tapes too" (which they sometimes offered to show us), apparently assuming that their tapes would exhibit a perspective very different from those in our collection. Others commented on how strictly they limit their own and their families' exposure to conventional television and films. In one typical example of the suspicion with which some women confronted prime-time television, a woman in a pro-life group, after viewing a clip from the made-for-television movie *Roe vs. Wade,* told us that she had consciously avoided watching the show when it was on television and that she found it "torture" to watch even the forty-minute clip we showed. [Suburban Group]

Although many of the pro-life women we interviewed appeared deeply involved in the television entertainment shows they watched during the group sessions, most were nevertheless able to maintain and express a more general, conscious distance from the lifestyles depicted in these shows and the values they represented. It appeared that pro-life women were accustomed to seeing—and at times enjoying—television entertainment that regularly contradicts some of their most basic values. If television serves our society as a marketplace of ideas, pro-life women know that many of their own ideas are not included in this market, or at least not accorded mainstream status. They took pains to protect themselves and their children against any effects of this exclusion.[13] Women repeatedly noted the pro-choice bias they perceived in most television, including the shows they viewed during the interviews, remarking on the inadequacy of the attempts at balance of content. They also noted as an accepted fact that the people who work in the mass media are overwhelmingly pro-choice, as in this quotation: "Most television shows are very pro-choice. Most . . . I have to say almost all media are pro-choice. Even the articles that are supposed to be unbiased are almost always pro-choice. You can tell just by the way they . . . just by the words they use." [Neighbors] Or this:

FIRST WOMAN: I have never read a pro-life article in the news or the [Detroit] *Free Press.* Even on Sanctity for Life Sunday they had a pro-choice article in there. To me that's appalling. Not one journalist in the newspaper is unbiased. Every single one of them is biased. Not one of them has ever fairly represented fairly the pro-life side. And then they make us look like a bunch of nerds. I resent that.

SECOND WOMAN: And I agree. Because I've looked for those articles. . . .

FIRST WOMAN: They're not there. And even in those articles where they think they're giving the facts, it's not even factual. One newspaper article they had the size of the fetus, I clipped it out, and I saved it, they had the size of the fetus as completely inaccurate. [Suburban Group]

Pro-life women often took issue with the accuracy of the way the abortion issue, and concomitant problems, was represented in the *Roe vs. Wade* movie and in the *Cagney and Lacey* abortion episode we showed them. One woman, for example, commented that she "thought there was a lot of misinformation" in the *Roe vs. Wade* movie.[14] In particular, she took issue with the way the movie painted a black-and-white view of the dangers of back-alley abortions compared with the safety of legal abortions performed in medical facilities. Although she conceded that perhaps abortions performed in hospitals under liberal abortion laws are indeed safer, she also argued that the movie minimized the dangers accompanying the procedure even when it is performed by a medical professional. This led to a more extended group discussion of the true dangers inherent in abortion, and of the way these dangers are often ignored in the popular media. [Suburban Group]

Pro-life women were even critical of the *Dallas* episode, despite their praise for the protagonists' decision to continue the pregnancy after they learned that the fetus carried the genetic marker for Down's syndrome. Some pro-life women felt the show oversimplified the demands of raising a child with Down's syndrome. Another argued that it did not present a balanced depiction of the abortion issue because most women who seek abortions do so not because of an abnormality in the fetus but because the pregnancy presents an inconvenience. Her comments implied that if more typical cases were depicted, the case for abortion would not appear as sympathetic. [Parents' Group][15]

Women also identified more complex forms of media bias in the television episodes they were shown. One informant, for example, presented a sophisticated objection to the depiction of the heroine of *Roe vs. Wade* as economically and socially helpless. This representation was constructed, she claimed, to invoke viewers' sympathy for her plight; she argued that viewers would not feel so sympathetic if the story featured a middle-class woman seeking an abortion for convenience rather than out of financial desperation:

WOMAN: Let's take you [to the group interviewer], for example; you're a professor. Do you have your doctorate?

ANDREA PRESS: Yes.

WOMAN: You have it. Are you married?

ANDREA PRESS: Um-hum.

WOMAN: OK, you're married. Do you have children?

ANDREA PRESS: No.

WOMAN: You're married and you don't have children, but this baby comes and you're just not quite ready because you're going to buy a house somewhere and you haven't purchased this house, so you decide to abort. OK? Do you think we're going to have pity on you? . . . People like you every day are aborting their babies because it's not convenient for them timewise in their life.

But we would not feel sorry for you, because we'd say, that woman probably would be a great mother. [Suburban Group][16]

This woman intimated that substituting a heroine like the White, middle-class professional interviewer for the invariably more disadvantaged women featured in television depictions of abortion would dramatically reduce viewers' sympathy for abortion. Pro-life women were very sensitive to what they saw as the manipulative use of relative helplessness, disadvantage, and poverty as rhetorical devices. They saw through this and protested it.

Many other women felt the narrative exaggerated the destitution and desperation of this character, who was presented as chronically unemployed and lacking family support. Some complained that she could have found a job had she tried hard enough; others objected that her father (a minor character in the film) would have offered more help had she chosen to give birth. [Suburban Group].[17] Many pro-life women thought these story lines remained underdeveloped, or were ignored altogether, because of the pro-choice bias infusing these fictional media representations.

Medical Authorities. At the most manifest level, women relate to television's images of doctors as agents of science and sources of objective fact. Consider their responses to a physician pictured in an episode of *Dallas.* The physician, a woman, is depicted counseling Ray and Donna, who have learned that their unborn child has the genetic marker for Down's syndrome and are undecided whether to continue the pregnancy. Pro-life women believe a doctor's job is to offer objective information, which in their view would point toward a pro-life decision for the couple. When women view the doctor as objective, they offer a positive assessment of her expertise. For example, one woman, in a group of two married, middle-class White women in their late thirties who met through a support group for parents, commented:

> I think she [the physician] handled [the consultation] really well. She had to give an unbiased opinion, no matter how she felt, because that was her job, not to recommend one way or another. And I think she handled it very well without going overboard one way or the other. I couldn't really tell what her true feelings on the situation would have been or how she would have reacted had it been her in that position, so I think she did real well. [Parents' Group]

Another pro-life woman went on to praise the same doctor specifically for being willing to offer information about the less commonly made decision to keep the child rather than abort. In essence, she was surprised and pleased that the doctor would offer information about alternatives to abortion: "I like the fact that she put it to Ray that a lot of families . . . [that] there is a waiting list for families to adopt these children, you know, there are people out there who would love them." [Parents' Group] In this respect the doctor was not judged to be biased toward the choice of abortion, as pro-life women generally expected, nor was she particularly regarded as biased against it. Instead she fulfills what these women see to be her more appropriate role, as the objective dispenser of information.

In contrast to this positive evaluation, women in another group could not overcome their suspicion of the doctor; in particular, they felt she was biased toward the pro-choice position. They interpreted negatively even her seemingly objective dispensing of facts, as evidence of the bias they suspected. For example, one woman in a group of married, working-class White women accused the doctor of overwhelming the couple with confusing facts, as physicians are wont to do, in a way that hindered rather than helped them in discerning the truth: "I almost felt like she was kind of showing just the really dark side of the whole thing [of giving birth to a child with Down's syndrome]. It seemed like she was hesitant and she was stating all these statistics that are overwhelming, you know." [Neighbors] In her view the *Dallas* doctor is probably biased against the pro-life position and consequently guilty of overloading clients with statistics that hide, rather than reveal, the "true facts." The same facts that led other pro-life women to praise the doctor as fulfilling their ideal of the objective professional led this woman to criticize her for bias.

There is other evidence that pro-life women doubt the veracity and good intentions, and certainly the pro-life sympathies, of the *Dallas* physician. Some directly challenged the information she dispensed. Although the doctor had said that when the fetus is known to have Down's syndrome, 99 percent of parents choose abortion, one woman's immediate response was that this statistic "didn't seem right to me." [Neighbors] She later amended this comment, realizing she had confused this statistic with information her own doctor had given her on the incidence of Down's syndrome itself. Her suspicion that in fact the television doctor was biased led her to immediately refer to information gleaned from her own doctor, who she knows supports her pro-life stance, and whom she therefore counts on to make the truth available to her.

Others in the same group interpreted the doctor's unspoken attitudes based on her mannerisms. One woman judged the doctor as pro-life— and therefore possibly objective: "I think I got the opposite impression, that she was in favor of keeping the child, but I don't remember why I thought that. She seemed real pleasant, she seemed like she was giving them all the facts about things." [Neighbors] She was immediately challenged by the other woman in the group, who claimed she disliked the doctor and thought the physician was in fact hostile to the pro-life position. This challenge quickly caused the first woman to recant her positive assessment. She was easily talked into rethinking, even belittling, her own former interpretation, adding, "Now, I feel like I want to see it again, because I'm thinking, Why do I think that? Was I paying attention or was I just wisecracking, you know?" [Neighbors] The power of the group to influence her own perception of television was so strong that her friend's doubts immediately led her to question her own interpretation, which had been less critical of the representation. Her friend easily "brought her into line." This incident may illustrate in microcosm a broader pattern of pro-life women's response to television.

Women in another pro-life group revealed even more clearly their cynicism about the medical profession. This was evident in their comments about the doctor Ellen consulted in *Roe vs. Wade*, who refused her appeal to perform an illegal abortion or to help her find someone who would. Several in the group immediately contended that, in refusing to help Ellen with the abortion, this physician was thinking primarily of his own interests, trying to protect himself against charges of wrongdoing:

ANDREA PRESS: Well, what did you think about the doctor that Ellen went to in the movie?
FIRST WOMAN: I think he covered himself well. It was against the law.
SECOND WOMAN: I don't think he wanted to take any chances.
FIRST WOMAN: No, I think he did just what he should have done. He felt sorry for her, but he said, "I'm not breaking the law. . . . "
ANDREA PRESS: So, do you think he treated her well? The doctor, I mean. Would you have had him react in another way?
FIRST WOMAN: He couldn't.
SECOND WOMAN: I think he just came out and he just said, he couldn't. . . .
THIRD WOMAN: To keep himself honest, that's what he had to do. [Pentecostals]

Their comments were particularly striking because, given their pro-life views, these women might have responded quite differently, denigrating Ellen's desire for an abortion and praising the doctor for the help he did provide (he told Ellen she didn't have to keep the baby and gave her the name of a lawyer who could arrange an adoption). Women could have praised him for his pro-life actions rather than noting, somewhat derisively, his fear of breaking the law. Instead, their comments censuring the doctor's unresponsiveness to Ellen's entreaties demonstrate starkly that pro-life women do not expect any real help from the professionals they encounter. These women expected professionals to think first of protecting themselves; whatever help they might offer would be strictly limited by these primary considerations.

Similar criticisms were leveled against the doctor in the *Cagney and Lacey* episode. This doctor works in an abortion clinic that has just been bombed. He angrily criticizes the pro-life protesters he believes are guilty of the bombing, mentioning that "twelve-year-olds" have sought abortions there. He questions the motives of those who seek to destroy his clinic, thereby forcing "children to bear children." One pro-life woman questioned the accuracy of his anecdote about twelve-year-olds, doubting that they would really seek care in a women's clinic. She measured his claim against her own experience working in a physician's office:

> This man [is working in an abortion clinic] because he's seen twelve-year-olds. . . . But twelve-year-olds are not going to these clinics. Generally speaking, twelve-year-olds are being taken to pediatricians, and they're being referred to gynecologists. [To her friend]: Wouldn't you agree pretty much with that? I know, where I worked at the pediatrician; that was how it was handled. [Baby-Sitters]

In her view, the doctor was using misinformation to justify both his role as an abortionist and the considerable financial gain she believed he reaped from it.[18]

One woman in the Volunteers group capped her group's discussion of media bias with a more extreme observation. She attributed an evil purpose to the political bias of the media, one specifically at odds with God's intentions:

> There's another reason [for media bias], too. The devil is subtle. He likes everybody to be not knowing and so when people have their evil things that they want, they go about them always underneath everything. Don't let anything be seen in the light or they will be found for what they really are. So that's why when things go on TV it's always the right thing is hush, hush, and the thing that they want is presented as being good and right for everybody. That's why.

Her remark was seconded by another group member, who added that what is on television is often merely "an advertisement for what *they* want, or propaganda." These are examples of the most extreme, and most concrete, attribution of evil purposes to the biases women noted in mainstream media.

Although most of the pro-life women we interviewed did not espouse such extreme views, most did expect to find bias and distortion among the mainstream professionals they encountered and in the news reports of conventional media. In response to these biases, women developed the sort of critical perspectives we have described. Often they developed their criticisms in consultation with alternative sources of professional authority, through the exposure to alternative media they actively sought.

CREATING AN ALTERNATIVE CULTURE: THE SEARCH
FOR LEGITIMATE AUTHORITY

Many of the pro-life women we interviewed lived strikingly insulated from mainstream authorities, including most doctors, network and cable television, and popular Hollywood films. Often this insulation resulted from a conscious strategy in which women sought out their own professional authorities, and their own sources of information, to counter what they considered the biased sources proliferating in the mainstream. They thus lived in what was in many respects an alternative culture. For example, several groups discussed the need to consult their own physicians when choosing among the various forms of birth control pills available. Their concern centered on whether certain formulas prevented implantation of the fertilized zygote, because to them this amounted to abortion.[19] Women relied on their own doctors for exact knowledge about the pill they were prescribed. One woman observed, "We have a Christian obstetrician, so we know he wouldn't . . . prescribe anything like that" (the pill that allows conception to occur). [Quakers]

At times women described their doctors as sources of moral as well as medical authority. One of the consequences of having a Christian obstetrician is that one's practices are closely monitored, and one has to think twice before engaging in potentially immoral behavior. Thus their doctors became a part of the moral policing apparatus in these women's lives. For example, one informant recounted how, when she became pregnant with her fourth child, she toyed with the idea of having an abortion despite her pro-life views.[20] The pregnancy was very difficult, and she spent several weeks in the hospital. She fantasized about having an abortion: "I thought, well, I could just go have an abortion and tell everybody I miscarried." She never acted on her fantasy, in part owing to thoughts about her doctor's opinion and how difficult it would be to hide the truth from him. She continued, "And then I thought, my doctor would know, and he's a Christian. In fact he's on the board on the Pregnancy Counseling Center; so I thought, no, I really wouldn't do that. Yeah, I had a hard time with this one, I really did." [Stay-at-Home Mothers] Of course, in addition to thoughts about her doctor's disapproval, her own pro-life sentiments entered into her decision against abortion. But it is clear that, for the pro-life women who carefully select their own experts, these experts then perform an important function. Not only do they dispense reliable information, but they also act as professional and moral role models who at times limit women's ability, and desire, to engage in behavior their moral community might find deviant.

Our informants consciously sought access to Christian authorities. Women in several groups invoked Dr. Wilke, a pro-life activist who travels nationally, lecturing on the misinformation he claims is dispensed about abortion and the pro-life movement, often through various mass media. One group of women discussed attending a Saint Patrick's Day rally where he spoke, and they cited facts about abortion they had learned from him. One of the ways they obtained information from such figures was by being selective about the mass media. Particularly popular among the women we interviewed was Christian radio.[21] Several groups mentioned listening to the *Dr. Dobson Show*. This radio program is narrated by a pro-life Christian educator who tells various stories and anecdotes to show that abortion is morally and medically wrong. One informant touted the educational value of listening to Dobson. She described one episode in which a nurse who had formerly worked in an abortion clinic "testified" on the show about her conversion experience:

> I listened to Dr. Dobson where one woman, she was a nurse [who worked in an abortion clinic]. See, God saved her from it. She accepted Christ and she realized what she was doing was wrong, and one night before she gave her life to God, she just heard a bunch of babies crying. She's got a tremendous testimony and she would look out in the hallway and she wouldn't see nothing and she would just continue to hear the babies crying. Thousands of babies crying and she gave her heart to the Lord. You'd have to listen to her, she really talks good about it. [Pentecostals]

The same woman went on to talk about educational literature by Dr. Dobson documenting the dangers of abortion that are denied by Planned Parenthood and often ignored in the mainstream press. At this another member of the group told why she thought Dobson a could be trusted:

FIRST WOMAN: I got magazines on it, by Dr. Dobson. I should have brought those.
SECOND WOMAN: Well, it's well documented then.

FIRST WOMAN: Yes, yes, it's very good. . . . I wouldn't be saying what I'm saying if it wasn't well documented. Even though I don't have it with me to show you, but I know for a fact [that] this stuff is very well documented, and I got things on it. I wouldn't be saying the things I said if it weren't.

The pro-life women we interviewed frequently cited the film *The Silent Scream* as another source of accurate medical information. Produced by a pro-life group to publicize what it considered to be the facts about abortion,[22] the film claims to depict a fetus in agony during the procedure. One informant described the power of the film:

> [Pregnant women considering abortion] should all be forced to watch the movie *The Silent Scream* which shows exactly what happens and how the tube comes up to get the baby and the baby moves off to the side. If it wasn't a living, breathing entity on its own, it wouldn't try to avoid the tube. But it is real life, and I feel that [lawmakers are] apart from it, they are living on a pedestal. And they make the laws, but they don't realize the effects. [Quakers]

A woman from another group cited *The Silent Scream* as evidence that abortion really amounted to murder:

> They stick something up there and they can't even see what they're doing, they're just probing up you to suck the baby out of you. Now, to me that does not make one bit of sense to me, and in my opinion it's murder, because I've seen a movie called *The Silent Scream* and they stuck that tube up there and that baby was crying. And it was moving away from the object. The baby knew what was happening. And they say that's not murder? [Pentecostals]

In this discourse we again see the female body referred to as essentially a mysterious hole, inaccessible to the eyes of science and man ("They stick something up there and they can't even see what they're doing"), a sharp contrast to pro-choice discourse stressing the need for women to have knowledge of their own bodies and thus control over them. Imagery in *The Silent Scream* clearly supports the first view. This woman concluded her commentary with the statement "these are true facts," a phrase aptly summing up the use of this and other alternative media products to lend medical and consequently moral authority to the pro-life position and worldview.

An informant in another group described how seeing *The Silent Scream* affected her own views on abortion, solidifying her opposition to the procedure. She recalled that she once disagreed with church doctrine, believing that abortion was justifiable in cases of rape and incest. Viewing *The Silent Scream,* in conjunction with her own experience of two miscarriages, radically changed her perspective. [Quakers] It is clear that viewing this film is a powerful and sometimes formative experience for many pro-life women.

WHAT UNIFIES PRO-LIFE WOMEN?

I just always had this vision of me being . . . well, Donna Reed, you know. [Laughter] Donna Reed, only I never had the pearls.

STAY-AT-HOME MOTHERS

Surprisingly, their common values powerfully drew pro-life women together, even across social class lines. Though our interviews included affluent, working-class, and poor pro-life women, there were more similarities than differences in the ways they spoke about the abortion issue itself and about the television shows we showed them.

Pro-life women were unified in their rejection of what they saw as materialist values, and they were well aware that this located them outside mainstream American culture. Many pro-life women expressed ambivalence about pursuing and acquiring material wealth. Several talked about tithing to their church. Thus their critique of the materialism of secular culture is seen to be part of their larger refusal to consume mainstream American media culture as well. Relatedly, they often had chosen to leave the paid labor force and stay home with their children. Although in many cases this choice considerably reduced family income, women strongly believed in a traditional family in which mothers stay home, at least with young children.

The middle-class woman quoted at the beginning of this section was among those who had decided not to work when her children were born. Her remark reveals both the power of television and its limits. Certainly she defined desirable family life according to the nostalgic norm depicted in situation comedies of the 1950s and early 1960s, like *The Donna Reed Show*. Her characterization of her general lack of affluence shows she is conscious of her material difference from the Donna Reed icon, yet her laughter suggests it is relatively unimportant to her. Indeed, although her decision to stay home reduced her family income, in the end, she remarked, "Bills always seem to get paid, and food always gets on the table somehow." Financial considerations have not prevented her from choosing the lifestyle she most desires.[23]

In general we did not find that financial status particularly affected the views of most pro-life women in our study. The pro-choice women we interviewed were not as unified across social class lines in their responses, however. In the chapters that follow, we consider separately the comments first of working-class pro-choice women and then of middle-class pro-choice groups.

CONCLUSION

We found that pro-life women often supported their convictions by appealing to commonsense notions of scientific documentation and fact. Their view of science, however, little resembled notions of science as they are constructed in the scientific and medical community. In a complex way, pro-life women's scientific facts were carefully selected and interpreted in order to exclude or neutralize evidence that might support the pro-choice position. They viewed medical experts and mass media products outside the Christian pro-life community critically and with suspicion. In this they developed both an oppositional perspective on our culture and an oppositional reading of its products. Pro-life women gathered their own evidence through careful screening of the experts they listened to and the media they consumed. They sought pro-life doctors and media products to scientifically document their own pro-life positions, which they contrasted to more mainstream sources that they perceived as distorted, biased, and ultimately unscientific.

In accord with the literature exploring the worldviews of abortion activists (Ginsburg 1989; Luker 1984), we find that pro-life women's views on abortion reflect a broader set of issues than those involving the construction of gender roles. The nonactivist women we interviewed in both opinion camps spoke more often about the proper role of government and scientific authorities in the lives of private individuals than they did about women's proper roles in the family and in child rearing. Through their abortion rhetoric, nonactivist pro-life women expressed seemingly paradoxical attitudes toward authority: they were critical of conventional authority figures in many ways but quite respectful of specific selected figures in others. In this, women invoked an alternative community set apart from the mainstream on important dimensions. For some of our respondents this community was one they could actually point to; for others it had a more imaginary existence. For all, it served to secure their worldview in a universe they often experienced as impersonal, immoral, and overrationalized.

More generally, nonactivist pro-life women's rhetoric referred to the discourse of scientific reasoning, yet it critically rejected that language as well, although women maintained their suspicions of the work of science as presented to them by many doctors and by the mainstream medical and media establishments. In their discourse, however, they chose to ground their suspicions in this very form of reasoning. Gordon (1982), Luker (1984) and Ginsburg (1989) all found that activist pro-life women resisted the market nexus dominant in many relations of modern life, posing their ideas about femininity as a counterpoint to this logic. Here we argue that the terms of rational debate—for example, of the rationalized life—in many respects form the basis for the way pro-life women understand their own identities, imagine their communities, and discover their truths. With this paradox, the pro-life women in our study poignantly illustrated some of the aspects of modern, secular life that are perhaps difficult to live with, yet even more difficult to live outside.

Some of the apparent contradictions in these pro-life arguments echo current tensions in our society between liberal and communitarian philosophies of life. The liberal ideal of the rational, critical individual remains a strong theme in the arguments made by pro-life women in our study. They were wedded to a belief in their own and others' critical ability to make crucial, responsible decisions concerning themselves, their families, and society. Yet at the same time, the pro-life women were clearly troubled by the too individualistic philosophy they felt undergirded the pro-choice position. One main pro-life argument is based on the individualistic premise of support for the life of the fetus. Others, however, such as those emphasizing the special relationship between mother and child and community responsibility to care for unborn children, are embedded within an ethic of community relatedness and social accountability.

Nowhere was women's belief in community more obvious, perhaps paradoxically so, than when they supported their positions with information presented as scientific truth. For without their vision of community and their belief in the hierarchies governing them, they would have been unable to select the "true facts"—those legitimated by these communities—that formed the foundation of their arguments.

For these pro-life women, scientific fact itself had acquired a unique character. Wrested from the impersonal authority of the rationalized society, it had become instead the property of a highly personalized community group. Their arguments and beliefs challenged the impersonal character of science. Although in some ways their redefinition of science resonates with Thomas Kuhn's invocation of the importance of the scientific community in legitimating fact (1996), in others it differed markedly. For Kuhn, this community is relatively universal, and certainly not the more personal set of authorities invoked in our discussions.

The groups of pro-life friends we observed supported one another verbally as they made these arguments. Together they constructed a critical semipublic sphere, governed by norms specific to their communities and beliefs and only occasionally engaging the broader society against which their criticism was largely directed. Women were able to maintain their convictions by associating with others who supported them.

Women's exclusionary media viewing, practiced within their families and throughout their communities, helped to maintain the integrity of their identity as distinct from the mainstream as they viewed it. This study illustrates the constitutive importance of media habits for those attempting to maintain beliefs they feel contradict those governing the mainstream. It also illustrates that pro-life women's views on abortion reflect deep-seated resistance to the norms and epistemological assumptions of the secular society presented in mainstream media in the contemporary United States. Their selective viewing habits are rooted in and reinforce the construction of a virtually alternative community of thoughts and beliefs. This community is positioned as oppositional to the secular mainstream, yet it simultaneously draws support and justification from secular society's scientific mode of argument, which is premised on the primacy of objective fact.

That women are able to navigate such a complicated path between science and faith is testimony to the resilience, and necessity, of both modes of being in the modern world. Contradicting Max Weber's dictum that continued scientific progress would lead to the ultimate disenchantment of the world (1946), the pro-life women in our sample appropriated certain forms of scientific argument while maintaining their nonsecular viewpoint. Indeed, they showed a striking ability to weave strands of the ideology of the dominant culture into their discourse at the same time that they remained in many ways outside it. They were able to appropriate, transform, and even co-opt outside discourses so that they validated their own worldview. By assimilating the language of science and technology into their arguments, pro-life women not only neutralized this powerful competing discourse but fueled their argument with the rhetoric of their opposition. When employed by those advocating the pro-life position, these transformed arguments may become seductive to mainstream audiences because they are supported with discourses that have broad appeal in the dominant culture. In this chapter we have examined such use of the concept of "science"; the rhetoric of pro-life activists makes similarly strategic appeals to popular ideas about "freedom" and "rights" (Condit 1990; Dillon 1993, 1995). More broadly, the political and religious right—in particular Newt Gingrich—has recently begun to adopt the discourse of "futurism," a variant of the discourse of science.

This argumentive style has important political consequences. Opinion polls continue to show that the majority of Americans favor legal abortion, with some restrictions (Correa and Petchesky 1994; Hildreth and Dran 1994); however, this rhetorical strategy may make the pro-life position more palatable to those outside the pro-life subculture. By appeals to the rational discourse of "science," advocates of the pro-life position appear to ally themselves with ideals of reason and objectivity as personified by doctors and scientists at the same time that they distance themselves from the irrational, deplorable, and emotionally motivated actions of "extremists" who assault these same doctors and their patients at abortion clinics. The abortion issue, readily amenable to both types of reasoning, continues to be important for pro-life women precisely because of its epistemologically hybrid nature. Engaging the most basic questions about life, science, and belief, it crystallizes the continuing interdependence of these factors[24] for most of us in the modern world.

Nicole and Ruby, friends since childhood, were White single mothers in their mid-thirties. Ruby had been poor most of her life and was currently supporting her children on payments from Aid to Families with Dependent Children (AFDC). Nicole earned a living for herself and her son by working as a waitress and selling used furniture and records at flea markets. In their youth both had been heavy users of recreational drugs, but they had overcome this habit. Neither had ever married.

Ruby and her children lived in a housing project, in a small apartment decorated with Elvis Presley memorabilia, including a striking portrait on black velvet. We had trouble hooking up our VCR to her outdated television set. As we began to talk about their views and experiences concerning abortion, the two vividly expressed irreverent, suspicious attitudes toward legal authorities. Nicole argued that if abortion were to become generally illegal, some women would still find legal means to terminate their unwanted pregnancies. In Nicole's vision of the post-choice future, judges would decree which women could have abortions, and women like her would certainly be discriminated against.

> What gives me the right to tell you, just because I'm a judge setting up here, and I just look at your paper, I'd never met you before, and I look at your

paper for two seconds and say, "You can't have an abortion." Now that's bull, because I'll tell you what's going to happen if they do this: each case is going to get up there, the judge is never going to see you again, he don't know who you are and he's going to know what's for you in a one-page sheet. The judge would look at that sheet and say, "Yeah, OK, she can't have one. This guy over here's got some money, though. . . . " [Single Mothers]

Ruby finished the thought for her: "She's on welfare, she can't have one. That's what it would be." Throughout the interview, Nicole and Ruby expressed the conviction that authorities such as lawyers and judges neither represented nor respected their interests. They anticipated that, almost inevitably, they would be disfranchised by those in power. They invoked arguments concerning justice and fairness that stemmed from their profound skepticism about the operation of justice in our legal system. They feared legal restrictions on abortion not because such laws would in principle abridge fundamental rights of women, but because they were convinced the laws would be prejudicially enforced. Nicole and Ruby believed, based on their experience, that to secure the rights that are legitimately theirs, they must successfully navigate an often unfair legal system. Consequently they supported liberalized laws they thought would optimize the choices available to them.

In the discourses surrounding the pro-choice struggles over legalized abortion in the United States, rights are a recurrent theme. The language of the *Roe vs. Wade* decision affirmed a "fundamental right to choose" grounded in the "right to privacy": this determination established the state's compelling interest in protecting these rights by making abortion legal (cited in Condit 1990, 103). Rights language is a unifying thread in much of the public discourse characterizing pro-choice actions as well, and it accentuates the individualistic tenor of public discourse about abortion.

Feminist scholars have discussed the political implications of activist rhetoric stressing the concept of "rights." Nancy Fraser (1989) argues that rights language serves the depoliticizing function of privatizing what are essentially public, political concepts. Public debate, constrained by the pervasiveness of this individualistic emphasis, focuses on the interpretation of needs and the question of entitlement: What needs are recognized, and which individuals "deserve" to have their needs met? Thus the abortion debate has come to focus on issues such as whether abortion should be available on demand or limited to certain relatively exceptional circumstances (e.g., cases of rape or incest). However, those who construe abortion in terms of individuals' rights to obtain services overlook the connection between women's life circumstances that lead them to choose abortion and their membership in larger groups defined by social class, race, or ethnicity. Framing the issue as one of individual rights disregards the differential access that various groups of women have to resources in our society. Needs do differ, not only because there are differences between individuals, but also because groups differ in their access to opportunities and resources. Denying women easy and affordable access to abortion affects poor and working-class women more directly than it does those who have the money to obtain safe abortions through alternative means, to travel long distances to places where abortion is legal, or to support unplanned children. Those lacking financial resources suffer the greatest hardship when restrictive abortion laws are enacted.

Recognizing that laws differentially affect different groups of women requires a level of group consciousness rare in mainstream American public discourse. But it is precisely this vision that was present in conversations with some of our informants. A surprisingly strong consciousness of social class membership emerged in the remarks of certain working-class pro-choice women. In this chapter we describe this consciousness in detail, looking at differences between groups of working-class women as well as their similarities.

As early as 1966, David Lockwood argued that because the working class encompasses workers in a variety of labor settings, there should be a corresponding variety of ideas about social relations within the population of workers. Since that time, others have developed the argument that differences in structural location within the working class should influence political and class consciousness. Notably, Erik Olin Wright (1985) argues that workers vary in skills and organizational assets. He presents evidence that class consciousness varies accordingly, and that those with fewer of these assets are more likely to identify with the working class. Because some individuals may have access to one type of resource while being poor in other types, Wright has characterized this complexity within the working class as a problem of "contradictory class locations." This position, though intuitive, is not without its critics. Gordon Marshall (1983) contends that this attempt to map class consciousness onto a structural definition of class is troubled by the "problem of the disappearing subject" (274): such an approach characterizes classes as objectively defined social locations rather than as groups composed of living actors who may themselves hold contradictory views.

Because television so often portrays those seeking abortion as financially needy, working-class women share the experience of seeing their own life circumstances reflected in television's depictions of abortion. In our interviews, however, we found that class consciousness among the working-class women who call themselves pro-choice is multifaceted. In this chapter we outline the important ways various groups of working-class women critique, challenge, and at times even accept these images, as they use their conversations to locate themselves in relation to television's abortion heroines. In this they implicitly articulate class consciousness and classed identities that are at times contradictory and shifting.

Across the pro-choice working-class groups, we observed an important commonality. Of all the women we interviewed, pro-choice working-class women were the most preoccupied with issues of rights, perhaps because they had the most at stake. These themes were manifested in complex ways. Working-class women repeatedly expressed concern and anger about whether laws would be differentially enforced, allowing certain privileged women access to abortion services, but the focus of this mistrust took different forms. Differences particularly coalesced around issues of legal and professional authority and the role authorities such as police, lawyers, judges, and others in the criminal justice system should play in enforcing restrictions against abortion or in preventing even lawful access to abortion by women of specific groups. In the discourse of rights, there is a recurrent tension between those who seek to safeguard the rights of individuals and those whose concern is to hold in check the exercise of those rights. Both of these themes are present in the discourse of working-class women.

In their assessments of fairness, working-class pro-choice women were divided in the level of their identification with or against institutions of power. Although some women saw themselves primarily as outsiders and identified with forces that resist attempts to regulate exercise of these rights, others identified strongly with the institutional authorities aiming at regulation. We coined the labels "working-class-identified" and "middle-class-identified" to differentiate these positions. These discourses mark deep divisions within working-class women's experience and in their attitudes toward middle-class life and societal authority.[1] Some working-class groups used one or the other of these positions exclusively. Conversations in other groups drew from both at different times.[2]

OUR SIDE OF THE WORLD: WORKING-CLASS WOMEN DISCUSS TELEVISION'S ABORTION HEROINES

As we discussed in chapter 2, entertainment television depicts abortion as a "classed" issue: only poor or working-class women choose abortion.

In this, television endorses a limited pro-choice position. Many of the working-class women we interviewed were sensitive to the classed narrative implicit in television treatments of abortion, and some criticized such representations of reproductive decision making, generally based on their own experience. For example, women in one group considered whether men should have the right to prevent their partners from seeking abortion. Although both women in the group were adamant that men were not entitled to this prerogative, they ultimately dismissed the debate as irrelevant to women in "their side of the world":

FIRST WOMAN: Chances are that don't happen very often . . . not in my side of the world anyway. We're both from the same side of the world. Men [who threaten legal action to prevent a woman from aborting], if they are, chances are, ninety-five out of a hundred, they're using it, thinking that the woman will stay with them, just like the women do to the men. Because how many men out there are going to say, "You're not killing my baby and I don't care what happens to you"?

SECOND WOMAN: I watch *Thirtysomething*, you know, and Michael is about the only man I know, TV relationships where it is discussed, "OK, honey, you go off the pill . . . OK, its time to have the baby. It's time to have a baby, honey." Give me a break! That doesn't happen in the real world! [Single Mothers]

Despite the general skepticism that working-class women sometimes expressed toward television, most who viewed the character of Donna on the episode of *Dallas* were fairly supportive of her and accepting of the show's characterization of her situation. Ray and Donna belonged to a minor branch of the prosperous Ewing family, subsidiary to the main events on *Dallas*. Some working-class women who watched the couple wrestle with whether to abort a fetus with Down's syndrome described them as "such loving people," who had "so much love to give" that it was sad to think of their having to make such a terrible choice. [Landlady and Tenant] Others praised Donna and her husband for deciding together whether to continue the pregnancy. [State College Group] This uncritical reception of Donna's character by working-class women is not surprising, given Press's (1991b) finding that such women tended to be less critical of middle-class or upper-middle-class characters on television than they were of working-class or lower-class characters.

More often, though, entertainment television treatments of abortion feature women facing extreme material difficulty. Consequently, working-class pro-choice women have a unique relation to the heroines of these narratives: characters like Ellen Russell and Mrs. Herrera are television's attempt to represent the realities of women like them. Working-class women's responses to these characters were complex.

Even among working-class women, it seems Mrs. Herrera is a relatively noncontroversial heroine. Working-class pro-choice groups were almost unified in their support for her. Pregnant within marriage, working hard in school, worried about her husband, and troubled over the morality of abortion, Mrs. Herrera faced her decision in a way that made her as acceptable to these women as she was to middle-class pro-choice women, and even to some pro-life women as well. Some working-class pro-choice women found it particularly easy to identify with Mrs. Herrera's struggle for upward mobility. They agreed with the television depiction of her plight, concurring that it is hard to finish school while caring for a child even with the assistance of welfare. This was true of the women in the Ambitious Mothers group. The two women in this group, both White and in their early thirties, were mothers of small children, and much of their friendship centered on doing things with their children. One was recently divorced, and the other was married to a man in the construction trades. Both had a high school education and at the time of the interview were homemakers; but, like Mrs. Herrera, they hoped to go back to school. One woman in this group drew on her own experience to illustrate the obstacles encountered by women who attempt to pursue higher education while raising children. She recalled her social worker's advice to delay her own education until her children were of school age:

> Well, in [Mrs. Herrera's] situation I could see why she'd want to [have an abortion]. She'd be better off doing it than to have the baby and have to give up everything and then, you know, not be able to take care of her kids in the future. It's really, really hard to go to school when you have kids, and people try to make it look like there's a chance and there isn't. There's almost this much chance . . . one in a million people make it. I'm trying right now to go to beauty school and get help from the state, and the lady from the welfare office is just telling me, don't even try it. The lady's saying, you won't be able to afford to pay the baby-sitter, you won't be able to do this. I don't want to give you such a negative aspect, but they told me not to do it. She said, "You're going to bury yourself in trying to pay for day care. You are only going to get forty-three dollars a week, which is not enough for the amount of hours that you are going to need day care. We don't like them to even try until their kids are in full-time school." That's what she said. [Ambitious Mothers]

Other working-class pro-choice women mentioned that the disabled Mr. Herrera might need care as well, expressing concern that Mrs. Herrera would be unable to meet the needs of her husband if she also had a child to care for. They viewed her desire for an abortion as understand-able in this light. Working-class women in these groups found that the character's situation presented a strong argument justifying legal abor-tion. Overall, working-class pro-choice women raised few objections to the depiction of Mrs. Herrera and expressed fairly unqualified support for her and her choice. A notable exception to this trend, however, were the remarks of one woman who discerned the criticism of financially needy women implicit in Mrs. Herrera's continual expression of her de-sire for upward mobility:

> Then the line that the Spanish [woman] said about "I don't want to go on welfare." I'm so sick of hearing that. You know, it gives welfare a bad name. I mean, it's nothing wonderful to be on, but it helps. I mean, it's there and I feel that if it's there to help you, do it. That's what it was formed for. You know, let your pride . . . starve your children just for your pride's sake. [Single Mothers]

This same woman expressed dissatisfaction with the show's relatively tame depiction of the controversy over abortion, which she felt down-played the conflicts involved. She challenged the portrayal of the Right to Life spokeswoman in the episode as stereotyped. "Well, the woman, they always portray the Right to Life people as mealymouthed, nothing better to do with their life. . . . If I were casting that show, I might have put Grace Jones (a flamboyant Black singer-actress) in that role, you know?" This suggests that even women who agreed with the bias they perceived were sometimes critical of television's tendency to flatten con-flict.

Ellen Russell's situation elicited a more complex and contentious reac-tion. Ellen's reception by pro-choice working-class women varied from lukewarm approval to extreme disapproval. Although working-class women did universally affirm her right to an abortion, they disapproved more generally of her lifestyle and the circumstances that led to her un-wanted pregnancy, as in these comments:

FIRST WOMAN: She was not the type to raise a child, definitely. Her lifestyle was not that. . . . I don't think it would be conducive to raising a child. Of course there are a lot of children who live with carnivals and things of that nature who are truly remarkable people. Her own personal lifestyle however, leaves something to be desired there. She's rather loose there. . . .

SECOND WOMAN: She needs to get a little more responsible with where she's sleeping around or what she's doing while she's there, though. A little more responsible sex. [Chain Store Managers]

Others criticized Ellen while recognizing that the character merely represented women who seek abortion:

SECOND WOMAN: Well, she [Ellen] made me feel that abortions only happen to roughnecks.

THIRD WOMAN: Yeah, that's what they made it look like too.

SECOND WOMAN: Yeah, she looked like a little slut. Like a little motorcycle mama to me. Somebody that's on the streets, you know. [Chain Store Workers]

In fact, some working-class pro-choice women objected that Ellen's case was used to illustrate abortion (even though the character was modeled after a real person). Like the pro-life women, they explicitly criticized the latent message in the television depiction. The woman quoted above went on to assert that it's not true that only women like Ellen have abortions.

> Doctors' wives can have one. Attorneys' wives, you know. You can be a well-to-do woman and still want an abortion. You don't have to be a street person, and they made it look like only the bad people, you know, [choose abortion]. Well, this [show] kind of made me feel that because she was from a rough part of town or she acted rough and tough and she liked to hang out in bars and all this . . . that's not reality. In reality any woman could need an abortion whether she's on the streets, in a $50,000 or $400,000 home.

In contrast to Mrs. Herrera, who aspires to middle-class status, Ellen Russell's character conspicuously rejects middle-class ideals and refuses to try to improve herself in hopes of achieving upward mobility. She is a working-class woman who appears to have no real prospects of leaving her class, nor does she actively seek them: she is extremely non–middle class identified. Among pro-choice working-class groups, there were two distinct types of responses to her character that led us to define distinct forms of working-class identity. Working-class women's evaluations of Ellen varied in relation to how they viewed themselves. Our terms "middle-class-identified" and "working-class-identified" describe different receptions of her character as expressed by women in the pro-choice working-class groups we interviewed.

THE WORKING-CLASS-IDENTIFIED POSITION

Many sociologists and other commentators on the American scene have noted that most Americans consider themselves members of the middle class (Ehrenreich 1989). This was true of some of the working-class women we interviewed, who saw themselves as no different from the middle class, or as aspiring toward that status. However, others viewed themselves as squarely outside the mainstream. These working-class women constructed a very different self-concept—in our terms, one more working class identified. This position is encapsulated by one woman who asked us what groups we were interviewing. Wanting to answer honestly but unwilling to explicitly use the terminology of social class, Andrea Press rather euphemistically said we were sampling various occupational groups. The woman responded, laughing, "Oh, you mean high class, middle class, and no class, like us!" [Chain Store Workers] Similarly, in another group a woman explained that we should feel free to use her real first name in our book rather than a pseudonym (though as a matter of policy we did not), because "no one who was a professor would know who I was." This lack of concern for anonymity contrasted sharply with the attitudes of middle-class-identified women; some were so concerned with protecting their identities that they took false first names from the very beginning of the taped interview, a position uncommon among the women we interviewed. The woman who made the "no class" comment acknowledged that she does not belong to the middle class and that she is clear, if not particularly comfortable, about that social location. Their remarks emphasized the assurance of invisibility these women experience, based on their feeling of discontinuity from the middle class and its hegemonic representations in the mass media.

Other women were even more articulate in expressing this class consciousness. One African American woman argued for a kind of practical solidarity based on commonalties of race and class, stating, "A support system. . . . I think that's what we lack in America period, in all races, not just the Black races. . . . I think we lack support everywhere." This group was organized by a woman who had taken part in another interview and offered to set up a second group composed of women from her neighborhood. She invited her mother, who was in her sixties, a family friend in her late teens who was single and had recently suffered a miscarriage, and this speaker, who was about forty. The interviewer asked a question to probe the limits of this solidarity: Did the speaker believe that the young White woman in the group, who before her miscarriage had considered having an abortion because she felt she could not afford a child, was also discriminated against?

> Yeah . . . because she's White, and she's a poor White, and that's what Martin
> Luther King called race discrimination. He didn't go out just to fight for the

Black. . . . If you follow his dream and his march, you will find that he fought for the people that was discriminated against and it was poor Whites as well as Blacks. Yeah, she's discriminated against . . . because she doesn't have that certain income level, so she's automatically put in the class with Black people. [Family Friends]

This woman's comments indicated a rather sophisticated class analysis that cuts across racial differences to acknowledge the common position held by low-income people in American society. Andrea Press, who was conducting the interview, then turned to the young White woman who had considered abortion and asked whether she believed she was discriminated against. "Yes," she replied.

"Why?" Press probed.

"Because I don't have any money."

Other working-class women made similarly frank comments about their economic standing. In this way it was not at all uncommon for working-class pro-choice women to acknowledge class difference in American culture and the kinds of discrimination low-income people might experience.

Working-class-identified women tended to be suspicious of members of the middle class, particularly those holding power in social institutions, in ways that middle-class-identified women were not. Their conversation was littered with references to their distrust of middle-class authority and, by extension, its societal representatives.

This distrust extended to authorities in the television episodes they viewed. For example, one group was harshly critical of the doctor who treated Ellen but also considered his behavior typical of what they expect from doctors:

ANDREA PRESS: What did you think of the doctor? When she went to see the doctor?

FIRST WOMAN: Scaredy-cat. My first impression was he just doesn't want to lose his license. You know how easy it is to sue a doctor right now, malpractice suits, I mean. It's just like in our hospitals today, you can go in for any kind of surgery and the first thing they have you sign is those arbitration or whatever they're called. So this guy is just covering his own ass. It's getting harder and harder to find a doctor that will deliver babies. It really is. *So I felt like he was just like any other doctor,* he's covering his ass. It's not legal in that state, so don't come to me for something. [Said with sarcasm; emphasis added]

SECOND WOMAN: [He's just saying] I don't know nothing about it.

FIRST WOMAN: Yeah, [he's saying] "I'll do nothing illegal." [Said in a scornful, derisive tone] [Chain Store Workers][3]

This same group derided other professional characters in *Roe vs. Wade* as well. The women strongly criticized Ellen's attorneys for using her to further their own careers. On the show the lawyers revealed that they were not entirely honest with Ellen, in that they never told her this was their first case. Indeed, after the first court's decision, Ellen accuses them of misleading her into thinking the case would be settled in time for her to have an abortion. However, the movie makes an attempt at balance by depicting Sarah Weddington's concern for Ellen in several conversations between the two. Yet the lawyer fails to call after Ellen, blocked in her efforts to get an abortion, finally delivers her baby, and in general she does not take much time out from her busy personal and professional life to be overly solicitous.

As in their assessment of the doctor, the Chain Store Workers again condemned the professionals for pursuing their self-interest at Ellen's expense.

FIRST WOMAN: I don't think they were very fair and honest with her right up front. I think they misled her. I don't think she realized in the beginning how long it really would take.

SECOND WOMAN: Well, they didn't tell her either, [that it would take] two months.

FIRST WOMAN: And then here you see her all of a sudden and she's got this big old belly. And I think they took this case on. . . . they believed in it and they believed in woman's choice, but I think they did it to set their career off. I think it was done selfishly on their part, because like they both said, "We're not telling her the truth, neither one of us have ever litigated."

ANDREA PRESS: So you thought the women lawyers were sort of misleading her?

SECOND WOMAN: I think so, I think they were just trying to further themselves. I don't think they really came down to the bottom line with her and I don't think she was really smart enough to question them thoroughly enough on the situation.

THIRD WOMAN: It was just any light of hope.

FOURTH WOMAN: They told her in May and it was March, she was just like. . . .

FIRST WOMAN: She was in limbo, she didn't know what to do. She was just believing what they told her.

SECOND WOMAN: Since there was nothing available at that point in time in Texas, that they would give her some alternatives. But they didn't even suggest anything. I think they did it to further their own careers and they're probably rich wealthy lawyers now.

Following these remarks, the group answered questions from Andrea Press about whether the lawyers should have helped Ellen obtain a legal abortion in New York. The women said the lawyers should have helped her, mentioning several other ways they might also have helped once they realized their case would not be resolved in time for her to obtain an abortion. Similar sentiments were expressed by the women in the Nontraditional Students group:

FIRST WOMAN: I felt that it was real empowering that they [the lawyers] wanted to do this [case], but I didn't think they told her the whole story, or if they told her they didn't. . . . they weren't able to get through to her what the total reality was. They may have said it, but that doesn't mean she heard.

ANDREA PRESS: You didn't think they were treating her quite fairly. . . .

FIRST WOMAN: They were excited about having the case and they needed a case. . . .

SECOND WOMAN: First case. . . .

FIRST WOMAN: Plus the fact that when she was getting angry with them, that part of me was going, "Yeah, get angry . . . you know, dammit, get angry for once!" And then she apologized to the authority figure about expressing anger and then they watch her walk out the door. And I'm sitting there thinking, it was empowering what they did [taking the case], but they weren't empowering women or they wouldn't have allowed her to walk out . . . just turn around and walk away. . . . Or, I don't know, maybe it's that, that part of me that would like to take care of somebody and say, "Listen, I'll pay it. My next case, I'll pay for you to do something. . . . "

ANDREA PRESS: Do you think . . . pay for her to do what? I mean, did you think that maybe they should have paid for her to go to New York?

FIRST WOMAN: Yeah.

This woman continued, elaborating her view that essentially the lawyers had won while Ellen lost: the attorneys benefited professionally from taking the case, while Ellen was left no option but to carry an unwanted pregnancy to term. She argued that the lawyers "probably got a lot of cases off from that or maybe they didn't, but let's say that they would. . . . They got some acknowledgment and it probably helped their career[s] a great deal. She [Ellen] should not have lost because of that." Working-class-identified pro-choice women were more eager to detail the ways the attorneys might have helped Ellen than were women in other pro-life and pro-choice groups, even though most agreed the attorneys had used her. This viewpoint follows from the generally critical attitude toward professionals and authorities of any kind held by the working-class-identified women.

In contrast, working-class-identified women were less critical of the character of Ellen than were other working-class women we interviewed. Although they did not hold any special affection for Ellen, they did see some redeeming qualities in her character. One complimented her tenacity, saying, "You had to admire her. . . . Whether I agree with her lifestyle or whatever, she had some fight in her." [Nontraditional Students] In contrast to the critical views presented earlier regarding Mrs. Herrera's pride, another woman praised Ellen's unwillingness to go on welfare, attributing it to her "pride" and independence:

THIRD WOMAN: You know, that one remark she made, "I'm not trash. . . . "
FIRST WOMAN: I tend to believe some people would just as soon live off the streets before they would ask for any kind of help. Maybe she [Ellen] was that way.
SECOND WOMAN: Too much pride.
FIRST WOMAN: Yeah, her pride stepped in before she would ask the state for help, or whatever the case would be. [Chain Store Workers]

Working-class-identified women were also more inclined than others to note parallels between Ellen's situation and their own experience or that of others in their families or among their friends. In this they showed evidence of identifying with Ellen. One woman, after viewing the show, told the story of a niece she had mentioned in the discussion before the show, noting at several points her similarity to Ellen. Like Ellen, her niece had a child as a teen that relatives had (almost entirely) raised, and she had become pregnant again soon afterward. Faced with the second pregnancy, this respondent had paid for her niece to have an abortion:

FIRST WOMAN: [My niece] had an abortion to keep from having another child raised by her mother and her aunt. Similar to this case.
ANDREA PRESS: Do you help out financially with her child?
FIRST WOMAN: Um-huh. We did, now we're not so much.
ANDREA PRESS: Is she working?
FIRST WOMAN: Well, she had jobs off and on, but now she's living with someone on a more permanent basis that he's financing them. He's taking care of her and her six-year-old. We don't have to help them anymore. But during her sowing her wild oats more or less, she got pregnant again and it was just a mutual agreement by all of us for her to have this abortion. I don't feel bad that she did.
ANDREA PRESS: Do you think she regrets that? Does she think she made the right decision?
FIRST WOMAN: No. She made the right decision. She wasn't very far along at all, she was maybe six, eight weeks. Just enough to know she was pregnant, it wasn't like the kicking and the moving and the feeling and the you know, it was like, "Oh shit, I missed my period, I'm pregnant, now what do I do? You know, I've got one kid that my mom's taking care of," similar to this girl here you know, real similar, except in my niece's case, she knew that it was not a permanent

thing. Now, she has her son, they have a wonderful life and things are working out for them. And she's grown up a lot. She's in her twenties, she's more settled, you know, but it took her a while. That's [how it is] with these girls, they don't realize when they're young and they have these babies, that life's not a bowl of roses here if they don't have a loving family to help them and to take care of these children for them and financially help them. [Chain Store Workers]

Working-class-identified women accepted *Roe vs. Wade*'s portrayal of Ellen's lack of resources. Unlike pro-life women in particular, who (as we argued in chapter 3) often insisted that Ellen had not fully tapped all family resources available to her, these women felt that at times such resources do not exist. One woman, a young single mother receiving financial support from her parents, recognized that her situation was very different from that faced by some young women: "Yeah, I know I'm lucky. I know a lot of people that have a baby and they don't get any help." [Chain Store Workers] Later in the conversation another person in the group offered this empathic statement about young women facing unwanted pregnancies:

Yeah, they're in a world of hurt. For them they need the choice of maybe being able to have an abortion. Because you're already struggling, you know, if you're a young girl and you're out there struggling your ass off to make ends meet, what's the burden of bringing another one into that struggle?

Working-class-identified women have had, either personally or through family connections, experiences that lead them to view television's abortion heroines sympathetically. They express their belief that their "side of the world" is often not mirrored by television's middle-class version of reality. When viewing television depictions of the working class, they acknowledge the genuine obstacles facing these heroines, and they challenge the societal authorities that seek to limit their choices in coping with them. In this their reading is oppositional to what we argue are television's preferred readings of the narratives. Most of the working-class groups we interviewed offered interpretations that were oppositional in some respects; however, not all constructed the same type of opposition to television's classed narrative of abortion.

THE MIDDLE-CLASS-IDENTIFIED POSITION

In contrast to the women we termed working class identified, working-class women who are middle class identified see themselves as essentially members of the middle class (though by our measures they were not).[4] This position was expressed much less frequently than the working-class-identified position, but one group, the Chain Store Managers, articulated the middle-class-identified position almost exclusively, and we quote them here extensively.[5] Women in this group took great pains to construct a picture of themselves in which they were completely separated from the members of their class who behave irresponsibly, such as those who do not work steadily, have no ambition, take drugs or drink heavily, and indulge in casual sex. For example, one woman in this group differentiated herself from those who would accept public assistance: "Many of us may have been in a situation at one time or another where we've struggled and we've made real hard attempts to avoid using those sources or may have been denied those sources for various reasons."

In contrast to their working-class-identified counterparts, middle-class-identified women were relentlessly critical of Ellen's character. These women criticized Ellen strongly for what they viewed as her lack of self-reliance. They saw her as looking for a handout, the very type of person most likely to end up with a free ride from the welfare system and probably the least deserving of it. They found Ellen's job search, and her continual complaints that she could not find work, unconvincing. A woman from this same group commented that Ellen "kept saying she kept trying to find a job, that there wasn't any work. Yet she could go out and have fun with her friends." Much of Ellen's unconventional behavior offended women in this group. They gave her no credit, as did the working-class-identified women, for her reluctance to go on public assistance (although in general they admired women who stand on their own). Indeed, some were even critical of this stance. For example, although some working-class-identified women interpreted Ellen's unwillingness to go on welfare as evidence of pride, a middle-class-identified woman attributed her behavior to ignorant "Texican" attitudes about who is trash and who isn't. [Chain Store Managers] For middle-class-identified women, her other irresponsible qualities completely overrode this virtue.

Middle-class-identified women filled in the narrative's "unsaid" portions, completing the character sketch of Ellen with qualities and background information that made her even more the object of their disapproval. One sketchily drawn but often-criticized aspect of Ellen's situation, for example, is the circumstances of her becoming pregnant for the second time. We never learn anything about the baby's father or her relationship with him. All she tells us is that he is "not interested," presumably in helping Ellen either to raise the child or to obtain an abortion.

Despite this limited information about Ellen's sexual history, one middle-class-identified woman articulated in some detail her belief that Ellen probably sleeps around: "I don't sleep with a man three days after I meet him," she ventured. Her remark implied that Ellen does precisely this, although the show gives no information except a similar accusation by Ellen's mother. Others in the group elaborated, imbuing the character with negative qualities not depicted in the television portrayal:

FIRST WOMAN: It just seemed it wasn't that she was in this long-term involved, stable relationship. [It was] not even necessarily long term, it seemed like it was just like a one night stand basically. Oops, I got pregnant. You've got to be a little more careful, you know.

SECOND WOMAN: She even said to her father and mother, he was just a guy. That's too bad.

THIRD WOMAN: I think it seemed like she was constantly in an environment where drinking might be available. She might have been drunk at the time of the pregnancy, you don't know. [Chain Store Managers]

These women reconstructed the details of Ellen's life in an extremely unfavorable light. Although many people we interviewed perceived Ellen as a working-class heroine, a prototypical example of the disadvantaged woman seeking an abortion on television, middle-class-identified women resisted this portrayal. The same group similarly constructed a hypothetical woman seeking abortion, attributing comparable qualities of flagrant irresponsibility to this "straw woman."

Those are the people who line up frequently, using abortion as birth control. There's a whole lot easier, cheaper, less painful ways to have birth control than to keep getting abortions. We have people at work that [say things like], "I think I'm pregnant again, I don't think I can go through my fourth abortion." You're twenty-two, what do you mean your fourth abortion? "Well, I didn't want to go to the drugstore. . . . " Well, then cross your legs and go home! [Several jokes made by group members here]

Others in the group expressed similar, if more extreme views. They argued that women who have had too many abortions are an unnecessary drain on the government, insurance companies, and the time and resources of physicians. Thus they used their construction of women like Ellen, real and imagined, as irresponsible, promiscuous, and lazy to justify draconian social policies, rationalizing their plan to construct a national surveillance system in order to sterilize women after a certain number of abortions:

ANDREA PRESS: Do you think that people like that should also have access to abortions?

FIRST WOMAN: I think they should have access to voluntary sterilization.

SECOND WOMAN: Precisely.

FIRST WOMAN: Have sex three times and you're out. . . . [Laughter]

SECOND WOMAN: There has to be some kind of control. We need a national computerized system here. Get an abortion in Boone, Kentucky, . . . and then if they move to Ypsilanti, Michigan, to get another abortion, that's it, chick. Twice and you're out! I'm serious, OK? *We are the government,* we have a responsibility to stop all this endless waste. It's a waste of money, it's a waste of good professional time. Why should some doctor spend all the time aborting some woman? I know one who has had seven abortions! I'm ahead of you. Why should some doctor spend good medical time and taxpayers' money or anybody's money to keep aborting the same person over and over again? [Emphasis added]

These women felt that under the current arrangements abortions are too readily available, and in response they constructed a vision relying on centralized authorities to promote responsible behavior by limiting women's access to services. Middle-class-identified women did not hesitate to invoke societal authorities to discipline women they feel take life too freely and easily. In fact, they identify with these authorities explicitly: "We are the government."

Most telling of the middle-class-identified women's particularly accepting attitude toward authority, and in sharp contrast to the views of their working-class-identified counterparts, is the way such women characterized Ellen's relationship with the attorneys who took her case to the Supreme Court. Although working-class-identified women criticized Ellen's lawyers for using her to get ahead, the middle class identified simply acknowledged this situation matter-of-factly, in a tone suggesting that this is the behavior to be expected of lawyers. When we asked if they thought Ellen's attorneys ought to have flown her to New York to obtain a legal abortion, one group chanted an indignant NO! in a unison that rarely occurs in group interviews of this nature. They argued that Ellen did not "contract" in advance for this kind of help, and thus no such help was warranted. Perhaps if she had been shrewd enough to demand it in the beginning, she might deserve it. But then, of course, Ellen was anything but shrewd. Rather than having sympathy for her naïveté, they implied that Ellen ought to pay for her lack of sophistication and strategy. In their view the attorneys did not owe her help, nor did she deserve any. In fact, the group was shocked that we would even mention this as a possibility, as though they couldn't quite believe anyone could take this position. It seemed to offend their most basic convictions about the importance of individuals' self-reliance.

The Chain Store Managers, in particular, constructed their own identities in opposition to Ellen and women like her. Their responses reflect their efforts to defend this construction. Their tendency to separate themselves from people like her was exemplified by their story about the daughter of one member, a narrative that contrasts markedly with the working-class-identified woman's story about her niece described above. In this case one woman's daughter, Arlene, had become pregnant while still in high school. She chose to have an abortion, and soon afterward she dropped out of school. Subsequently she became pregnant again, this time deciding to keep the baby, although she was still single. She later married the father briefly and was now divorced. She was currently working, caring for her daughter, and planning to attend school part time at some point in the future.

When talking about this young woman's experience, the group collectively assumed an almost reverent tone that stood out clearly from the rest of their discussion and was particularly remarkable compared with their attitude toward Ellen and her choices (between us we came to refer to their comments as the sainthood of Arlene):

FIRST WOMAN: Arlene is a very mature young lady, always has been. Her actions at that time may not have been considered mature, but her decisions were correct for her at that time. . . .

SECOND WOMAN: She has an unusual confidence and responsibility. I think a lot of that comes from the support that she's received. It's an unusual circumstance in that she has a real friendship, I think, with her mom and with Pete [her stepfather]. [Chain Store Managers]

Group members repeatedly commented on Arlene's maturity. No one criticized her character, despite her behavior. Ellen, on the other hand, strongly disliked by all group members, was disparaged as morally "loose" and irresponsible for actions strikingly similar to Arlene's.

Although the group's regard for her mother's feelings certainly accounts in part for their reluctance to criticize Arlene, their comments appeared to be offered sincerely. Our interpretation could of course be mistaken, but the women seemed to genuinely like Arlene and to admire her strength in surviving and making the best of difficult circumstances. The divergence in this group's feelings toward Arlene and Ellen may spring from their desire to separate themselves from "those immoral" working-class people like Ellen, the ones who are depicted on television and in the news.

This "us versus them" distancing is further illustrated by the group's view of welfare abusers as people who take advantage of the system that people like themselves work so hard to support:

THIRD WOMAN: Of course, the trade that we're in, we get to see misuse of welfare money, continuously.

FIRST WOMAN: Oh, they misuse food stamps like you wouldn't believe.

SECOND WOMAN: If you've ever read food stamps, if you ever looked at the books or actually read what you can do with them food stamps, you can buy lobster if you wish and they frequently do. . . . You can't buy soda, you can't buy tobacco, of course you can't buy alcohol, but if you wish to have a lobster dinner for your friends and you can all come up with enough welfare money, you can have a lobster dinner. You can buy steak.

In general, this group strongly disapproved of the "lazy, irresponsible" people who receive government assistance. Their comments suggested that they believed the system is flawed, giving people no incentive to work, and that ultimately they would like to see it wiped out altogether.

These abstract, theoretical views on the subject, however, contrasted sharply with their descriptions of the actual people receiving welfare they meet at work. One woman, for example, in her job as an assistant manager at a discount store, took employment applications. With seemingly uncharacteristic sympathy, she described seeing applicants who "should have been paid yesterday," single fathers whose children haven't eaten in days, for example, and others in extreme need of aid. She and the group strongly agreed that these people deserve assistance. They criticized the welfare system for not being generous enough, for not helping quickly enough. The same woman described the decisions she must make in evaluating applicants' potential as workers. She argued that often such people "need a chance"; they could be efficient workers despite their lack of experience, high school degrees, or other paper qualifications. These attitudes toward the people she encounters, many of whom become her coworkers, contradicted the way she and her friends characterized the scheming masses on welfare, and also their placing Ellen in this category despite her insistence on remaining off welfare. Again, such contrasts might be explained by this group's desire to separate themselves and those they work with from the bulk of working-class and poor people "out there," thereby strengthening their construction of, and identification with, a middle-class-identified subject position.

In sum, in their responses to television, middle-class-identified women discounted their personal experience in favor of expressing their commitment to more abstract principles. They judged the characters they viewed against their abstract code of conduct rather than making comparisons with the people they encounter in their everyday lives. When experience and principle conflict, they often favor abstract values reflecting what they would like to believe is true rather than practical knowledge based on their own lives.

AFRICAN AMERICAN WORKING-CLASS WOMEN

The proportion of African American respondents in our total sample roughly reflects the proportion of African Americans in the United States (see appendix A); however, only two Black women answered our solicitation, and the groups these contacts organized were composed entirely of African American women (other Black women in the sample took part in groups that were otherwise entirely White). Our experience reflects the difficulties of recruiting African Americans to participate in research, particularly qualitative research, that have been reported by other scholars (Cannon, Higginbotham, and Leung 1988; Reid 1993). The first, the Young Mothers group, was composed of three women in their middle teens and early twenties, two of whom had small children themselves, and one of their mothers, who was in her mid-thirties. The women in this group had trouble scheduling a full three-hour meeting; to accommodate them, and because of our problem in recruiting African American respondents generally, we conducted two shorter interviews with them, one day apart, and showed them both the *Cagney and Lacey* episode and the clip from the *Roe vs. Wade* movie. The two women in the second group, the Greek Organization group, were also young, in their early twenties, and were working toward bachelor's degrees at the local state college. They met through a women's group associated with a fraternity on the campus. One had a child and considered herself a homemaker as well as a student; the other was not a mother and worked at a convenience store.

All six of the women who attended the groups organized by these two African American respondents were themselves African American and poor or working class. Four expressed consistently pro-choice views; the other two, a mother and her daughter, were more ambivalent, but in many cases they too acknowledged the necessity or desirability of abortion. All but one of the women in these groups was younger than twenty-five, four of the six had become mothers by age twenty-one, and half reported in the interview having had at least one abortion. Only one was married. Thus this is a small and very select sample, representing a subgroup of African American women who have been made emblematic of a variety of American social and economic problems by the mass media and policymakers alike (Collins 1990; Luker 1996). Although their responses should by no means be considered to reflect attitudes held by Black women generally, the views expressed by women in the two groups composed exclusively of African Americans may illuminate the perspective of young, financially disadvantaged Black women who have themselves been the focus of one of America's culture wars.

None of the women in these two groups made comments specifically locating themselves in a social class, as did several of the working-class-identified women in predominantly White groups. Neither did they discuss race explicitly.[6] One Black woman did make a subtle allusion to her classed view of the world as she criticized *Roe vs. Wade*'s heroine, Ellen, for her unwillingness to accept welfare: "That excuse about she didn't want to be on welfare, well what makes you better than everybody else?" [Young Mothers] In this she implicitly compared the character with herself and women like her, as she suggested that for some women public assistance is a necessity of life, however unwelcome.

Yet in some important ways the positions expressed by the working-class Black women were very similar to those of their White working-class-identified counterparts. Black women shared their distrust of professional authorities. In particular, they were critical of lawmakers attempting to curb the availability of Medicaid abortions:

> This is what I don't understand, particularly in the state of Michigan . . . how can they tell you that they don't want you to have an abortion, but yet still, if you're on welfare, they don't want you to add more than two kids on it? I mean, that don't make no sense. So what are you supposed to do, I mean, are you supposed to keep having kids and not be able to afford them? I mean, that don't make no sense, you know, if you're going to stop one, you got to give somewhere, you can't just try to put bars on both doors, you know, something's got to give. [Young Mothers]

Her vivid metaphor of lawmakers putting "bars on both doors" of the options available to women makes clear her feeling that political authorities have little concern or respect for the freedom of women like her. However, unlike the attitude of White working-class women, working-class Black women's distrust of authorities was most marked toward doctors and the medical establishment. Women from both African American groups repeatedly expressed wariness and skepticism toward generally accepted medical practices. For example, one woman described how she inadvertently became pregnant:

WOMAN: I'd been taking the birth control pills for five years, so I just wanted to stop for a year.

ELIZABETH COLE: Why did you want to stop?

WOMAN: Because I'd been taking them for so long, it was just like . . . you know, you take a certain thing for so long, it's like your body just gets messed up and like I had just been real sick the year before, so it's like I just want to stop taking all kinds of medicine . . . and get my body resistance built up on its own. That's basically why I stopped. And then when I stopped, I didn't have no money to go get anything else. That's what the problem was. Because I had been out of work for a while, too. [Greek Organization]

This woman believed that birth control pills, and indeed most medication, interfere with the human body's natural ability to defend itself. Her comments are representative of the particular wariness toward contraceptives we found among the working-class African American women we interviewed. Although all reported using birth control, they also discussed their fears about the general effects of these technologies on women's health. In the Young Mothers group, for example, a sixteen-year-old mother of a new baby said she intended to begin using Norplant.[7] Her mother, who was also in the group, expressed concern and worry ("How do they know how your system will act toward it?") and wondered whether pregnancy was still possible after the drug was implanted. Others offered information to reassure her, but she concluded, "I'm overprotective of my oldest daughter. . . . I'm scared to hear her say something like that, you know. . . . I don't want to see her hurt. . . . And she's going through all these experiment things, she hears more things than I can think of you know, than I see on the news." Similarly, women in both groups repeatedly mentioned that multiple abortions could "mess up" a woman's body, perhaps making it impossible for her to bear children in the future. As another woman put it, "You hear all these stories about what happens to people."

This distrust of medical professionals extended to the doctors in the television episodes we showed. For example, one group vividly described both the contempt with which they believed the doctor viewed Ellen in *Roe vs. Wade* and their belief that doctors routinely perform illegal procedures:

FIRST WOMAN: I guess he didn't want to break the law, though, you know, because that's his license, but you know, it's just like, he had one of those . . .

"well I don't really care how you feel" attitudes, you know, I mean, it's like he could have made. . . . I mean even though. . . . I don't know, it's like he couldn't suggest [anything] besides that back-alley abortion. I'm pretty sure that he knew doctors that did some underhanded stuff under the table. He could have suggested something other. . . . I mean, it was just like he looked at her and right there figured that she ain't nothing but a slut. . . .

SECOND WOMAN: He didn't care what happened to her, [whether] she had the baby or not. [Young Mothers]

In the tone and content of their remarks, these women expressed a deep mistrust of the entire medical profession. In this their comments are reminiscent of those made by the pro-life women we interviewed (see chapter 3), but their skepticism springs from different sources. Working-class African Americans' reservations about the medical establishment may be understood in light of the fact that women from both groups claimed to have become pregnant while using contraceptives, however inconsistently. For example, one woman said she conceived her son while using "over the counter" contraceptives (spermicidal vaginal suppositories); later she was told she should have used two inserts at a time, although the package directions said to use only one. Black women's wariness may also be related to evidence that researchers have at times abused African Americans under the guise of offering them medical treatment (Jones 1981), a report that is well known in Black communities.

Indeed, some working-class Black women manifested particular distrust and even bitterness toward members of the pro-life movement. They felt that pro-life activists refused to understand the realities faced by poor and working-class women and thus were doing a grave disservice to those they counseled to carry their pregnancies to term. One young woman, a student and the single mother of a toddler, told how she had approached a pro-life organization for financial help after she gave birth to her son:

FIRST WOMAN: I was like, I don't have any money for food, I don't have any money for diapers. . . . Well, they're like . . . "you can get government assistance," and I'm like, that's not enough. . . . I said, I can't even afford to live by myself with the baby, because I was staying with my mother and I mean, even now, I have to have a roommate. . . . And then the cost of living in this area is so high because of the universities, you know, no one can live by themselves unless they're working full time somewhere. And that's hard to work. . . .

SECOND WOMAN: You need a good job.

FIRST WOMAN: Yeah, a decent job, full time, and it's hard to work full time when you have kids to take care of because you got to get full-time day care for them if they're not in school. . . . So, you know, it's hard to say, you know. I'm telling them I don't have any money for this and they're telling me to do this and do that. At that time if I went to a clinic and decided to have an abortion when I . . . was pregnant with him, and they changed my mind, because they made me change my mind, they're not there helping me. They're not doing anything to help you. All they're doing is making you have a baby that you're not sure that you want or that you're not able to take care of, you know. [Greek Organization]

She concluded, "It's hard for me to have any sympathy or to kind of, you know, understand what they're trying to do because they're not really helping anyone." Working-class Black women expressed similar hostility toward the pro-life activists depicted in the *Cagney and Lacey* episode. In the Greek Organization group, the woman who was first to speak after the tape ended criticized these activists, arguing, "I still think the people who are like picketing in front of the [clinic], they really shouldn't have done that because it was the person's choice of whether or not they could go to the clinic. Besides, going in for an abortion isn't the only thing they could go in there for." Although most women we interviewed, both pro-life and pro-choice, felt that Mrs. Crenshaw, the leader of the pro-life activists, was an unsympathetic character, women in the Young Mothers group were uniquely distrustful of her, arguing that when the police questioned her "it seemed like she was hiding something, so I did kind of think she had something to do with [the clinic bombing]."

Thus the poor and working-class African American women we interviewed were in some important ways similar to their working-class-identified counterparts: although they rarely made explicit reference to their social class membership, all distrusted societal authorities, particularly medical authorities. Although it was never addressed explicitly in our interviews, for Black women this criticism of authority may arise out of racial consciousness rather than class consciousness, which may be less salient to African American members of the working class (Gurin, Miller, and Gurin 1980).

Other comments made by women in these groups, however, more closely resemble those made by the middle-class-identified White women. Like them, poor and working-class African American women were critical of other working-class women, whom they perceived to be lazy, irresponsible, and abusing social welfare programs.

For example, some women made distinctions between those who received welfare temporarily, as a means toward independence, and those who sought to garner higher welfare checks by having many children. In one group a young woman, herself on welfare, harshly criticized Monique Davis (a pseudonym), a woman from her neighborhood, for having more children just to raise her welfare check:

FIRST WOMAN: This is just hard to believe, you know, I pay taxes for people . . . and I am on welfare, but it's hard to believe that I pay taxes for people who lay up for each year and have a kid. You got to stop somewhere.

SECOND WOMAN: But you always have a job. She [Monique] don't try to help herself. . . .

ELIZABETH COLE: This woman doesn't work at all?

SECOND WOMAN: She never works . . . she don't know what work is.

FIRST WOMAN: She never worked . . . never worked in her life. Monique has never had a job. . . . She feels her work is laying down having children, collecting welfare, that's working. [Young Mothers]

They joked harshly that this particular woman bred "like a roadrunner" and was trying to "populate Ypsilanti [a small Michigan town] with the Davis name." The group continued, expressing their opinion that the state should be able to regulate repeated childbearing by women on welfare.

ELIZABETH COLE: So, this is interesting to me. So you think . . . the government shouldn't be able to tell you whether you could have an abortion or not, but you think that after a certain point they should tell you [that] you can't have more babies?

FIRST WOMAN: Yes. Because it's like, you know . . . if you use welfare as a matter of a job, like she is, you know . . . her job is like going to the hospital and having a kid, you know, you're using. . . . Welfare's not a job, welfare to me is like a temporary source to help you out until you can do something better. And in her case, she don't want to do nothing better, she just wants to collect money. . . . Especially if you're not even taking care of your kids, you know, you let your kids run around dirty, nasty, filthy, and whatever else. I mean, yeah, I think after four kids, you know, and you still ain't got no husband and you still ain't got a job, and you're not trying to better yourself . . . yeah, why . . . don't you go ahead. . . . Why can't the state make you get your tubes tied? You know, it's better than keep having kids and it's also better than keep having abortions. [The state should] just force you to have birth control or take birth control or something besides having all those kids.

Women in the Greek Organization group made similar disparaging remarks about the sister-in-law of one of the group members, who had borne three children by age twenty-two. "Two of her sisters have five children . . . and they don't believe in birth control or abortion. . . . She's one of those that don't do anything to prevent getting pregnant, and she either keeps having kids or keeps having abortions. I think, you know, that's just, you know, irresponsible. . . . You can't just keep getting pregnant over and over again." Although this particular woman did not use AFDC to support her children, the respondent believed she had let herself become pregnant with her second child in order to "trap" the respondent's brother into marrying her. Her comments seem particularly ironic because the respondent herself had had several abortions and was now raising her toddler-age son as a single parent. However, it was clear that she saw her situation as different from her sister-in-law's because she had used contraception.

The African American working-class women brought similar attitudes to their judgment of the women seeking abortion on television. Like other working-class women, both groups were sympathetic toward *Cagney and Lacey*'s Mrs. Herrera, considering her motives for seeking abortion appropriate and unambiguous. The remarks of one woman, who watched this show as well as *Roe vs. Wade*, were typical:

> Yes, it's easy to understand Mrs. Herrera's case, I mean, you know, she had a real big flat-out opinion why she wanted to get an abortion. She wasn't trying to, you know, have everybody in the world feel sorry for her, you know, because she wanted to get an abortion, you know. When the clinic got burned down, she got up and made an appointment someplace else. [Young Mothers]

She and other women approved of Mrs. Herrera's motivation and goal directedness. Most agreed that in her place they would make the same decision. This is in direct contrast to their opinions about *Roe vs. Wade*'s Ellen, who received scorn similar to that leveled against other poor women who experienced multiple pregnancies. Working-class Black women in the group that viewed *Roe vs. Wade* found Ellen irresponsible and looking for a handout. One woman, herself pregnant with her second child at age twenty-one, remarked,

> I didn't like her. I mean I can understand the fact that she was poor and she didn't have any money, blah, blah, blah, but it's kind of like hard to understand, you know, even though I'm for abortion, it's kind of like hard to understand that she done had one child, [and] her father said he'll take, help her take care of this one, you know, and I'm pretty sure that her father is not going to lie to her. I mean, it didn't seem like he was a drunk or alcoholic or he was on drugs, I mean, he seemed like a pretty decent person, you know, at least from what I saw. And I think he would help her to take care of her, but she just have to realize that sometimes in life you have to take responsibilities.

I mean, I'm pretty sure at the time, you know, she could have thought of contraceptives or something, you know. She especially, considering that she done had a child, she should have been using something, you know, condom or whatever, you know, or abstinence or whatever. [Young Mothers]

Another summed up the group's general reaction, saying "she seemed like she was a pitiful case." They challenged Ellen's claim that she could not find a job, calling it an excuse. They speculated that her repeated appeals to doctors and lawyers stemmed from a reluctance to pay for an abortion herself and argued that she should have "caught her a job right quick" to get the money to travel to New York where abortion was legal. After all, "Things don't always be handed to you on a silver platter." Despite—or perhaps because of—the similarities between their own circumstances and Ellen's, these women found her claims of material hardship tiresome ("blah, blah, blah") rather than compelling (or even heartrending, as one pro-life woman did). Notably, the solution they offered Ellen is the same one preached to women like them by conservative politicians and pro-life activists: "condom or whatever, you know, or abstinence or whatever."

Jennifer Hochschild (1995) has argued that certain psychological rationalizations are necessary in order for poor African Americans to cling to the American dream, the myth that no matter what disadvantaged circumstances one is born to, one can achieve some amount of upward mobility through hard work. By making downward social comparisons with others who are even worse off, some can maintain the belief that they themselves may do better in the future.[8] Hochschild cites surveys reporting that up to two-thirds of poor Blacks agree that "most people on welfare could take care of themselves if they really wanted to" and that "poor young women often have babies so they can collect welfare." Indeed, poor Blacks are seven times more likely to agree that most poor people prefer government assistance to hard work than are middle-class African Americans! Hochschild argues that poor African Americans attempt to distance themselves from others who are in worse circumstances in order to maintain their own self-esteem.[9]

That these particular women cling to their version of the American dream is clear: all the college-age women in both groups were attempting to earn college degrees (or intended to do so), despite delays related to childbearing. Similarly, the oldest woman in either group, who was thirty-five and a grandmother, lamented that her unplanned pregnancy at age nineteen had prevented her from enlisting in the army and "stopped me from completing my life. . . . I'm thirty-five years old and I still don't have nothing in my life but two kids and a grandchild." Yet she blamed only herself for her current situation, noting, "It was meant for me not to have nothing in life because what I had, I throwed it down the drain." Her construction of her life story is particularly noteworthy in light of Kristin Luker's (1996) analyses suggesting that poverty is a cause rather than a consequence of teen motherhood. Luker's data suggest that poor women who bear children early in life do not have significantly different life outcomes from other women in similar social and economic circumstances who delay childbearing. Yet the respondent, like many other Americans, believed she could have overcome her poverty if she had not had a child as a teenager. Thus her comments suggest that this faith in the American dream may not come without a cost: because she believed the system allows people to achieve upward class mobility, this remorseful speaker attributed the failure of her own ambitions to what she perceived as her individual shortcomings.

It appears that the poor and working-class pro-choice Black women we interviewed may at times distance themselves from other poor women by condemning them as irresponsible and lazy. In this they are similar to the middle-class-identified working-class White women. However, there was no evidence that working-class African American women also identified with sources of professional and political authority; indeed, these women were as critical of social authorities as were their working-class-identified White counterparts.

CONCLUSION

Entertainment television readily captures both a moralistic attitude toward abortion and a rights-oriented defense of the pro-choice position in what we argue is the preferred reading of its portrayal of generally acceptable abortions. The characters of both Mrs. Herrera and Ellen Russell are painted sympathetically, as poor women who find they must make the extremely difficult decision to abort an unplanned pregnancy. These media depictions of women like themselves afforded working-class women the opportunity to respond to middle-class perspectives on working-class life and to resist these depictions by putting forth their own interpretations and evaluations of such experiences. In this way, some women constructed oppositional readings of television's narratives based on alternative notions of working-class identities.

Some working-class women recognized that their class position rendered them vulnerable to the social control imposed by legal and professional authorities. They readily described personal encounters with police, lawyers, judges, and physicians in which they felt they were unfairly judged or mistreated. These working-class-identified women feared that more restrictive abortion laws would make central control of women too easy for the authorities, whose interests are inevitably at odds with their own. Working-class-identified pro-choice respondents also opposed television depictions of the representatives of societal authority as well meaning and compassionate. They were suspicious of both the professional and family authorities Ellen comes in contact with, including the doctor, her lawyers, and her mother. In their view Ellen's salvation lies not in obeying authority and conforming to society's rules, but in learning to navigate the legal and medical systems to the best of her ability, as these women have done in the course of their own lives. Their criticisms exposed television's sanctioning of authorities' right to control the options available to poor women.

Many working-class-identified women, despite their pro-choice stance, did not personally condone abortion; however, they were reluctant to invoke societal authority to prohibit it. They were unwilling to support the power of legal and professional authorities to govern their society and their communities and to make decisions that affect their individual lives. This wariness was expressed clearly in the Landlady and Tenant group. The woman who organized this group invited her landlady and a friend. Two of the women were White, the third was African American. They ranged widely in age, from mid-forties to mid-sixties. The two younger women had low-level sales jobs, and the third was retired. One was married to a man who worked in security; the others were single. Their ambivalence was captured concisely by one respondent, who argued:

> I think the law sticks its nose in too damn many things, pardon my French, into too darn many things as is. I don't think it should be necessary to have a law on [abortion]. Because it seems to me that it's almost divisive. Of the two, I'm far more pro-life than I am anything else, but I am to some extent antiabortion. . . . I think we should be teaching more to our children about the sanctity and beauty of a soul, a human life.

Working-class-identified women challenged judges' authority to make decisions that would affect women like them living in social contexts that judges neither recognize nor respect. In the words of a woman from the Single Mothers group, "What gives me the right to tell you, just because I'm a judge setting up here. . . . [that you] can't have an abortion?" Indeed, this respondent feared that should access to abortion become more highly regulated, poor women like her might be forced to abort wanted pregnancies. On their "side of the world," such authority is more likely to persecute them than to secure their rights.

Working-class-identified women expressed a deep skepticism that justice as practiced by the courts is blind. Some offered vivid first-person accounts in which a middle-class or wealthy person was treated more leniently than they were. Others were more generally suspicious that laws, particularly those concerning abortion, are not enforced impartially:

> We don't have much of a middle class left anymore; we're getting the have-nots, a very small middle class, and the haves. . . . And it wouldn't surprise me to find that abortion . . . happens more in the wealthy people than we know. It wouldn't surprise me at all. Oh, just fly off to Rio de Janeiro for the weekend when she felt, I mean, long before the baby starts to show. And unfortunately it does tie in with money on that. . . . To some extent, there are two sets of rules there, because it takes money for an abortion, I mean, let's face it. [Landlady and Tenant]

The propensity of working-class-identified women, then, was to support policies designed to limit the authorities' reach, as do those taking the pro-choice stance on abortion. Women in these groups expressed similar distrust toward medical professionals. They did not put their faith in the notion that societal and community authorities must uphold the good. Consequently their liberal support for the right to free choice was less qualified, because they were reluctant to allow authorities any more control over their lives than the considerable amount that, in their view, they already exercise.

In contrast, other working-class women identified with these sources of social and political power. These women, satisfied that their interests were the same as those of government and professional authorities, argued to expand their jurisdiction. Their reading of television was different in content and detail from that offered by the working-class-identified women, but it was also an oppositional one. These middle-class-identified working-class women resisted the sympathetic constructions of women like themselves that pepper the mass media. Rather than acknowledging the limitations imposed by class status, they steadfastly denied the existence of any limits at all. They resisted the liberal, therapeutic worldview[10] that acknowledges with sympathy the personal problems and handicaps faced by many in American society. Instead, they embraced more conservative themes in our culture. They opposed the welfare state, insisting that government ought not rescue the irresponsible from the consequences of their actions. In their view, people should earn what they deserve by hard work and perseverance. These women endorsed generally pro-choice tenets concerning abortion, yet in a qualified way. In their view the right to abortion did not extend to unlimited freedom for women. They believed those who exercise their freedom irresponsibly ought to have that freedom curtailed. Although the middle-class-identified position represents a minority in this sample, the discourse of these women recalls the idea that the working class is inherently more authoritarian than the middle class (Lipset 1963), whose greater exposure to education has afforded a broader and more tolerant worldview (Gabennesch 1972; Grabb 1979; Middendorp and Meloen 1990).

The middle-class-identified women invoked notions of the good in their moralistic interpretation of Ellen and in their prescriptions concerning how immoral behavior ought to be controlled. This is the "communitarian" strain in their thought (Sandel 1984). Communitarianism contrasts community-based notions of what is "good" to the Kantian liberal rhetoric of "rights" most often used to support the pro-choice position in our public political discourse. A qualified, communitarian pro-choice perspective better describes these women's position than does our more customary, undifferentiated use of the pro-choice label to construct a pro-choice political subject.

The communitarian strain evident in the middle-class-identified group resonates in some ways with that displayed in pro-life rhetoric.[11] But in contrast to the utopian pro-life vision of a society in which all families are stable and each sacrifices to care for others in the human community at large, these pro-choice women were much less idealistic. They envisioned a hierarchical social order where the smarter and more able must necessarily care, however unwillingly, for those less intelligent and responsible. The burdensome qualities of the "lower" groups therefore must be contained. Their remarks suggested that if abortion, welfare, and unemployment benefits were too easily accessible, some in our society would use these resources profligately, draining the pocketbooks and compassion of those who contribute to society: they themselves and the authorities with whom they feel interchangeable.

These positions with respect to the role of authorities were reflected in responses to television as well. Working-class women were divided on the sources of Ellen's problems. Working-class-identified women who acknowledged the ways Ellen's life resembles their own placed the blame for her predicament largely on a legal system that sought to exploit her and a medical system that puts its professional interests ahead of the patient. Middle-class-identified women blamed Ellen for her careless behavior and then charged these same legal and medical authorities with imposing the control that she herself could not manage.

For working-class-identified women, their real-life experience with authorities overshadowed the images they see in media. Accustomed to continual clashes with authority, they have come to believe that their interests fundamentally diverge from the goals of those in power. Their image of themselves as "other" colors their reception of television's normative language, which paints working-class women as either powerless or striving for membership in the middle class. Their own self-image matches neither characterization and in this sense is defined in opposition to television's categories.

Other working-class women aspired to middle-class status and consequently rejected a fixed working-class identity for themselves or those in similar economic circumstances. If easy access to abortion for all women must be sacrificed in constructing this alternative identity, the middle-class-identified women were willing to pay this price, in part because they believed such draconian measures would not affect "sensible" people like them. Middle-class-identified women's responses to television images, in these instances, can be seen as evidence that they resist hegemonic interpretations of abortion dilemmas and hegemonic constructions of their own identities as subjects. But the basis for this resistance is an ultimate conformity to authoritative notions of what upward mobility, middle-class identity, and membership in the middle-class really mean. In this sense, then, working-class women in this subgroup were ultimately thwarted in their attempt to truly resist dominant meanings and definitions of their identities, their actions, and the parameters of their world.

The views expressed by the working-class pro-choice African American women we interviewed cannot be neatly captured by either the working- or middle-class-identified label. Like the former, they were critical of societal authority, particularly the medical profession, both in their own experience and in the television depictions they viewed. Like the latter, they were quick to castigate other poor women if they perceived them as unwilling to work or unable to use contraception effectively. Neither did these respondents explicitly frame their positions in terms of their social position or identity as Black Americans. Nevertheless, we argue that their views are best understood in the context of African American experience. As members of a minority group with a long history of both discrimination and resistance, it is hardly surprising that they brought skepticism to their interactions with authorities and an oppositional reading to television images of benevolent professionals (Bobo 1995; hooks 1994). However, African American culture is also rife with exhortations to overcome systemic obstacles to success through individual and collective perseverance and hard work (particularly through educational achievement; see Farley and Allen 1987). As Hochschild (1995) has observed, the belief that individuals' life circumstances are a reflection of personal merit may bolster self-esteem through downward comparison. But for other working-class Blacks this belief in the possibility of upward mobility and its corollary, that the poor are to blame for their own plight, may be a two-edged sword: without a corresponding identification with the powers that regulate a hierarchical society, some may be forced to conclude that they have failed to achieve economic success because they themselves "threw their chances down the drain."

Fraser (1989) argues that the language of needs in our culture "reprivatizes" its public dimensions, recasting the public needs of groups as the private needs of individuals. The language of working-class women we interviewed, however, resists this repackaging. The conflict between their needs as individuals and the privatization of public thinking about these needs emerges distinctly in their speech, breaking through the silence that conceals such contradictions in our society's more dominant and audible discourses, such as those of the mass media, that are accepted by the middle class. In the following chapter we discuss the ways middle-class pro-choice women invoke an ultraindividualistic therapeutic language that, to paraphrase C. Wright Mills (1959, 9), reframes "public needs" as "private troubles."

Even before we walked in the door of Diane's house, the toys strewn about the yard showed that children lived there. Her large, open family room had a comfortable disorder that made it feel welcoming and lived-in. Like the friends she invited for the interview, Diane managed to combine work and family by running a small business out of her home. Two of the other women at the session were old friends from college, and the third had been a classmate of Diane's husband in graduate school. All were in their early thirties, but they could have easily been mistaken for college students, dressed in jeans and sweaters and with their hair in ponytails. As the interview ran into the afternoon, it was punctuated by the demands of young children.

After viewing the *Roe vs. Wade* television movie, Diane compared her own situation with Ellen's, describing how difficult it had been to start her own business. "I had to pay for a certain number of hours of day care a week, and it was like, 'No, wait a minute, not only am I not drawing a salary here, I'm going in the hole.' And *I* had [my husband's] income to diddle away, you know, and then say 'hey, we're going to pay the mortgage late.' This woman had nothing."

"So, your feeling is she had no choices," Andrea asked.

Diane's friend Chris replied, "Yeah, I don't think she did."

Diane, less willing to view Ellen as helpless, said, "She had choices. . . ."
But Lori argued, "Not very many of them."

Jessica agreed, adding, "And she didn't perceive herself as having any, and so therefore she had none. . . ."

Diane clarified what she meant by choice, articulating a distinctly psychological version of the concept. "But someone in her situation who thought differently would have choices. Maybe she could have begged. [But] she wasn't a beggar. See, I think I probably would have [begged], even though I wouldn't like to see myself in that situation. I would probably sit down and beg those attorneys to take me somewhere. OK, I don't have money, [but] I'd have hitchhiked, I would have done something if I didn't want that baby." [Entrepreneurs]

Although Diane recognized that Ellen faced serious obstacles because of her background, she conceptualized these barriers in individual, psychological terms rather than seeing their systemic, social origins. Sociologists have repeatedly discussed the power of the therapeutic ethos in American culture, locating its evolution within the various strains of individualism characterizing ideological developments in this country throughout the nineteenth century (Lasch 1979, 1984; Rice 1996; Rieff 1966; Wilkinson 1988). As industrialization and its attendant economic and social changes weakened the ties that traditionally both connected people to groups and constrained their actions, social intercourse came to be constructed as taking place between autonomous individuals with few ties to others and with few guidelines to shape their behavior. As people became less scripted by traditional roles, interpersonal relations required more work and entailed more anxiety and uncertainty. Rather than being guided by group norms and social roles, interpersonal relations became increasingly centered on individuals and their qualities. Robert Bellah and his colleagues recount how in this situation, individualism came "more and more into its own, with ever weaker restraints from older biblical and republican traditions" (1985, 118).

Simultaneously, the Progressive Era's optimism about the power and potential of science influenced the rising therapeutic ethos in American society, infusing the processes of social regulation throughout the twentieth century (Brint 1994; Kirschner 1986; Kolko 1976; Weinstein 1968). One of the most significant effects of this movement toward scientizing was on the popular concept of the individual. As dominant ideas of proper socialization changed from stressing the need to inculcate correct moral values and beliefs to emphasizing the conditions necessary for development of the healthy personality, moral categories gave way to medical ones (Bellah et al. 1985; Rieff 1966). Guidelines for behavior that once were dictated by moral standards or were implicit in the notion of "character" increasingly came to be measured against an ideal of psychological health: that of the autonomous, self-esteeming individual who makes choices and sets goals at the urging of his or her own conscience, independent of the social dictates of the community, if need be (Bellah et al. 1991; Grodin 1991; Simonds 1992). This ideology assumes that the problems individuals encounter are appropriately addressed with psychological help from a professional. Through therapeutic intervention (including the support of therapists, social workers, or self-help groups), those who are unlucky or disadvantaged can be strengthened to better meet the expectations of a society predicated on the effort of, and competition between, strong, autonomous individuals.

With changing ideas about the nature of the good person came the rise and institutionalization of the therapeutic professions (Herman 1995), which many have linked to the more general development of a therapeutic ethic in our culture (Bellah et al. 1985; Rieff 1966; Simonds 1992; Veroff 1981; Veroff, Douvan, and Kulka 1981; Wilkinson 1988). The use of therapeutic language to frame ideas about individuals and personal relationships is prevalent among the more affluent and educated in our society, although it is at times invoked by members of other groups as well. Members of this segment of society in particular experience stressful demands to produce and otherwise distinguish themselves in their occupations, unaided by the support from family and other social institutions that once was available to everyone (Bellah et al. 1985; Veroff 1981; Veroff, Douvan, and Kulka 1981). Eventually the characteristics of the therapeutic association came to be seen as describing the normative relationship for women in the middle class: focused on intense emotional disclosure, isolated from the larger fabric of social connections, bounded in space and time, and contractual in nature.

Thus the therapeutic ethos asserts as its primary goal the good, or health, of the self. It is characterized, first, by its placing the goals of the self before the good of the community, and second, by its scientific orientation toward measurement, or diagnosis, of mental health. In both respects the therapeutic ethos heralds specifically modern attitudes about personal "evaluation," determining ideas about the proper relation between individuals and society. In the mass media, and in American culture generally, therapeutic discourse has been disseminated virtually without challenge (Herman 1995; Livingstone and Lunt 1994; Rapping 1996).

The middle class embodies our culture's hegemonic perspective on many social and political issues (Baritz 1989; DeMott 1990; Ehrenreich 1989). Thus it is hardly surprising that we found therapeutic language common among economically and educationally privileged women—our middle-class pro-choice groups. In this chapter we focus on their comments and note the prevalence and importance of the therapeutic outlook implicit in their language and attitudes.

The study of the middle class has particular significance given that middle-class opinions resonate with the perspectives toward abortion articulated in television representations. We argued in chapter 2 that a specific pro-choice discourse is the preferred reading of most prime-time television, one that tempers the idea that abortion is acceptable by emphasizing the tragic dimensions of abortion choices and showing only women in desperate financial straits choosing this option. Middle-class women often share this viewpoint and consequently are particularly unconscious of it in television images. This contrasts with the other groups we studied, who were more apt to recognize and criticize these encoded perspectives because television's implicit ideological stance differs from their own. It is important to understand the construction of abortion in the discourse of pro-choice middle-class women because their views reflect our culture's hegemonic position on the issue. Women's discourse in these groups reveals the workings of the insiders in our culture, the thinking that bolsters insider identity and the general logic of liberal culture.

We discerned several dominant themes in the pro-choice position as expressed by middle-class women. First, they justified the right to abortion on the grounds of individual privacy and liberty: in this their discourse is similar to that of the working-class women we interviewed and to that of television and even resembles the language of the *Roe vs. Wade* Supreme Court decision that legalized abortion. This version of the pro-choice position assumes the sovereignty of the individual against the state (as in the slogan "Keep your laws off my body").

But in contrast to their working-class counterparts, middle-class pro-choice women privileged therapeutic authority, which in one sense can be seen as social control by middle-class professionals. Therapeutic activity seeks, through contact with professional authority figures, to "strengthen" the autonomous individual by shaping him or her according to a middle-class mold.[1] Thus middle-class pro-choice women in many cases have internalized societal authority, distinguishing them from pro-life women and certain working-class pro-choice women who reject its legitimacy. Consistent with the therapeutic ethic, the middle-class version of pro-choice identifies assistance at the level of individual dysfunction as the key to helping women, rather than legislative or economic change intended to benefit women as a class.

Third, the middle-class pro-choice groups we interviewed were distinguished by the degree to which they incorporated liberal feminism into their everyday worldview, similar to current perspectives on prime-time television (Dow 1996). Of all the groups we studied, the middle-class pro-choice women were most likely to express overtly feminist sentiments. They accepted certain tenets virtually universally, particularly in discussions of abortion: women's need for autonomy from men, for example; the rhetoric of "choice" expressed as women's right to make their own decisions about their own bodies; the importance of women's education and careers; and the high value placed on women's physical and psychological health. They focused on individual rights for women, couched in the language of a more general liberal discourse based on the primacy of individual rights. In this their brand of liberal feminism showed the influence of individualistic and therapeutic beliefs as well. They invoked none of the radical discourse of group identity and feminist critique of conventional social norms heard in the language of more extreme feminist positions, which we also discerned in the speech of some working-class women. In this they echoed the early language of feminism's second wave, which—stressing that "the personal is political"—urged women to raise political consciousness by analyzing their interpersonal relations and private life. In line with a therapeutic ethos already gaining popularity among middle-class women at the inception of feminism's second wave, the categories of individual, personal life were exalted as emblematic of a new form of consciousness, with a new epistemological power.

The therapeutic-feminist ethos is a powerful analytic and linguistic tool used by middle-class women in our culture. It is present in mass media directed at women, such as the tremendously popular television talk shows, which have been widely analyzed for their individualistic-therapeutic biases (Livingstone and Lunt 1994; McLaughlin 1993). It also permeates best-selling essays and memoirs by popular feminist authors such as Gloria Steinem (1992), Jane Tompkins (1997), and Naomi Wolf (1997). This ethos strongly influences the thought and language of ordinary women, particularly those of the middle class. Our interviews with middle-class women illustrate how these forms of feminism meld with the therapeutic ethos to form a system of values and beliefs that contrasts markedly with those we discussed earlier.

MIDDLE-CLASS VERSIONS OF CHOICE

We heard the most overtly contradictory positions on abortion from middle-class pro-choice informants. These women claimed to be passionately pro-choice because "no one should tell someone else what to do" about abortion. Paradoxically, most were also adamantly opposed to abortion for themselves. This is the essence of a liberal perspective on abortion: in the abstract, each individual's *right* to have an abortion is defended, while abortion as a personal decision is categorically rejected. Although women defended abortion rights, many who believed in such rights also felt that for them abortion would be out of the question.

We encountered this logic many times in our interviews. Speaking of the marked divide she saw between the law and her personal ethics, one respondent argued:

FIRST WOMAN: I think that the law of, you know, having a law saying that "No, you cannot have an abortion," there's just no way. I mean, of course you can have an abortion, of course there should be free choice, but me personally, I could never have an abortion, I mean I just know that. That would just not be possible for me to do that.
SECOND WOMAN: I feel that way too.
FIRST WOMAN: But damn it if anybody's going to tell me I can't. [Presbyterians]

In conjunction with this firm expression of her support for abortion rights, this woman later justified her personal aversion in terms of therapeutic concerns. Abortion was not a choice she could make because "it wouldn't help her," given her "fragile" personality. This discussion, grounded in a definition of health based on individuals' unique personalities, contrasts sharply with pro-life women's expectations about the universal good health and well-being that those renouncing abortion will inevitably enjoy. Middle-class pro-choice women believe abortion must remain available to those who feel that, in their particular cases, it would benefit their health and well-being.

The relation between theory and experience, between an abstract theoretical position on abortion and concrete life circumstances, was problematic in the abortion discourse of middle-class pro-choice women.

Their concrete actions and reactions in the course of their own experience sometimes contradicted their stated theoretical viewpoints. For example, one woman who supported pro-choice laws wholeheartedly and felt it would be wrong to tell any other woman what to do described how her position *for herself at that moment* shifted the instant she believed she was pregnant:

> I did not have [an abortion], by the way, but I really did contemplate it one time when I thought I was pregnant. . . . I said, "Oh my God, I'm pregnant!" and suddenly all this nice liberal talk we'd had about "Oh sure, if we had another kid it would be fine" vanished. I wasn't worried about being pregnant, I wasn't worried about having an infant, I just didn't think I could handle the dates with the cooperative nurseries once again, and another game of Candyland. I just thought, "Oh, I just can't do this." It's the mothers, it was the tricky little mothers and these cutesy people. I just thought, "I can't do this, not at thirty-eight years old." [Presbyterians]

Yet in the next breath she weighed her reservations about the pregnancy against a list of evidence testifying that she could easily have borne and raised a new baby. "It wasn't any of those issues like the chances of bringing into the world an unhealthy child. . . . I'm really blessed with good health and I like to have kids . . . and our economic status wasn't that grim and the child would have been loved." Her analysis suggests that she didn't judge her own reasons for wanting an abortion as legitimate according to her own beliefs about what could justify that choice. She had the physical, financial, and emotional resources to raise another child and therefore was not a candidate for either medical, economic, or therapeutic help. Because she did not "need" an abortion, she evaluated her own reasons, her feeling that she "didn't think [she] wanted to handle it," as not justifying an abortion. Such an action would have been a transgression of her beliefs about abortion, and she was vaguely ashamed for having contemplated it. Yet her moral views did not prevent her from considering the option seriously when faced with her own unwanted pregnancy. The unanticipated situation demanded unprecedented decisions, and although some choices were perhaps morally unjustified to her mind, they could theoretically be defended in particular situations such as the one she had experienced. She later found she was not pregnant and was consequently spared the difficult decision. We heard many middle-class pro-choice informants navigate a seemingly contradictory course between the legal and the personal, the abstract code and the specific case.[2]

We call the middle-class pro-choice women's comfort with these apparently paradoxical positions the "shifting context of justification." These women expressed one opinion about abortion when speaking abstractly and another when discussing their own actions or experience. They repeatedly stated that abortion should be legal without restrictions. Their logic often took the following form: No one can really know what someone else is going through; therefore no one can make a valid abortion decision for another. When discussing whether abortion could ever be right for them, however, such women often said that they personally could never have an abortion, that in fact (surprisingly, given their otherwise pro-choice stance) they believed abortion was wrong. At times it would surface that they had considered abortion or even had had abortions earlier in their lives, usually when their material circumstances were different. Their logic of justification for abortion shifted, therefore, depending on whether they were discussing their own abortions, those of other women, or their own decisions at other phases of their lives.

The tension between moral reasoning at the level of the abstract and the particular recalls the work of psychologist Carol Gilligan (1982), who has often been criticized for the middle-class bias of her work.[3] She contrasted women's moral reasoning, which she characterized as privileging concern for maintaining relationships, with another form, more often seen in men, based on abstract reasoning about fairness. In our interviews, middle-class pro-choice women moved between abstract and relational levels in constructing their moral positions on abortion. Although they were firmly committed to the abstract principle of choice and the belief that abortion can be a legitimate option in specific situations, when discussing their personal choices they often retreated from this position to substitute a more relational type of logic in which abortion was construed as something close to murder. As one woman said, since the birth of her daughter, Karen, the idea of having an abortion seemed as if she would be "doing away with a Karen." [Presbyterians]

In middle-class women, then, the pro-choice opinion was often qualified. As in their attitudes toward television abortions, they rarely considered abortion legitimate for themselves and others who do not face serious material, medical, or psychological difficulties. They spoke of themselves as very different from women who were poor, very young, or under extreme psychological stress, whom they viewed as optimal candidates for abortion. They identified abortion with people who are "other" either materially or psychologically, whose existence they acknowledged but whom they spoke of as inhabiting a world far from the lives of the privileged. When they did contemplate abortion for themselves, as in the case of the older woman who found herself pregnant or the women who had abortions when young and single, the moment when that choice was made or considered was seen as "apart" from their "real" life, a temporary aberration from which their return to material or psychological "normality" was swift and the break was clean. In one middle-class woman's words, "abortion isn't a nice thing" [Presbyterians], meaning that she would consider it only if a desperate lack of alternatives precluded other choices. From middle-class women's own perspective, abortion has little place in the relatively privileged world they inhabit.

There are situations, however, that make abortion legitimate in this mode of thought. Sometimes middle-class women found themselves in such a position temporarily. In such cases, even those who considered themselves unable to make such a choice sometimes contemplated abortion. In retrospect, however, women often criticized their own situational thinking as a flawed analysis. Thus, in one of the cases cited above, although the woman made no decision because she was not actually pregnant, she analyzed her circumstances differently from the perspective of the present. Looking back, she argued that in fact she was healthy, the pregnancy would probably have gone smoothly, and having the child would really have placed no undue financial or even emotional burden on her family.

This position suggests a belief that although situations *truly* necessitating abortions do occur, they befall other people. The middle-class pro-choice women in our study felt genuine compassion for those who, in their view, might require an abortion to resolve their problems; however, it was a distanced type of compassion that did not require a close identification with the person who was its object or with her circumstances. Consequently, because their empathy for such women was so distanced, they did not apply their acceptance of abortion to themselves as well. In this way middle-class women maintained a pro-choice position in which the option of abortion remained remote, even though many had had abortions before they were married. For these women abortion never came too close, and their pro-choice philosophy was relatively abstract.

The middle-class pro-choice women we interviewed were committed to the idea that there are no hard and fast rules about the rightness or wrongness of particular abortion decisions, yet they did not believe that all such decisions have the same moral or ethical standing. Their liberalism was coupled with the strong conviction that some choices are responsible ones while others are morally ambiguous. This is a second way the context of justification of abortion can be said to be shifting. The middle-class women clung to the pro-choice conviction that abortion is a woman's right, and consequently they insisted that they could never judge another's decision; at the same time, women in many of the groups told stories of others' abortion decisions in which they felt that the pregnant woman's previous actions made her desire for an abortion morally questionable. These two attitudes existed side by side.[4] Behaviors that rendered the choice of abortion suspect included a history of unintended pregnancy, poor judgment in relationships with men, or, most often, failure to use birth control consistently. This position was expressed particularly well by the members of one group who described several abortion decisions they felt were irresponsible, including those of a friend who had not used birth control and of another acquaintance who had used it carelessly because she wanted a child but knew her husband opposed it. One woman in the group offered a more unusual example to make her point that some abortions are morally problematic:

> I actually know someone who . . . had a couple of abortions. She was a pretty freaky person. And then [she] was pregnant again, and deliberately waited because she wanted to see what it felt like to be pregnant before she got the abortion. Now that one got to me, and I do think that's where we all run up against the kind of squeamish thinking this isn't something you fool around with. This was not an all bad person, by the way, or even an all freaky person. [Presbyterians]

Even in this case the respondent defended her friend's character and her right to choose abortion. Yet it is clear that middle-class pro-choice women's staunch support for the availability of abortion does not mean they believe that every abortion choice can be justified. Yet their liberalism sometimes leads members of the same group to make statements that suggested this was so. In response to the pointed question, "Under what conditions do you believe it would be justified to have an abortion?" they replied:

FIRST WOMAN: For me personally or for my decision for other women?
ANDREA PRESS: For other women.
FIRST WOMAN: Any.
ANDREA PRESS: But for you personally the answer would be different then.
FIRST WOMAN: Yeah.
SECOND WOMAN: The whole idea of whether the embryo becomes a human, or whether it's immediate upon conception, or at birth, that's an intellectual question for me. That embryo is my child from the moment it's conceived and so I can't afford that. I don't think I felt that [during] the first pregnancy as I did the second, because part of it was that second was . . . it was really special.

ANDREA PRESS: How about you. . . .

THIRD WOMAN: I'd have to say that I'm probably against abortions like in the last trimester or so, because somehow that seems awfully rough for me. I mean you see premature babies at six months who live all the time. That seems very hard for me, but as to who could have an abortion I don't have any real restrictions at all. *I think everybody should be allowed to have one if they wanted one* [emphasis added]. I don't think it's something everybody necessarily will choose to have. [Presbyterians]

Note the similarities between the last woman's remarks and some pro-life rhetoric about the possibility that some fetuses are aborted at such a late stage of development that they could survive independent of the mother's body. The women in this group steadfastly insisted that the rules for *themselves* would be different than the rules *should be* for others. Other women should be allowed to have abortions whenever they want to in the pregnancy, for whatever reason. But these women felt that they would—and for varying reasons related to their own beliefs, should—impose more stringent restrictions on their own decisions.

A woman in another group confronted this contradiction in her own thinking even more directly:

Individuals struggle. . . . Right now, I can say, "Yeah, I would do it". . . . [But that] doesn't mean I wouldn't struggle making the decision and for years struggle over it. . . . I don't know if I was married and had two children already and, "Whoops!" . . . Maybe it would be easier then. But being single. . . . It's very hard to explain why I feel like that. But I'm absolutely 100 percent behind anybody who wants an abortion, and I can't explain why I'm so free about anybody else and not about myself. [Bowlers]

Again, for these middle-class women, an important variable in their judgment regarding the legitimacy of others' abortion choices is the emotional anguish and somber deliberations they demand that others experience in coming to such a decision. They believe abortion should not be taken lightly. Only considerable personal reflection can justify such an act.

We conducted one group interview with pro-choice activists in order to discern the ways their views were similar to and different from those of ordinary women espousing pro-choice views. Demographically they were similar to the middle-class women. In our conversations with activists, however, a markedly different position on abortion emerged. Rather than stressing the emotional pain necessarily involved in making abortion decisions, the activists minimized the need for mental suffering. Instead they argued that particular situations mandated the decision to obtain

an abortion. But like their nonactivist middle-class counterparts, they implied that in general they themselves would never be in a situation where
they would choose abortion. Although their rationale was different from
that of nonactivist middle-class women, the outcome of their arguments
was essentially the same: abortion was justifiable for other women, perhaps those who were poorer, of lower social class status, and therefore
more vulnerable than themselves; but for them, and for women in similar
circumstances, it would rarely be necessary or desirable. The activists'
attitudes recalled the research of Faye Crosby and her colleagues (1989),
which found that even in a sample of politicized feminist women who
believed strongly that sex discrimination exists, most refused to believe
they had ever been victims. As in our interview with activists, even those
who perceive social injustice may be reluctant to acknowledge that they
themselves suffer any disadvantage.

TELEVISION AS MIDDLE-CLASS RHETORIC

The middle-class pro-choice women differ from the other groups we
studied because their own perspective on abortion, deeming it legitimate
in dire financial circumstances, is closest to the perspective of the television representations they viewed—to what we argue is the preferred reading of these shows. In the programs we showed them, as in television
generally (see chapter 2), poor and working-class characters were depicted choosing abortions although the upper-middle-class protagonist
did not, even though her fetus had an abnormality that, when identified,
in reality most often leads women to choose abortion.[5] The preferred
readings of the shows we examined are very similar to the distanced,
abstract support for the pro-choice position that we discerned in the discourse of middle-class women.

Thus the pro-choice perspective seen on television was a qualified one,
paralleling the reservations many middle-class women expressed. In both
television dramatizations and the discourse of middle-class women, abortion is sanctioned in cases of extreme personal suffering, brought on
more often by material circumstances in the case of television abortions
and by emotional-psychological ones for the middle-class women and
their friends (although they can imaginatively describe all sorts of cases
that might cause such mental anguish for other women).

Irrespective of the details of their particular situations, however, each
of the protagonists in the shows was depicted as making an individual

decision, effectively unsupported by networks of friends or community or often by spouses. The social dimensions of the conditions each faced were diminished by television's simplified narrative presentation. Thus when Mrs. Herrera is shown as unable to turn to her husband and unwilling to rely on public social support such as welfare, these are portrayed as individual problems rather than those common to her social group. Ellen's itinerant lifestyle is presented as the result of her personality rather than of her lack of opportunity owing to the scarcity of affordable child care or well-paid employment for unskilled workers.

Middle-class women's responses to these representations illustrated the way they believed their own world was set apart from the spaces in which abortion was most likely to occur. In fact, it was in response to television's abortion heroines that they most fully expressed their therapeutic perspective toward less privileged individuals. Observing these characters at a distance, they focused their empathic stance on the pregnant women's personal lack of coping resources; this perspective occluded their view of the more systemic obstacles that blocked their access to genuinely free choices. Middle-class women's therapeutic orientation toward these characters paralleled television's own treatment of the issue.

Accepting the Message, Rejecting the Medium. Although middle-class pro-choice women were more likely to assert their distance from television in general than were working-class pro-choice women (though neither group was as distanced as the pro-life women),[6] their more specific comments about the content of the shows attested to their general agreement with the perspective they viewed. Television's own viewpoint, therefore, was less visible to this group than to any other, and consequently they were more likely to take these depictions at face value than were members of the other groups. They accepted television's characterization of the material reality underlying the plight of the upwardly mobile Mrs. Herrera, the less mobile Ellen, and the well-off yet indecisive Ray and Donna. Their own notions of class, power, and upward mobility paralleled those infusing these representations. Their perspective on abortion was similar as well: although few were willing to condone the act of abortion or to accept it for themselves, none were willing to condemn others for it, particularly those perceived as psychologically or materially needy. Liberal sympathy for and tolerance of—even identification with—less fortunate "others" was apparent throughout the discourse of these groups.

Although the other women we studied illustrate different types of resistance cultures with respect to television representations, the middle-class pro-choice women were a mainstream or hegemonic culture, sharing in the basic values of the media. What they viewed on television, in fact, were representations of working-class or poor women created by middle-class writers and producers. Television itself mimicked the detached sympathy with which middle-class women received its images. There was little in the content of the television portrayals that they disagreed with or felt inclined to criticize.

Rather than acknowledging the systemic differences between the heroines and women like themselves, middle-class women looked for the similarities, finding some on interpersonal, individual levels and emphasizing those in their descriptions of the television images. This enabled them to identify somewhat with the television characters. In one group, for example, a woman answered the interviewer's question about her views on Mrs. Herrera's actions by saying that if she were Mrs. Herrera she would get an abortion. Other groups echoed this reaction, talking about the problems of having an unemployed husband and of wanting to continue her education, and about how difficult it would be to manage this with a child. [Bowlers] Ellen called forth somewhat more complex reactions, as in the discussion of the Entrepreneurs, who felt empathy toward her character and her view of her choices while at the same time believing they would see more options. Yet they did not challenge the depiction of Ellen as an accurate portrayal of how a woman in her situation would have felt and acted. As one woman in the Entrepreneurs group said, Ellen "probably feels like a lot of lower-class women."

Middle-class women, although espousing many feminist values, rarely questioned the underlying values and biases of the status quo; theirs was a mainstream, domesticated feminism, on the surface fully compatible with hegemonic social beliefs about individuals and their rights. Although middle-class viewers might find Mrs. Herrera or Ellen to be strong, feminist heroines in certain respects, they did not challenge their inability to confront their difficulties by applying a broader, sociological critique recognizing the ways women are systematically disadvantaged by an inequitable social system. For example, the quotation above from the Entrepreneurs was preceded and followed by many remarks illustrating the group's overall belief that Ellen was "wrong" not to see her other options:

ANDREA PRESS: If you were in [Ellen's] position, would you have made the same decision that she did?

FIRST WOMAN: No, I would have gone to a state where they had it.

SECOND WOMAN: I would have gone to a state sometime. . . .

THIRD WOMAN: I wouldn't have said I didn't have the money; I would have found a way.

FIRST WOMAN: But she didn't have the money. . . .

SECOND WOMAN: So what, you hitchhike. . . .

FOURTH WOMAN: She hitchhiked everywhere else.

THIRD WOMAN: Yeah, but what about when she got there? . . .

Even though it was agreed that many women would see their situation just as Ellen did, overall the group felt that this perspective was mistaken, and that a rational, aware person (e.g., a middle-class one) could ferret out the hidden opportunities that did exist (although this was debated and there were some dissenting voices).

Another woman's comments illustrate the way television reflects and confirms the middle-class worldview. Comparing the show's depiction of Mrs. Herrera's struggle with that of her friend Terry, who was much more affluent, she nevertheless found the group members' indecisiveness about abortion to parallel the themes of the show:

> Well a lot of [the *Cagney and Lacey* show] was sort of the same things we were saying before we even watched it. And even Cagney was saying, sure she's pro-choice, but she says, "I'm also pro-life." I mean [Mrs. Herrera's] having the same kind of a struggle that [our friend] has. . . . [It's the] same thing Terry said, she's pro-choice, but if it were her [who was pregnant] it would be a hard decision. [Bowlers]

This woman recognized herself and other members of the group in the show. What particularly sparked this identification was the way abortion dilemmas, and the characters' struggles with them, are framed.

Of special interest was a scene in which Cagney and Lacey argue in the police locker room. Cagney, who was raised Catholic, maintains that although she is pro-choice ("I've never lived my life any other way"), she is also pro-life. Lacey pressures her, saying, "Are you on everybody's side?" insisting that women must take a stand on this issue. Four out of the five women in the Bowlers group noted that they identified much more with Lacey's character than with Cagney's (the fifth didn't identify with either). Cagney's doubts about abortion, framed in religious terms, seemed foreign to them. Almost paradoxically, they all emphatically disagreed with Lacey's admonition that "you have to take a stand on [abortion]." The women agreed that the issue is not one on which women must take some firm, specific stand, except in personal, individual terms—as one woman put it—if a woman is pregnant and has to decide about abortion. They were quite comfortable with its portrayal as something about which women experience conflicting emotions and make conflicting judgments.

A member of the Presbyterians group also firmly disagreed with Lacey's remark as she defended her own position of being both pro-choice and, in some ways, pro-life: "I think that's very descriptive of the way I feel, and I really resent the pro-life movement for saying that I'm not pro-life by being pro-choice." Other members of the group supported her. One respondent said that probably a woman should make a decision about abortion before pregnancy has progressed to the point of fetal viability, but she qualified even this opinion, noting that there may be legitimate exceptions:

> But there are a few times when the fact [is], that a woman might get to the sixth month and for reasons I don't know, they need to make a decision to have an abortion. They ought to be able to make that decision. . . . I just think that decision is so personal and even though it might not seem so anguishing to me, it could easily be that for the woman who is having the abortion. It's not my right to make that choice.

Another group member immediately chimed in with an example of a legitimate exception, illustrating the pro-choice women's unwillingness to make any hard and fast rules about which decisions were right and which were wrong:

> That makes me think of a friend of a friend who went into kidney failure late in her pregnancy. I think she actually miscarried before they took the baby, but it's one of those things you can't predict, and you're right you can't just say, well, never after a certain point, because there are always those cases.

The convergence of middle-class pro-choice women's shifting context of justification for abortion with the perspective offered by television became evident more generally in their responses to the heroines in the shows they watched. Unlike the pro-life women and many of the working-class pro-choice women, they refused to condemn either Mrs. Herrera or Ellen, finding valid reasons for each to choose abortion. In fact, women often compared their own situation favorably with those of the television characters, looking sympathetically at the difficulties they faced. One woman, for example, painted Mrs. Herrera of the *Cagney and Lacey* episode as almost a role model for independent, feminist women, noting her autonomy and independence as a Catholic woman from a traditional background seeking an abortion in secret:

I think she was a pretty rare individual to break away from her religious and her family convictions to even go to the clinic in the first place. I think that she would be a very, very small percentage of the type of woman who would go to a clinic. As she was saying, all of her friends were pregnant at her age, and then they never went anywhere from that point because they were always home with the kids. [Sisters]

The group of mothers who worked at home supported Ellen's desire for an abortion in *Roe vs. Wade.* They had the following dialogue over Ellen's decision:

ANDREA PRESS: Well, do you think she should have had an abortion. . . . Ellen?
FIRST WOMAN: Absolutely.
SECOND WOMAN: Absolutely should have had the right.
THIRD WOMAN: She really wanted one.
FOURTH WOMAN: She didn't ask you that, she said do you think she should have had it.
THIRD WOMAN: Because she wanted one, she should have had one.
SECOND WOMAN: Yes, yes. . . . She should not have had to go through giving up a second child. It had already ruined her life that she gave up the first one, she should not have had to go through it again.
FIRST WOMAN: And anybody with that kind of self-insight, who knows where their limits are that clearly, I mean, I think she made a perfectly healthy decision. [Entrepreneurs]

One woman in the group went on to deny that the abortion was justified by Ellen's material circumstances. Rather, it was Ellen's "state of mind"— that she perceived herself as having no choices and thought having the child would ruin her life—that legitimated her desire: "It wasn't her situation, it was her state of mind. It was how she felt about it and the fact that she definitely wanted [the abortion]." Almost simultaneously, though, the group debated whether Ellen had acted too irresponsibly, and with too little forethought, to deserve an abortion, even though her desperate wish for one was obviously sincere. Here the respondents disputed whether Ellen had acted responsibly and became pregnant through no fault of her own or whether she had carelessly failed to use birth control. In this exchange, the context of justification for abortion shifted yet again in a different sense; the group supported Ellen's right to an abortion at the same time that they were skeptical about whether her past behavior legitimated her current choice. The group members seemed untroubled by this contradiction.

Women in the same group had a complex discussion about whether Ellen could have found other ways to obtain a legal abortion. Several argued that they would have hitchhiked to a state where abortion was legal. Another intervened, questioning whether Ellen really did have other choices, given her limited financial resources and lack of social support:

FIRST WOMAN: Yeah, I mean, just like her class . . . her lack of money, the fact that she was poor, practically a vagrant, you know, eliminated her having any choice at all, not only about having [an abortion] in her state, but also somewhere else. I mean, when I paid for my friend's abortion, she had to go to New York, it took five or six of us, and we were teenagers, pulling together.

SECOND WOMAN: But that's my point, [your friend] had no money, but she found a way.

FIRST WOMAN: She found a way because she had friends around her. . . .

FOURTH WOMAN: You don't know what it is. . . . I mean, I don't think any of us know what it is to not have family, to not have income, I don't think we can put ourselves in her place. . . . The only thing that I could totally relate to with her was the rage; you could just see it.

Generally, the women felt empathy toward Ellen. Some thought that if they were confronted with the same circumstances they might have found other options; however, they were unwilling to condemn Ellen, recognizing that her social class and family background were unfamiliar to them and may have set limits they had not experienced. Although at several points the conversation veered dangerously close to a negative judgment of Ellen's decision, unlike the working-class pro-choice women this group quickly moved away from this condemnation. They checked their impulse to judge someone so different from them and kept themselves open to the most sympathetic interpretation of her actions. In this respect middle-class pro-choice women's therapeutic orientation toward poor or working-class television heroines was evident.

Others could not read the show as a representation of reality, because its terms were confounded by the easily recognizable stereotypes characteristic of television entertainment. One woman talked about how distracting she found the exaggerated dramatics of the *Cagney and Lacey* episode:

I was watching it as someone who is sort of interested in drama, and all these television shows are sort of pared down and everything is pretty stereotyped, and so it was all pretty predictable. It was sort of hard for me. . . . Well, we're getting away from the issue of abortion and into the issue of art. And this kind of sitcom [*sic*] sort of has to have a dramatic ending and has to have its dilemmas. . . . There's nothing very subtle about this show. And, ah, that isn't really, it doesn't really deal a whole lot with how people really deal, or how one really deals with the issue of abortion. Things do not get resolved by a nutty lady trying to blow somebody up and a pregnant lady sacrificing so. . . . I kept getting caught up in the sort of all too overt presentation of the issues. [Presbyterians]

For her, this overstatement prevented any real involvement with the characters' supposed dilemmas; she even found it hard to assess the show's treatment of the abortion issue.

Therapeutic Attitudes. Other studies have shown that middle-class women highlight the emotional in their responses to entertainment television (Brown 1994; Heide 1995; Press 1991b). Similarly, the middle-class women we spoke with attended to the emotions depicted in the programs we showed them, and their responses often privileged emotional concerns. One example is the woman quoted earlier who identified with Ellen's rage. Another said that for her the highlight of the *Cagney and Lacey* clip was the part where Lacey, in an intimate conversation with her husband, describes her feelings about the abortion she had in her youth. She stated, "I guess that just the nicest piece of the whole show for me was her talking about her own experience and her own feelings about that [her abortion]."

This emotionality of response lent itself to a distinctively therapeutic attitude toward the heroines of the stories. Although they often acknowledged that these working-class characters' problems stemmed from a lack of financial resources, they just as often located their source in the characters' personalities: these women needed professional help.

The character of Ellen in the *Roe vs. Wade* movie evoked the most directly therapeutic responses. Because Mrs. Herrera aspires to middle-class status and has definite plans for attaining education and employment, middle-class informants were comfortable attributing her plight to external circumstances, such as her husband, her extended family, or cultural norms prohibiting abortion. Notably, not a single group raised the possibility that Mrs. Herrera had failed to use birth control or was in some other way personally to blame for her unwanted pregnancy.

The circumstances surrounding Ellen's life and her abortion dilemma are presented quite differently. She lives a rather itinerant life, floating aimlessly from one job to the next, with no definite plans for improving her situation. What is shown is her frustration and helplessness because she cannot find and hold a stable job. She wants an abortion not because she believes it will help her better herself, but because she feels entirely unable to care for a child in these economic circumstances.

Ellen's situation called forth a decidedly therapeutic response from middle-class pro-choice women. In contrast to the working-class pro-choice women, who often showed disbelief over Ellen's complaints about her unsuccessful job search, the middle-class women spoke of aspects of Ellen's home environment that contributed to her low self-esteem. Many mentioned the poor treatment she seemed to receive from her mother, as did this woman in the group of work-at-home mothers: "I was shocked by her mother in the first scene. She obviously wasn't raised in an environment that esteemed her or helped her to feel that she was going to go somewhere or do something." [Entrepreneurs] Women doubted that Ellen's daughter Cheryl could be receiving adequate care from such an abusive parent. Based on their view of her mother, they suggested that Ellen must certainly have suffered a difficult upbringing, and they believed this had contributed to her facing "some very hard choices" in adult life. These attitudes contrast sharply with those of the working-class and pro-life women, several of whom criticized Ellen's lack of respect toward her mother.

Although many middle-class women believed that in Ellen's place they would make other choices and would perceive more options and opportunities, they were reluctant to criticize Ellen for painting her own alternatives as so limited. The Entrepreneurs phrased their comments in particularly therapeutic language, noting that "[Ellen] didn't perceive herself as having any [choices] and so therefore she had none," in marked contrast to responses from nearly all of the working-class and pro-life women.

Others talked about Ellen's material problems, pointing out the social barriers that faced a woman of her class in the 1970s. Yet even this discussion concluded with a focus on Ellen's personality:

> You said she had some choices. Well, in 1970 women were really just starting to come out strongly to the workplace. There really was not that much opportunity for somebody of her social standing. . . . Now if she had gone to Sarah Lawrence and gotten a degree, yeah, she would have been out there with the Gloria Steinems of the world, but *she wasn't that kind of a person* [emphasis added], so it's a little bit different. [Entrepreneurs]

This remark reiterates the common idea that there are "kinds of people," and that one's "type" determines or limits one's behavior. Often this thinking seemed to us a shorthand for a conscious terminology of social class groups, which was rarely expressed explicitly.

In sum, a therapeutic language, which supports the shows' preferred readings, dominates the way middle-class pro-choice women perceived the heroines of television abortion dramas. Although women carefully distinguished their own circumstances and personality characteristics from those of the characters facing abortion decisions, they nevertheless remained unwilling to criticize or condemn those characters, even though their actions were very different from what the women felt their own responses might be. Instead, they responded empathically to the depiction of these women in difficult circumstances. They described the characters with sympathy and sometimes attributed their need for an abortion to the low self-esteem caused by their early lives. This treatment of abortion was consistent with middle-class women's general attitude that although abortion should be legal because many women face trying material and psychological conditions, they often could not envision themselves ever being in such desperate straits that an abortion would seem necessary.

Thus the pro-choice stance of middle-class women is a tempered one, in which they carefully distance themselves from those women, usually lower class, who may feel they need to choose abortion. According to this position such women need help, not criticism or judgment. These attitudes support and legitimate the therapeutic orientation of the entire helping establishment that often intervenes in the lives of poor women—from social workers to clinic staffers to psychological professionals, who are often themselves middle-class pro-choice women similar to those we interviewed. Although such professionals often mitigate the distress of particular women, a more systemic analysis of their plight in socioeconomic or feminist terms may be sacrificed to individualistic analyses and solutions.[7]

When the working-class women we interviewed used therapeutic language, the speaker was usually someone whose life had been touched in some way by helping professionals. Thus the Cousins, who had both been in psychotherapy, at times talked in therapeutic terms, as did the Nontraditional Students, several of whom had also had therapy. One woman from the latter group, who had gone back to school for a bachelor's degree in counseling and planned to become a therapist, explained that Ellen "had tons of options, but she didn't believe she had them, so it doesn't matter." Later in the interview she used even more explicitly therapeutic language in discussing the movie:

What I believe is that women themselves . . . we have a lot more options than . . . once we feel a certain way about ourselves, the whole world opens out in a different kind of way and we see options that we didn't see before and choices that we can make that protect us from decisions that aren't the best decisions, I guess, is how I see it. But if that person doesn't believe they have all these options, it's like my counseling battered women. There are options available, but if they don't believe . . . and if they're not ready to . . . if they're not at a certain place to work or to move in those directions, there are not options for them. . . .

Another woman in the group seconded this vision of reality as perception driven: "Well, it's their own reality, what their own reality . . . how they perceive their reality is how their reality really is." The first woman continued speaking in therapeutic terms about Ellen's life, labeling the lawyers' intervention with the term empowerment. That these groups incorporated therapeutic discourse into what is an essentially working-class experience of the world is testimony to the power of the helping professions when their practitioners intervene in the lives of working-class women.

CONCLUSION

Middle-class pro-choice women's relation to television in particular, and to our culture in general, is distinctive: insiders rather than outsiders, they are unlikely to see themselves as challenging the status quo. Instead, whatever political passion they display derives from their adherence to the individualistic principles they believe underlie our society. Alone among the groups we studied, they are the true believers in our system, supporting its hegemonic values. Although this status may make them less motivated to work for political change, we speculate that they nevertheless might be politically mobilized more easily than members of the pro-choice working-class groups, whose outsider status leads to a more alienated group identity. We speculate that women's outrage at the violation of rights they confidently expect to be granted could become a salient force. Yet their potential for political mobilization has its limits, as long as their perspective masks the contradictions between liberal ideals of freedom and equality and a society increasingly splintered along the lines of race, class, and often gender privilege.

Middle-class women's adherence to a feminist outlook and to the tenets of therapeutic thought reinforces their inability to move from an individual level of analysis to one based more on group position. Their tendency to view the dilemmas of television's abortion heroines as individual predicaments resulting from accidents of fate rather than from the characters' membership in less privileged social groups made it unlikely that any critical social analysis would enter into their discussions. Indeed, there was little evidence of such analysis in their assessment of these characters. Instead, they tended to focus on their qualities as individuals with whom they could empathize (though from a distance) and to whom they could offer advice based on an underlying therapeutic feminist ethos valuing individual empowerment and strength, particularly for women, and even more particularly for women facing such distinctively feminine dilemmas.

Middle-class pro-choice women's discourses well illustrate some of the most contradictory aspects of the ways the academy is currently characterizing the liberal/communitarian debate and, more generally, debates about the public sphere, its conversations, and the possibility of consensus. The middle-class women express a type of liberalism Christopher Lasch has described as interested in protecting privacy rather than in ensuring that acts done privately are in accord with the public good (1988, 183–84). According to Lasch, this discrepancy is the main problem with liberalism as it is practiced in our society. The dilemma expressed by many of the middle-class women we spoke with illustrates their problem in finding words capable of expressing a judgment about what takes place in individuals' private lives. Although they firmly believe that every woman should have the right to choose an abortion, or not to choose one, they argue with equal passion about whether a particular decision is "correct" or "wrong." Yet their liberal language gives them no vantage point for connecting these two perspectives. They argue a radical position of individual choice that it is clear they do not fully embrace when it is moved from the abstract level and applied to an issue as concrete as particular abortion decisions, taking place in specific circumstances. They shun the vocabulary of consensus in their "public" rhetoric, protesting that there is no problem, that many people believe as they do, and that their position is ultimately coherent. Yet they find themselves searching for the consensual grounds of their belief in the "private" language they invoke to discuss their own lives and those of other real people they know. In the end, they argue that in each case there are right and wrong abortion decisions, but that rightness or wrongness can be determined only by the individuals who make these decisions. In their view, only a woman choosing abortion can determine whether the decision is "right," and the legitimacy of her judgment—applying to her case alone—is not generalizable.[8]

These stresses and contradictions within the middle-class discourse expose a fault line in the logic of legitimation underlying the pro-choice movement in the United States. Certainly the need to attend to the considerations that undermine unity among pro-choice advocates has become apparent in recent years, as pro-life forces have gained ground in ongoing political struggles. Ultimately, we hope this book will be useful both to those seeking clarification of American women's political rhetoric, on abortion and other issues, and to those seeking direction in the political struggles surrounding abortion. In our concluding chapter, we discuss the ways this book more fully contributes to and, we hope, illuminates this debate.

The abortion issue encompasses a spectrum of concerns ranging from women's relation to their own bodies and reproductive processes to their more general relation to various institutions of power and authority in our society. We argue that it is this latter aspect of abortion—the way the issue helps to develop ordinary women's sense of their relation to structures of power—that has been ignored in discussions of women's abortion opinions. The previous chapters explored how discourses of authority permeate television's representations of abortion and women's discussions of the issue. This analysis revealed many ways the abortion issue implicitly taps our culture's attitudes toward social hierarchies, the rights of individuals, and the legitimacy of authority. In our interviews, women's discussions of abortion quickly transcended the issue itself, opening out onto these broader themes, particularly in response to the television treatments of abortion they viewed. Yet women differed widely in the concerns that preoccupied them and in their critiques of the abortion controversy and its depiction in entertainment television.

Today the mass media are active participants in our social conversations about political and cultural matters, influencing our ideas, opinions, and values. Individuals engage in public dialogue not only with other citizens but also with these mass media representations, and television plays a powerful role in these debates (Fiske 1987; Gitlin 1980, 1983). Consequently our informants' readings of television's treatment of abortion helped us understand both the ways they made sense of the issue and the ways different women see themselves in relation to the political and cultural mainstream. In the preceding chapters we have attempted to convey the concerns that animated groups distinguished by both socioeconomic status and ideology (pro-life and pro-choice). In this concluding chapter we briefly summarize our analysis and then take a step back to make broader comparisons across groups. Finally, we speculate about the implications of this study for the future of the abortion debate.

READING TELEVISION'S CLASSED SUBTEXT

We have argued that television depicts abortion as a classed issue in which some women, lacking social support and money, are depicted as worthy candidates for abortion while others, rich in these resources, are regularly spared such decisions through manipulation of the story line. In this construction of abortion, those who produce entertainment television present a worldview in which financial reality defines individual choice in a deterministic way, dictating the spectrum of available alternatives and serving as perhaps the most important consideration in evaluating which of the options is most appropriate.

Pro-Choice Women. Pro-choice women differed in their readings of this subtext. Because their life circumstances often closely matched those of the destitute heroines of these television treatments, many working-class and poor pro-choice women offered oppositional readings of the text. They were quick to criticize these representations of women as helpless victims with little choice or agency in their own lives. They rejected scenarios in which the protagonist was presented as incapable of raising a child, and they were particularly critical of characters who saw lack of money as a reason for abortion. They were personally well acquainted with the options available to poor and working-class women and understood that choice may mean selecting options others find distasteful. As one working-class young mother asserted derisively: "That excuse about she didn't want to be on welfare? Well, what makes you better than everybody else?" [Young Mothers] This rejection of television's class-based version of choice, expressed by many working-class women, constituted a powerful critique of the middle-class worldview in which rational actors strive for upward mobility.

One working-class woman with pro-choice views poignantly expressed a sense that the divergence between life on the screen and her own family life sprang from discrepant worldviews. "If we were the type of people, it's hard to talk about . . . if we were the type of people that came from the Ozzie and Harriet type family, you know, our whole issues and beliefs would be different. You know, I'm sure." [Single Mothers] She was troubled by television's inability to represent her own experience, and her comment conveyed impatience with the medium. Her remark was made during a longer discussion in which she defended her decision to have children even though she was not married and therefore was not part of a traditional family. Her own mother, who had married an abusive man, had been compelled by economic hardship to work outside the home while her children were growing up. Vowing never to repeat her mother's mistakes, this respondent had forgone opportunities to marry, and she elected to stay home with her own children even though it meant collecting welfare payments. For her, television families like those on *The Ozzie and Harriet Show* were a vision of a "normal" life that she had never experienced or even witnessed at first hand.

Our findings regarding working-class women's views build on conclusions made in Andrea Press's earlier book (1991b). She found that working-class women accepted television's depiction of middle-class life as "normal," and as normative, in that many made a middle-class lifestyle a goal of their own lives. In contrast to middle-class women,[1] working-class women in Press's earlier study valued what they defined as "realism" in television, and they judged images of middle-class life to be acceptably lifelike. But they were extremely critical of television depictions of the working class, judging them unrealistic. Consequently it came as no surprise that many working-class women we interviewed rejected television images of women making abortion decisions, permeated as they are with television's particular focus.

Pro-choice working-class women, who more often than not are the heroines of television's abortion narratives, become accustomed to what they see as television's misrepresentation of their world. This ensures their critical reception of these stories and their position as "other" to those most often depicted. Their attitudes toward authorities, particularly those representing the legal system, are those of outsiders as well; these attitudes constitute the crux of their oppositional reading. Fearful that their rights and interests will not be safeguarded, many working-class women carve a path for themselves through the injustice they have come to expect. Forced to confront this continual prejudicial treatment, some construct an identity that stridently acknowledges their status as outside what is universally respected.

However, not all groups of working-class women shared this critical stance toward middle-class values and the social authorities that enforce them. Women taking a position we termed middle-class-identified similarly objected to television's portrayal of working-class women as powerless and disadvantaged victims; like their working-class-identified peers, they rejected these depictions. But middle-class-identified women felt that those who carelessly engage in unprotected sex ought to pay for their errors, that they should not be allowed to depend on the state to solve problems they themselves have created. Their support for the prochoice perspective was qualified by their fear that granting irresponsible women too much freedom and support would perversely enable destructive behavior. They responded to the television they viewed by criticizing the working-class characters rather than the media depictions themselves. Their readings were in some ways close to what we argue are the preferred readings of the television texts, yet they were inflected with their own concerns given the status anxieties particular to their situation.

Similarly, middle-class women did not object to the content of the television episodes we showed them. Indeed, their comments demonstrated that they took this content largely at face value and that their own interpretations also concurred closely with what we argue are the preferred readings of the texts. Their critiques were external to content, focusing on television as an artistic medium. As one woman complained, "It isn't that I don't think the issues brought up [by the show] are not real issues. It was just that watching them in this situation you [can] call all of them, you could kind of call what the screenwriter was going to write, and that was interfering for me, in dealing with the issues of the show." [Presbyterians] Considering herself a discerning viewer, she analyzed the form of the medium, disparaging its formulaic predictability. Yet her comments do not imply a similar distance from television's content, which, as the creation of middle-class writers, producers, and others, mirrors many of her most basic values and perspectives. Critiquing the medium rather than the message, this respondent illustrates that prochoice middle-class women have the least problematic relation to cultural authority because they are most closely identified with it. Almost paradoxically, they also have perhaps the most complex relation to television of the three groups we examined. Rejecting the medium as predictable and repetitive, they nevertheless turn the least critical eye on its treatment of the abortion issue and its characterization of women making abortion decisions.

Instead, many middle-class pro-choice women asserted that the material poverty of television's working-class heroines had stunted their psychological outlook, limiting them as surely as any tangible obstacle. As one middle-class woman said of Ellen in the *Roe vs. Wade* movie, "She didn't perceive herself as having any [choices], and so therefore she had none." [Entrepreneurs] They asserted that the television characters needed some type of therapeutic intervention, which might strengthen their self-esteem and possibly help them rationally accept the limits to their choices posed by poverty or encourage them to "better" themselves through education or training.

Pro-Life Women. Pro-life women take a critical and distanced stance toward the dominant values represented on television. In effect, they constitute an alternative culture. Because the pro-life vision of the world, which includes utopian hopes that families and communities can come together to support women in need, is essentially absent from television, these women feel excluded by its images, as they are in so many ways excluded from mainstream society in the United States. Their absence on television and in other widely disseminated societal narratives fosters their general rejection of accepted hierarchies and of the powerful, encouraging them to turn to other sources of authority. Consequently they seek alternatives to mainstream mass media and to societal authorities generally. Their approach is well illustrated by one woman who keenly criticized the class- and race-specific dimension of television representations of abortion. "Right at the beginning of the show they showed this poor little old Spanish girl," she said. "It's always poor little Spanish girls that get pregnant. It's never, you know, middle-class White girls like my friend Melissa." [Baby-Sitters] In this she displayed her dissatisfaction both with television's pro-choice bias, as she perceived it, and with the classed dimension through which this bias is customarily expressed. Her comment also revealed her fundamental detachment from television as she chided the medium for its customary misrepresentation of issues important to her.

In contrast to the very different perspectives of working-class and middle-class pro-choice respondents, pro-life groups representing disparate economic circumstances engaged in markedly similar discussions of the abortion debate and mainstream media treatments of the issue. Pro-life women of different socioeconomic status also expressed comparable values concerning the appropriate attitudes toward earning and spending money. Whatever the economic circumstances of their own households, pro-life women felt strongly that their family income should not be spent thoughtlessly to gratify frivolous desires. Instead, they were acutely conscious of the power of money to support businesses and institutions that furthered their religious values, and they presented themselves as prudent custodians of that resource. One middle-class woman, married to a man with a professional career, expressed this conflict:

> I just bought new carpeting . . . and [I wondered] did I spend my money on the right thing or should I have given it to this cause or should I have put it in the bank or should I have done this kind of thing? You know, we're all Christians and I guess I feel free to say that we're fairly conservative and we believe in tithing, you know, and giving our money to church and helping people when they need it. And now, when you go around and buy things that are nice to have, you always wonder, "Well is this something I really truly needed to spend the money on, or am I just indulging my own personal whim?" [Stay-at-Home Mothers]

In another group composed of working-class women who became friends through their church, a single woman who had worked as a file clerk but now supported herself on disability payments made a similar argument about why she chooses not to go to the movies:

> What it comes down to is . . . when we go to the movie, where's our money going to when we pay the theater. . . . Where's it going to? Is it going to a good movie or are they going to make a movie perverted and all this and that? I guess that's what . . . the preachers and everything, they get down on, because where is that money going? You know, instead of putting my money in something like that, I want to put it to a good cause. [Pentecostals]

Although the first woman ponders how to make the best use of several hundred dollars while the second is concerned with a much smaller sum, these pro-life women of different class backgrounds express strikingly similar concerns.

Many of the pro-life women of both classes we spoke with had money problems, often because women with young children chose to stay at home rather than to work outside it. Nevertheless, many mentioned that they regularly donated to religious and pro-life groups. They were committed to marshaling whatever resources they could to support these organizations because they felt that their own values and way of life not only were remote from the mainstream but were under assault from secular society and consumer culture. A Catholic pro-life woman expressed this view poignantly:

The bias is so overwhelming. . . . I think pro-life [people] tend to hold a whole array of values together, and a lot of those values are under attack from all different directions, not just the pro-choice direction. You just kind of feel like you really have a hard time, feeling like you just have to fend for your values in every direction. [Christian Community Group]

Because pro-life women have consciously decided to reject the dictates of secular consumer culture, their views were not differentiated by socio-economic class. Among the pro-choice, certain working-class women were similarly well aware that they live outside the commercial culture depicted on television, in which patterns of consumption are among the most valued forms of personal choice (Giddens 1991; Warde 1994). Thus their reception of television's version of abortion, in which choice is justified primarily by economic desperation, was markedly different from that of pro-choice women who enjoy middle-class privileges. Although many middle-class pro-choice women expressed their misgivings about entertainment television as an art form, they did not level the same kinds of criticism as did pro-life women and certain working-class women because the worldview presented closely mirrored their own. Yet even though the groups we interviewed brought very disparate readings to the classed subtext of these abortion stories, they all responded to television's implicit framing of the issue as primarily concerned with an individualistically based and economically driven version of choice.

LIBERALISM VERSUS COMMUNITARIANISM

Broader debates between liberalism and communitarianism help make sense of these different ways of thinking about abortion. In particular, they help us understand the importance that different groups of women placed on notions of individual rights relative to traditional community standards and clarify their concerns about the appropriate roles of various types of social authority. Earlier we argued that our interviews shed light on the fissures naturally occurring in the various structures of authority that constitute our society; framing our findings in terms of the liberal/communitarian debate reveals the specific locations of these potential challenges as well as the ways women of different social class backgrounds make sense of, and at time struggle to confront, the authorities that govern their lives.

Certainly the pro-life women best exemplify communitarian thinking as discussed by a variety of theorists (Barber 1984; Bellah et al. 1985;

MacIntyre 1984; Reynolds and Norman 1988). Pro-life women invoked spiritual and correspondingly scientific authority to justify their basic antiabortion orientation. Overwhelmingly, pro-life women identified with this vision of their community and maintained that its standards were justified by the authorities they deferred to. Such a vision made it difficult for their objections to be generalized into a principle that might lead to a more radical, essentially critical perspective.

Occasionally pro-life women recognized the desirability or necessity of abortion in certain cases where women faced overwhelming hardship. One such incident occurred when a group of otherwise staunchly pro-life women viewed *Roe vs. Wade.* In discussing the television clip, one woman in the group said that Ellen probably should have the abortion because she so dreaded giving up another child for adoption. [Suburban Group] Such instances were rare in our interviews, but they occurred often enough to prove that community standards mandating a stance against abortion were not total for everyone in the community and were not closed to criticism in particular cases. However, the shocked reaction of other group members immediately showed that to them this opinion was outside acceptable bounds. The incident quickly passed, and of course we do not know whether the speaker would have defended this position against sustained criticism by others in her social world. No one, including the woman herself, generalized this critical perspective. It was offered as an exception, a worst-case example of the possible limited acceptability of abortion in some truly outlying cases, a case to be passed over quickly with no lasting impact on their thinking about abortion decisions generally.

The homogeneity of the pro-life perspective we encountered contrasts dramatically with the heterogeneity we found among women endorsing the pro-choice position. We heard several varieties of pro-choice arguments in our interviews, corresponding to women's social class positions in both a material and a subjective sense. The pro-choice working-class women, as a whole, stood in contrast to the pro-life women, who were actively constructing a community, with its own alternative authorities, as the source of their standards and beliefs. The former derived their identities not from identification with a real community, but from the way they saw themselves in relation to the wider society. Two types of identities were invoked by women in this category. That of working-class-identified pro-choice women was theoretically based on opposition to dominant authority. In this respect the working-class pro-choice women drew on their experience to generate a critique of what they saw as the mainstream society and the authorities that maintain it. Their sense of identity was inherently connected to their sense of being "other" to the authorities regarded as legitimate by the larger culture; but unlike that of the pro-life women, their identity was not connected to any real community. These women were more likely than members of other groups to have fallen through the cracks of society in their marginal work lives and their material status, and they used this outsider vantage point to construct an identity that questioned authority and sought to navigate outside it. For them the pro-choice stance was based on this general opposition to authorities that might encroach on them. Their experience was permeated with cases where the institutions of liberal society failed to make good on their stated ideals; they recounted stories in which judges treated them unfairly or school authorities penalized their children but not others. These experiences helped them construct a position in some ways individualist, as when they challenged the right of authorities to regulate their personal behavior, and in others communal, as when they talked about the perspectives shared by people in "their side of the world."

The individualist aspects of their identity drew on the dominant language of individualism, though the communal standards implicit in this thinking broke through some of the limitations of individualist thought. These women were aware of a need to protect the voice and autonomy of individuals and groups falling outside the approval of generally sanctioned authorities. This concern was reflected in their responses to television's abortion heroines, as they recognized a social space very familiar to them. They objected to the way these women were pictured largely through the lens of individualism. They at times recognized that this view was biased, often invoked in judgment against people like them, and they richly objected to the unfairness of these criticisms.

The "us against them" orientation that often surfaced among working-class-identified pro-choice groups paradoxically offers a strong potential for group solidarity, similar to that found among the pro-life women, who considered themselves outsiders as well. But the latent cohesion of this group is largely unrealized. The capacity for political activism among the segment of the population these groups represent has been largely overlooked by pro-choice activists seeking to broaden their base of support; yet it may be difficult to politically mobilize these women, given the exigencies of their lives (Fried 1990).[2]

Women taking the middle-class-identified position invoked their own vision of community as well. Such women, however, envisaged a society in which government authorities closely guarded women's access to abortion and made the final decisions. They felt that the community from which they derived the basic character of their identity was sanctioned by authorities generally recognized as legitimate by the broader social system. Their strength lay in their confidence that many aspects of this identity, as they expressed it, are dominant in our society. Pro-life women felt strongly the community-based nature of their standards as well; but they also felt keenly the outsider status of this community, which was evident in that many of their practices were designed to navigate the broader culture. The middle-class-identified women also differed from the pro-life women in that their standards of belief and evaluation stressed the liberal tenet of individual responsibility. In this way their thinking drew more on the dominant language of liberalism than on the community-based standards of communitarians.

Finally, the discourses of pro-choice middle-class women well illustrate some of the most contradictory aspects of the ways the academy is currently characterizing the liberal/communitarian debate and, more generally, debates about the public sphere, its conversations, and the possibilities for consensus. The middle-class women embody the pluralism often seen as the essence of liberalism (see in particular Lasch 1988, 183), with their shifting context of justification for abortion decisions. Although they firmly believed that every woman should have the right to choose an abortion, they argued with equal passion for the potential rightness or wrongness of particular abortion decisions. But their language of liberalism gave them no vantage point from which to reconcile these two perspectives. For the most part they relied on their notions of the individual as the legitimate basis for making such decisions. Rather than the ideal of the "responsible individual," however, they espoused an ideal derived from therapeutic constructions of the person. Middle-class pro-choice women looked to the "suffering individual," the person in anguish, to guide their decision making. This is why their abortion language at times seemed relativistic. Although they argued an extreme position of individual choice, we see that in fact they measured the legitimacy of a decision according to the anguish the woman suffered in making it. With regard to abortion, they believed that no norm can be enforced across the spectrum of individuals, because no such abstract norm could take into account the richness of each person's experience as she lives through the specific circumstances that lead to her choice.

Middle-class women uniformly marshaled these arguments to defend the pro-choice position. The language they used for their evaluations is deeply rooted in therapeutic ideals about the self, individual lives, and the role emotion plays in constituting the "authentic" self. In this respect middle-class women shunned the vocabulary of community and consensual values in their "public" rhetoric, protesting that abortion is an individual decision whose logic is not generalizable. The language they used to discuss the nature of these decisions was inherently bound to a notion of the individual in which social connection is primary. The content of the anguish centers on thoughts of relationships—often their own with the fetus, with extended family, with the father, and with other people with whom their lives are intertwined. Carol Gilligan (1982) elegantly summarized the nature of individual middle-class women's discussions of abortion decisions, emphasizing this theoretical perspective. She explained that many women facing unwanted pregnancies consider the impact of the choice on others in their lives to be critical in their decision making.

Bernard Yack (1988, 168) argued that liberal practices and institutions do not "live down" to the limitations that many contemporary communitarians have found in liberal theory. By this he meant that there is a significant and undertheorized gap between liberal theory and liberal practice. Liberals speak in the terms of radical individualism, abstracted from community context and standards, and this makes them vulnerable to communitarian critiques claiming they have ignored the importance of community. They argue for a position of individual choice that—when moved from the abstract level and applied to an issue as concrete as particular abortion decisions being made in concrete, particular circumstances—it is clear that they do not fully embrace, because when they discuss choices they or other women have made the qualifications they place on this concept quickly emerge. Yack and others argue that liberal theorists face a problem of justification. As a consequence, universal values may be used to generate theory; but socially constituted criteria have given rise to these values.

The contradiction between liberal thought and practice is particularly evident in the language middle-class women chose to express abortion dilemmas. It seems they employed a vocabulary of extreme individualism, because they offered "individual anguish" as the primary criterion by which abortion decisions can be evaluated and justified. On closer examination of what this standard means in practice, however, it is evident that the women making these decisions experience this anguish in a social context and use a complex set of social standards to govern their judgments of which practices are right and which are unjustifiable. The equivocal position on abortion expressed in the prime-time television shows we used, with which middle-class pro-choice women for the most part agreed, illustrates these contradictions as well.

Discussions of the coexistence of liberal and communitarian thinking in our society help to illuminate the different logics invoked by women in each of the groups we studied. Framing our discussion within the terms of this debate helps explain the relative ease with which pro-life women can mobilize politically as a group. This analysis also offers some explanations for the difficulties pro-choice women have in coming together as a political coalition, given the differences in thinking and life circumstances that characterize them. In the next section we discuss differences and similarities in the way feminist thinking is invoked by the different types of women we interviewed.

FEMINIST VISIONS

The women we spoke with sometimes expressed both explicitly and implicitly feminist views. These attitudes revealed much about their beliefs concerning community and individualism as well. Consequently we find it important to explore the meaning of feminism both analytically and in the minds of our informants. Although a feminist perspective is most often identified only with the pro-choice perspective on abortion, women from each of the groups we have described here espoused what might be considered feminist viewpoints.

In both the political arena and the academy, debate over the content of a "feminist" perspective is long standing (Albert 1988). Even in its third decade, the political and intellectual movement called second wave feminism resists frequent attempts to cleave it into neat taxonomic categories (see Donovan 1985; Jaggar 1983; Tong 1989; Warhol and Herndl 1991). At the very least, most feminists would agree that women have special needs because of their sex and that they simultaneously experience discrimination for this same reason. Yet these two beliefs lead, in Nancy Fraser's perceptive terms (1997, 23–31), to a clash between those stressing the socioeconomic necessity of redistributing resources that women may be denied because of gender discrimination and those who emphasize the cultural demand to recognize women as a group with special needs. In the discourses and movements that constitute feminism today, confusion clearly abounds. There is no clear consensus about the sources of gender inequities or about appropriate remedies (Delmar 1986). Moreover, even the label feminist implies some commitment to political action, a standard that most of the women we interviewed could not meet owing to our sampling criteria. Yet in their dialogue clearly audible strains of feminist thought were focused on topics that are currently contested within intellectual and political feminist movements, and such remarks serve as windows on women's broader moral and political beliefs. Despite common stereotypes about the liberal and individualist basis of all feminist rhetoric (Albert 1988), we heard a range of feminist beliefs that fit within both communitarian and liberal frameworks.

Paralleling the individualist emphasis in their conversations generally, middle-class pro-choice groups were most likely to use the liberal feminist rhetoric that characterizes the most familiar feminist discourse. Middle-class women were comfortable employing such rhetoric to defend the right of individual women to free choice in decisions governing their personal and professional lives. Implicit in this belief is a construction of choice in which each autonomous individual has the opportunity and personal resources to pursue those options that will further her own happiness and well-being. This feminism, based on hegemonic social beliefs about individuals and their rights, cannot challenge the underlying values of the status quo.

Not surprisingly, the vision of feminism articulated by the middle-class pro-choice women is limited in its practicality and appeal in the same way that the liberal feminist political movement has been. Because it constructs a very specific type of privileged individual as the universal, this approach cannot address the concerns of many women whose material and social circumstances connect them to networks of other needy individuals, as is true among racial and ethnic minorities and the poor. Middle-class pro-choice women acknowledged that the working-class heroines seeking abortion in the television shows were financially disadvantaged; however, their feminism failed to recognize the political importance of the very real material differences between women like themselves, whose only disadvantage is their gender, and those whose choices are constrained by many other aspects of their social location and economic resources. Ironically, it is the tendency to homogenize differences among women into an imagined universal of "woman" that has stalled efforts to build a broad-based feminist movement. Since the mid-1980s, many political and academic feminists have worked to generate theory and practice built on a more inclusive vision; but the responses of our middle-class pro-choice women suggest that these efforts at a new kind of consciousness raising have generally not yet reached mainstream women outside the movement.

This recognition of difference does not come without a price, however. Once the unitary concept of "woman" has been discarded, feminists must struggle to reconstruct an understanding of gender that is sensitive to other relations of power and the multiple subjectivities of gender that are created through its intersection with class, race, and other social categories (Collins 1990; Hurtado 1989; Valdivia 1995). This version of feminist rhetoric was clearly audible in the views of the women we termed working class identified. Acutely aware of the differences that separated their material reality as well as their outlook from those of television producers, officers of the law, and university faculty, these women clearly articulated their particular standpoint as defined by their social location. Their remarks suggested a consciousness of both their socioeconomic location and their gender identity. Women in these groups defended their pro-choice position based on a general appeal to justice that was informed by their very specific reality of both gender- and class-based discrimination. This potentially communal discourse based on group identity shared with other marginalized groups offered a compelling challenge to prevailing social norms. For example, one woman in a working-class group said that viewing the *Cagney and Lacey* tape had made her think about the women's movement in ways that had not occurred to her for quite a while:

WOMAN: [The tape] made me think we need to fight hard to keep abortion as an option, and I think that women's movements are just kind of died down and they died down too soon.
ANDREA PRESS: You're real worried that people are going to start telling women what to do.
WOMAN: Yeah. I don't want to see that happening.

Her ambivalent support for feminism was evident as the discussion continued:

ANDREA PRESS: So, the more you think about abortion, like having this discussion, the more you start thinking it's important to keep the options open for women?
WOMAN: Yeah, and keep fighting for it. Yeah, there's a lot of areas that I'm kind of mad that women's lib thought up and stuff like that, but in some areas they did a lot of good. [Ambitious Mothers]

When questioned about what "women's lib" issues angered her, this woman mentioned two in particular: the acceptability of her boyfriend's having women as "friends," which she found threatening and confusing, and the increasing tendency for judges to award custody of children to fathers in divorce cases:

It [the women's movement] makes life a lot harder, like, ah. . . . It just makes life kind of confusing because a lot of areas were . . . where it was really black and white . . . what was right for a woman to do and what wasn't. . . . I like a guy to hold a door open for me and stuff like that, and a lot of men won't do it anymore. You just go walking . . . bam . . . they're walking in front of you and they just let go of the door. And ah, like, I suppose that ah, that my boyfriend having girlfriends like this is kind of a women's lib type thing and these women are very liberal. I don't like it so much. I don't understand it, I can't really cope with it, but in another way, I really like it because I think he's a lot more. . . . He's not a brutey type guy. You know, that doesn't care about emotions and stuff like that, so we're able to talk about a lot more. I think that it's taken away from mother's rights a lot with [what] the women's movement did. A lot of fathers are fighting to get their kids now, and they've done some good by saying, well, fathers are just as good as mothers, but a lot of times mothers gave up their career to marry the father and then they take care of this man for years and he's got more money so the judge says that's better for the kids. He ends up with the kids and she's got nothing and she actually gave up her career to marry him. I have this going on with my girlfriend.

Clearly she felt ambivalent about the impact of the feminist movement on herself and her friends. Her own close friend had lost her children in a custody dispute after putting her husband through school, because in the end he could support them financially better than she could. The unfairness of this situation was evident to our informant. Yet she also was partly in sympathy with many of the aims of what she termed "women's lib." Her feminism was ambivalent owing to her multiple identifications not only as a woman, but also as a member of a disadvantaged class.

Most pro-life women may be reluctant to describe themselves as feminists because of the long-standing connection of the label with the pro-choice stance. Yet in the discussions of pro-life women we heard clearly the twin acknowledgments that women have special needs and that they face discrimination. Their version of feminist rhetoric invoked the larger image of themselves as women belonging to a clearly established social group, marked as oppositional to the wider society by shared moral, religious, and often political convictions. Rather than turning to the feminist movement for redress, pro-life feminists seek to better women's situation through their allegiance to this oppositional community. In these respects those we talked with did not see feminist insights as goals in themselves, but instead made such critiques part of a more general effort to create and maintain an oppositional community that, through the moral strength and insight of its members, would be able to remedy many of the socioeconomic and cultural inequities women experience.

In particular, pro-life women we interviewed were confident that the mainstream biomedical establishment is not concerned with the best interests of women. They argued that many women are kept from the knowledge that abortion may cause physical injury and emotional distress that can persist indefinitely. Many recounted examples to document their view that abortion causes such severe and continuing mental trauma. In this their discourse did reflect common feminist themes emphasizing the importance of safeguarding the health and well-being of women and skepticism about the claim that mainstream medical professionals have women's best interests in mind (e.g., Ehrenreich and English 1978). Yet their critique stopped short of a more sweeping feminist pro-life position, asserting that abortion does not solve the larger problems, such as sex discrimination, that disadvantage pregnant women and mothers in a male-dominated society. This argument, articulated by the organization Feminists for Life (Sweet 1985), contends that pro-choice feminists have accepted a sexist society on men's own terms. Rather than embracing feminist identifications, pro-life feminists seek by their more general group allegiances to transcend the sexist aspects of mainstream society.

In sum, the many feminist visions articulated by the women we interviewed not only expressed their views about women's place in society and its attendant injustices, but reflected their broader beliefs about social justice and how it may best be achieved. In particular, their feminist rhetoric revealed their larger reliance on notions either of the individual or of particular social groups as their main level of identification and as the source of the important social changes they see as necessary to achieve their visions of the just society.

THE FUTURE OF THE ABORTION DEBATE

Our work posits the central importance of the mass media in framing, disseminating, and influencing our culture's central value systems. Women's attitudes toward television and their discussions about the medium illustrate the mass media's influence both on their vision of our culture's central values and norms and on the way women at times resist these norms and values as they conceive them. But the television landscape is changing. The development and growth of such technologies as cable television and pay-per-view, and the prospect of interactive viewing through collaborations between television and Internet providers, are eroding the market shares held by network programming while simultaneously isolating more and more specific viewing audiences. In this new arena we may expect to see programming increasingly designed to mirror the sensibilities of the target audience.

With respect to abortion, this trend is exemplified in the HBO made-for-television movie *Absolute Strangers,* broadcast in 1992. *Absolute Strangers* is the story of Sherri Finkbine, who decided to obtain an abortion in 1962 when she discovered that the thalidomide she had taken during her pregnancy was likely to cause gross deformities in her baby. Finkbine is depicted as ambivalent, and in the end she opposes the abortion foisted on her by the joint decisions of her (male) doctor and her husband. The episode highlights male conspiracy, including scenes in which Sherri explicitly accuses the two men of manipulating her and refusing to take into account her opinions and feelings. The episode clearly implies that women as a group have such sensitivity that the act of abortion is almost never their own idea or their own choice. The political tenor of this representation contrasts sharply with the more individualized prime-time television narratives we have discussed, which view abortion decisions, and the obstacles to abortion, in much more individualized terms.

A similarly political feminist consciousness was depicted in *If These Walls Could Talk,* broadcast on HBO in 1996. This project was conceptualized as taking a politically neutral stance on abortion; however, the movie sympathetically depicted the stories of several women who faced abortion decisions during various periods over the past fifty years. Although each faced wrenching emotional circumstances that led her to consider abortion, none of the subplots attempted to justify the characters' choices based on financial hardship. In this the movie, produced and directed by a well-known feminist actress, broke with the network television tradition of the "generally acceptable abortion." HBO was able to produce, broadcast, and widely publicize such a potentially controversial depiction of abortion with little fear of the repercussions by pro-life groups faced by the networks, because their audience is composed of subscribers who differ demographically from network audiences. In fact this was the most highly rated original movie ever produced by HBO/Cinemax.[3] Taken together, the treatments of abortion in these shows suggest that the current proliferation of nonnetwork programming will give a public voice to more diverse positions in the abortion debate.

The struggle over abortion in the United States does not appear to be reaching any conclusion. Our conversations with women suggest that this is so not only because of what is at stake over the manifest issue of abortion itself, but also because the topic crosscuts larger questions that are deeply contested in American society. What is the appropriate role of medical and scientific authority as our medical knowledge proliferates? How can we administer justice through the legal system in a way that will be fair and unbiased toward people in every social stratum? In a society that values individual autonomy over collective social mores, by what standards can the behavior of individuals be evaluated, and how shall we manage those who deviate from these standards? That these themes in turn reflect historic political struggles over liberal and communitarian values may in part explain why abortion is a more contested political issue in the United States than it is in most industrialized, democratic nations.

Previous literature on abortion attitudes has focused on the way individuals' views on the subject are connected to their ideas about women's roles and identities in our society (Ginsburg 1989; Luker 1984). In contrast, our research highlights the centrality of visions of hierarchy and authority implicit in the terms of the debate. However, women vary on which of these areas are of most concern to them. Consequently we find that women who hold different attitudes toward our culture's hegemonic ideas—who occupy different places in its hierarchy—often take different positions on abortion or defend their stands in fundamentally different ways. These distinctions are not adequately captured by the customary terms of pro-life and pro-choice used to characterize positions on legalized abortion. This is particularly true of the pro-choice label, which we argue is an umbrella term encompassing many disparate beliefs about the abortion issue.

Normally the pro-choice position is defined simply as one of a bipolar set of opinions seen to characterize the abortion debate. In general this construction does not recognize the various subject positions possible under the rubric pro-choice. In particular, it excludes explicit reference to the ways members of different social classes articulate the position. "Pro-choice" as we commonly define it, and as it is depicted on television, derives from middle-class conceptions of the world, of individuals, of the experience of "haves" and "have-nots," and of pregnancy and childbearing and women's related dilemmas. In this construction of "pro-choice," poor and working-class women are silent outsiders in the abortion debate, as they so often are in the American political arena.

Women of different class backgrounds may articulate very different ideas about the complexity of abortion at both the private and public level while espousing similar views about the legal status of abortion. This suggests there are profound causes for the problems the pro-choice movement has had in presenting a unified political front during the ongoing struggle to keep abortion legal. No solution to the rift within the opinion group labeled pro-choice may be forthcoming until the movement finds a way to address the broader concerns of power and authority inherent in the concept of choice.

APPENDIX A: THE ETHNOGRAPHIC FOCUS GROUP

Abortion is an issue that involves both our most private realm of experience and our most public and political domain of social interaction. The topic is therefore well suited to our interdisciplinary collaboration between a psychologist (Cole) and a qualitative sociologist (Press). In fact, Press's background as a sociologist prepared her to collaborate with a psychologist, and to use interdisciplinary methods, because in sociology qualitative research is often augmented by collaboration with quantitative researchers as well as by theoretical dialogues with humanist critiques of empirical research and its limits. The method we used in our project combined elements of research traditionally labeled qualitative and (to a lesser extent) quantitative, but it was also informed by the insights of postmodern theory, which are critical of all attempts at empirical research and the classificatory schemes on which such research so often depends. We used this combination of methodologies and theoretical orientations to probe the relation between opinions on abortion and social class membership. This study is an example of the new tradition of feminist research investigating popular culture audiences. The ethnographic focus group method we employed allows researchers to observe women as they engage in semipublic discourse, in both the presence and the absence of television. Unlike more traditional audience research, this method aims to collect data as women speak for themselves, and with each other, in the context of responding to questionnaires, viewing television, and being interviewed.

Both our choice of method and our analysis of the resulting data have been influenced by the qualitative studies of media reception that have flourished over the past two decades (Hobson 1982; Liebes and Katz 1990; Long 1988, 1994; Lull 1990; McRobbie 1978, 1981, 1984; Morley 1980; Press 1991a,b; Radway 1984, 1988; Seiter 1993; Seiter et al. 1989; Willis 1978). However, students of the mass media audience, influenced by postmodern theorizing about the concept of the subject, have criticized these efforts (Ang 1991; Fiske 1989a,b, 1990; Grossberg 1988). They challenge the existence of unified, reflective "subjects" in any traditional post-Enlightenment sense, substituting a more diffuse (but less easily researchable) notion of "subjectivity" (Baudrillard 1988; Lyotard 1984; Radway 1988; Scott 1988).[1]

Of course ethnographers have also criticized traditional social scientific epistemologies, particularly for their often ethnocentric assumptions about the nature of the subject. Yet on another level ethnography requires faith in the possibility of creative activity by the subject and in the ethnographer's potential to come to "understand" her "subjects," which is often difficult to maintain in the face of postmodern theoretical challenges to our customary notions. This paradox has led to a widening split in the field between those embracing the postmodern critique of research and conventional knowledge generally and those more interested in the new research techniques and emphases the critique has spawned.[2]

This seeming contradiction between theory and practice has particularly affected scholars using ethnographic techniques to study the popular culture audience. Most centrally, the question of the way mass media audiences at times resist cultural hegemonies and at other times accept them has preoccupied researchers in this field, continually foregrounding challenges to traditional notions of the subject (Fiske 1989a,b, 1990; Grossberg 1988, 1989; Radway 1988). Increasingly these scholars attempt to accommodate the postmodern critique by eschewing notions of the unified subject. But scholars have not been very successful in altering the working notion of subjectivity that informs most current research in the field. Those in the vanguard have produced theoretical critiques of earlier works, theoretical tracts, and calls for ethnographic research based on these new ideas. To date little research has been done that might make a convincing case for the power of the postmodern critique to deepen our understanding of the construction of subjectivity in our time.

Feminist cultural researchers have been particularly sensitive to the construction of the subject in research. They have attempted to respond to this postmodern critique as well as to the related theoretical development of feminist theory discussing the masculinist bias of traditional notions of the subject (Flax 1990; Harding 1991; Nicholson 1986; Scott 1988). Feminists theorists have also cautioned researchers against an essentialist construction of the female subject that is abstract and ahistorical.[3] Feminist studies of popular culture audiences have generally led away from essentialism, because ethnography, the study of specific, historically situated cultural subjects, has been the method of choice among feminist researchers looking at female audiences (Hobson 1982; McRobbie 1978, 1981, 1984; Press 1991a,b; Radway 1984).[4] Nevertheless, the temptation to construct an equally essentialized, resisting "female subject" who can be effectively contrasted to the "male subject" more customary in cultural theory has been a continuing problem in some feminist ethnographies.

For example, Janice Radway's (1984) influential work constructs a rather undifferentiated, perpetually resisting female subject, owing her continued existence and re-creation to female popular culture genres such as the romance novel. The book, based entirely on interviews with White middle-class women and directed toward a similar audience, universalizes the qualities of these women as inherently female qualities. Although Radway herself has since retreated from the extreme position this work represents (Radway 1988), the tendency to essentialize the attributes of some women as representative of women as a class remains a danger in feminist work. The new direction in feminist cultural studies is toward more historically and geographically specific research on particular groups of women. The pitfalls of essentialism are effectively avoided as studies become increasingly specific in scope. Yet this complicates the subject identity researchers must refer to, as ever narrower categories of race, class, age, location, occupation, political affiliation, and generation are invoked in the effort to avoid unwarranted generalizations.

Of course this approach in turn invites criticism such as Ien Ang and Joke Hermes (1996) have leveled against Andrea Press's earlier work. They criticize attempts by Press (1990) and by Ellen Seiter et al. (1989) to make connections between informants' interpretive statements about television and their social class position. Although they acknowledge that Press qualified her conclusions by warning against overgeneralizing from small samples, Ang and Hermes nevertheless admonish that attempting to classify respondents according to class and to interpret their responses in light of their classed experience may open the door to "creeping essentialism" (1996, 116), which not only threatens to reify differences between class groups but also groundlessly implies that these groups are homogeneous.

Elsewhere in the same volume (Ang 1996), Ang more fully explicates the problem of essentialism in ethnographic audience studies and describes its potential consequences. She charges that mainstream sociological research treats demographic categories such as gender, class, and race as "self evident pregiven factor(s) that can be used as 'independent variable(s)' to explain" (49) any observed differences between groups defined by these categories. These demographic categories thus come to be seen as "clearly defined, fixed, static 'objects' in themselves as it were" (49). Ang presents three criticisms of this research approach. First, she rightly points out that such an analysis is reductionist, failing to recognize that every individual encompasses multiple identities, any of which may be more or less salient during a given viewing. Second, analyses premised on group differences are primarily descriptive and have little explanatory power. Thus Ang urges critical researchers to focus on the structures of power underlying social relations between groups, because these relations, rather than innate or essential group differences, give rise to the observed differences between groups. In the absence of such attention to power, the net effect of the group difference paradigm is to depoliticize audience research. Finally, Ang reminds us that the promise of ethnography lies in its close attention to the historical, the contextual, and the specific: in this it allows researchers to be receptive to data that challenge our theoretical assumptions, thus avoiding the problem of "abstract empiricism" (Mills 1959). Approaching the data with sociological constructs such as gender and class in mind may prevent us from being receptive to exceptions to our theories posed by the data.

Although the construct of class is central to our work here, we maintain that we have not succumbed to the pitfalls Ang describes. We began our inquiry with an interest in whether women of different social classes might use different strategies to make sense of abortion as both a political and a personal issue, but we were willing to abandon this paradigm when it did not prove useful for understanding our informants' discussions. Within our sample, we found that other identities often took precedence over class in women's discussions of television and abortion. This is well illustrated in our analysis of the conversations among the pro-life women we interviewed. Their discussions suggested that their identities as members of a religious and cultural minority, distinct from the secular mainstream, were more pertinent to their interpretation of the television shows they viewed than was their social class. Moreover, our conversations with working-class women led us to conclude that class membership is not a unitary construct. Much of our chapter on working-class pro-choice women, for example, was concerned with explicating the variations we observed within working-class identity. We propose that these differences are rooted precisely in individual women's own identification with and against institutions of power and authority in our society. Our work suggests that although Ang's criticisms are well founded, it is a failure of the imagination, and a severe limitation on thoughtful work of all kinds, to conclude that constructs such as race, class, and gender cannot be used to make sense of ethnographic interview data without essentializing the people we study. Indeed, our close attention to the specific experiences of class expressed by the women we interviewed points not toward a reified, fixed, or unitary picture of social class, but toward a more nuanced understanding of this important sociological construct in which social class identity is not a demographic category but is constructed by individuals themselves out of their own experience and worldviews.

Other work heavily influenced by postmodern theory challenges traditional notions of the subject in the quest for specificity. For example, in an interesting attempt to put into practice theoretical insights into the fragmented nature of the postmodern subject, Radway (1988) recommends that researchers observe and describe sets of conflicting practices in abstraction from the subjects producing them. Many see these transformations of more traditional feminist theoretical goals as an emerging strength of a field reconstituting itself at a new level of theoretical and historical specificity (Scott 1988). In this vein, feminist inquiry has much in common with research being done from a series of other critical perspectives including queer theory and research, as well as research motivated by questions involving the importance of racial and ethnic identities and social class positioning. Although we have not been able to incorporate the insights of all these perspectives, we locate our work in this multifaceted emergent critical tradition.

SURVEY RESEARCH AND THE ETHNOGRAPHIC FOCUS GROUP: ISSUES IN INTERDISCIPLINARY RESEARCH

A major part of what we know about public opinion on abortion is gleaned through survey research using standardized instruments administered to large-scale random samples of individuals. But what do these statistics reflect? How valid are statistical survey measures of Americans' beliefs about this complex issue, and how are we to interpret their findings? Although we did not set out specifically to investigate this topic, our study sheds some surprising light on the discrepancies between subjects' answers to written survey questions and their more in-depth personal opinions about this issue.

There is a body of research that explores the limits of survey research methods. Howard Schuman and Jacqueline Scott (1987) presented compelling evidence that survey respondents may give very different responses to the same question depending on whether the item is presented as open-ended or closed-ended. This implies that surveys sometimes fail to tap important aspects of respondents' views, perhaps overlooking the complexity of opinions on social issues. Similarly, research by Hope Landrine, Elizabeth Klonoff, and Alice Brown-Collins (1992) suggests that items that constitute classic measures enjoying widespread use in psychology are interpreted differently by members of different cultural groups. In the absence of more qualitative data from respondents, this discrepancy casts doubt on our ability to interpret with any validity the meaning of responses to these items.

Conventionally, public opinion research has attempted to measure attitudes toward abortion on a continuum ranging from the most pro-life stance to the most pro-choice, attitudes that have largely been defined by activists on the issue. Although some researchers have tried to capture the nuances of Americans' ambivalence toward abortion through sophisticated statistical models (Alvarez and Brehm 1995) or by identifying the conditions under which attitudes toward abortion are least ambivalent (Hildreth and Dran 1994), even these analyses are still hampered by the method used to collect data. We argue that survey research methods may be particularly inappropriate for studying women's opinions on abortion because the issue crosscuts the political and personal spheres. Forced-choice questions cannot tap the nuances of opinion held by many women, who feel abortion is justifiable in some cases but not in others. Moreover, response categories used in survey research can give the misleading impression that a consensus exists within opinion categories, although respondents may endorse the same opinion for different reasons. Finally, because the anonymous situation in which survey data are collected is very different from the settings in which people actually discuss abortion, the ecological validity of surveys is questionable.

We find opinion to be a complex phenomenon, more complex than the categories captured through conventional survey research methods. Most relevant to this dimension of our work is William Gamson's (1992) qualitative study of public opinion among working-class people. Gamson challenged those who portray ordinary people as passive and nonevaluative consumers of media accounts of social and political issues. He argued that people form their views and their conversational approach to social issues through several levels of analysis, weaving media discourse together with experiential knowledge and "popular wisdom" (117). Moreover, people navigate these three sources of knowledge in part through what Gamson calls "cultural resonances": symbols that draw on larger cultural themes are particularly powerful in conversation (135).

By examining variations and nuances of opinion within the discourse of particular groups of women, and the differences between groups, we sought to illustrate the complexity and fluidity of such discourse. Women's ideas about abortion, the family, and their own identity as individuals are formed in dialogue with each other and with cultural images such as those they see on television and in other mass media. It is these dialogues that we sought to understand through analysis of our focus group discussions.

The Ethnographic Focus Group. Our project looked closely at the discourse of ordinary women as they discussed their positions on abortion. In some ways our work is an extension of work by Kristin Luker (1984) and Fay Ginsburg (1989) investigating the worldviews of abortion activists and by Carol Gilligan (1982), who studied moral reasoning in the narratives of women facing unplanned pregnancies. However, our project explores the significance and meaning of abortion in particular, and reproductive decisions in general, in the lives of women who are more representative of the larger population of the United States: we look primarily at those who are not politically active concerning the issue and who are not currently facing a decision about an unplanned pregnancy.

We chose to examine women's discourse as it occurs in a collective context. In this choice we were influenced by the notion that the important political dimensions of discourse are those expressed in public settings.[5] The literature about women's abortion opinions either examines the private views of individual women (Gilligan 1982) or looks at the views of abortion activists (Luker 1984; Ginsburg 1989), who take part in a very conventionally defined political realm. We drew from feminist literature that questions the contours of the political sphere as it has been defined to describe what has largely been male political activity. Seeking to expand these boundaries, we assembled groups of friends so we could listen to them discuss public issues in a part-private, part-public setting—the home of one of the group members. We call this the "ethnographic focus group" method, because it modifies traditional focus group methodology in several respects. Groups consist of friends, not strangers; they are somewhat smaller than traditional focus groups (two to five versus five to nine); and rather than an institutional, impersonal environment, our groups met in a nonneutral setting, a member's home, to make participants more comfortable. Additionally, we attempted to ensure some homogeneity of opinion within groups by asking women to invite like-minded friends. Conventional focus group methodology welcomes dissent and disagreement within groups; but we felt that because abortion is, for some, such an emotionally heated topic, groups in which pro-life and pro-choice friends were forced to confront their disagreements might have led to less open and forthcoming conversations and might have been ethically questionable as well.[6]

Sampling. To recruit a sample of women who were not active on the abortion issue, we solicited respondents through newspaper advertisements and announcements at Parent-Teacher Association meetings at schools in our area. Each contact agreed to host a group meeting in her home, inviting female friends or relatives (or both). During the first telephone conversation with the contact respondent we stipulated that the other group members should hold attitudes about abortion that were similar to her own so that everyone in the group would feel comfortable sharing her views openly. That groups were composed of friends of our initial respondents in some ways mitigates the biases of self-selection; although the contact person may herself be more interested and informed about abortion than the general population, the other members of each group were not self-selected advertisement responders. Of course, because the groups were composed of friends, information from each member is not independent in a statistical sense, but because we intended to look at opinion expression and formation in groups who ordinarily talk to one another outside the research setting, this was unavoidable. Before the group interviews, respondents completed a short questionnaire that included items on demographic information, media use, and opinion on the appropriate legal status of abortion, as measured by a version of an item from the National Election Study (Miller, Kinder, and Rosenstone 1993).

Generally, researchers conducting survey research have the resources of staff and funding to conduct systematic random samples of their population of interest. Too often, researchers practicing ethnographic methods do not have these resources at their disposal. And even with adequate funding it may be insurmountably difficult to collect a truly random sample in focus group research because of the large commitment of time and effort required from those who organize groups and host them in their homes. For example, Gamson (1992), who also used focus groups to study opinions on current political topics, attempted to collect a probability sample but failed because so few respondents were willing to organize focus groups.

Participants. From 1989 through 1993, we conducted thirty-four discussion groups, ranging in size from two to five members. Additionally, we interviewed three women individually at the start of this project as a pilot study for the focus groups; including these interviews yields a total sample of 108 women.

Appendix B lists the groups, briefly describes the relationship between the women, and gives their demographic characteristics. Based on self-identification of abortion opinion by the contact respondent, 53.7 percent of our sample were pro-life and 46.3 percent were pro-choice. The vast majority of the women were not involved in activism related to abortion; however, we did interview two groups of activists (one pro-life, another pro-choice; see descriptions in appendix B). Respondents indicated their year of birth using a categorical scale: the midpoint of the median response category corresponded to thirty-four years old at the time of the interview, with a range of nineteen to sixty-six. At that time 53 percent of the women were married, 14 percent were divorced or separated, and 31 percent were single.

Classifying participants as middle-class or working-class is notoriously thorny, particularly for women (see Baxter 1994; Press 1991a,b; Rubin 1976, 1994). Groups were described as middle-class if most members had completed four years of college, held professional positions, or were married to professionals or executives. In working-class groups most members had no more education than two years of college; if they were married, their husbands had a similar educational background and held "blue-collar" jobs.

Such perfunctory classification of the groups was relatively simple because the groups of friends were strikingly homogeneous not only in abortion opinion, but also in socioeconomic status and race. Most of our contacts were White women, who invited predominately White friends. Of the total sample, 11 percent were African American; the rest identified as White. Because very few Black women responded to our advertisements, we conducted only two groups that were entirely African American. No other races or ethnicities were represented in our sample.

As a validity check on this relatively informal method of classification, the occupations of the respondents, and if applicable their husbands, were coded using the categories described by Hollingshead and Redlich (1958). The coder was blind to the class categories we had assigned to the respondents. On this scale, a score of 1 corresponds to unskilled worker; 2 is semiskilled worker; 3 is skilled laborer; 4 is sales/clerical/technical worker; 5 is administrative worker; 6 is minor professional; and 7 corresponds to major professional occupations. Occupations of women in our sample ranged from 1 to 6. Compared with the middle-class groups, groups classified as working class by the criteria above scored significantly lower on their own occupational status (means of 4.4 and 2.8, respectively), educational level (slightly more than a bachelor's degree and slightly less than some college work, respectively), and family income ($55,000 compared with $25,000). Additionally, among those who were married, the occupations of working-class women's husbands scored significantly lower on the Hollingshead and Redlich scale than did those of middle-class women's husbands (2.4 and 5.3, respectively).[7]

Group Interviews. The focus group method, based on semistructured interviews with small groups of respondents, approximates the casual and intimate settings in which television is most often watched and discussed. Additionally, small groups of people who knew each other provided a supportive and nonconfrontational atmosphere in which respondents could discuss the personal, controversial, and potentially emotional issue of abortion. As David Morgan states, "The explicit use of the group interaction . . . produce[s] data and insights that would be less accessible without the interaction found in a group" (1988). Peers talk to each other far more freely than they would talk to an interviewer. Some have theorized that the use of focus groups mitigates the role of the researcher in directing the discussion (Gamson 1992).

Of course our use of focus groups departed significantly from convention in the ways already mentioned. We believe that our practice of interviewing in homes whenever possible avoided the influence of a "bureaucratic" setting and, particularly for working-class groups, neutralized the sometimes intimidating institutional atmosphere. In addition, we felt that our method increased the ecological validity of our data, since groups of friends were conducting their discussions in a seminatural environment. A serious drawback of the focus groups method is confusion about whether the appropriate level of analysis for the data it yields is the group or the individual. Following Morgan (1988), we used the group as our basic unit of analysis, although at times we highlight the contribution of individuals who were noteworthy in some way.

The interviews were loosely structured by a fixed protocol (specific questions are listed at the end of this appendix); but the group setting fostered interaction among respondents, who were quick to ask their own questions both to probe and to clarify each others' positions. Thus, although the setting was not completely "natural" owing to the presence of the two researchers, to our ears the groups seemed forthcoming and lively. Andrea Press led most of the interviews, beginning with questions about decisions the participants or their acquaintances had faced regarding unwanted pregnancies. She then encouraged them to talk about the factors they believed women weighed in making such reproductive decisions and to describe their own thoughts on how such decisions ought to be evaluated. The respondents then viewed a thirty- to forty-minute segment of a prime-time entertainment television program treating abortion decision making. After the tape, the interviewer asked the respondents to discuss the segment they had viewed in much the same way, evaluating the decisions made by the characters and the opinions expressed in the show. The interviews generally lasted about three hours and were audiotaped and later transcribed. Each respondent was paid twenty dollars for participating.

Analysis. As in the grounded theory method pioneered by the sociologists Barney Glaser and Anselm Strauss (1967), rather than approaching the transcripts with hypotheses, we sought to discover the emergent themes in the women's narratives. However, it would not be accurate to say that we had no expectations about what we would find and no thoughts on what the relevant issues were. In this sense we were influenced by what Michael Burawoy[8] calls the "extended case method" (1991, 1998). According to this method, researchers approach a project guided by a specific theoretical framework that leads them to frame their study, and their interview questions, in particular ways. Because Press had previously raised the problem of social class differences in responses to television, we approached the current study with class differences in mind. In addition, to the extent that both authors were steeped in social science literature about qualitative methods, feminist literature about standpoint theory, and postmodern literature interrogating science itself (the latter was particularly true for Press, in the communication field), these conflicting traditions influenced the way we structured our study and analyzed its results.

Using a statistical package for the analysis of qualitative data, we coded the transcripts thematically, then excerpted the recurring themes from many hundreds of pages in order to view them simultaneously (Morgan 1988). In this way we distilled several main themes present across the interviews and identified themes common to particular categories of women. Both authors coded each interview for these themes.

It was our use of the grounded theory method that allowed us to see the importance of social class in structuring participants' expressions of abortion opinion. Although we did not begin the study thinking of social class as central to the expression of abortion opinion, we quickly became convinced of its importance in dividing women who conventionally were collectively categorized as pro-choice.

What we were not prepared to find was the extent to which the women we studied viewed the abortion issue in relation to power and authority. In this sense we found that the labels pro-choice and pro-life as defined by activists were inadequate to capture the subtleties of their positions. Our close attention to the views of nonactivist women has led us to challenge the usefulness of the pro-choice and pro-life labels that currently organize our culture's commonsense views of the topic and much of the academic literature as well. We argue that most women who would conventionally be identified as members of either camp are ambivalent about abortion in a manner not captured by these labels because the issue cuts across larger philosophical and ideological questions that continue to be deeply contested in American society: What is the appropriate role of legal authorities in regulating the lives of individuals? How can we understand life, death, and health when technology and those who control it seem to redefine these concepts daily? What is the relevance of the ideal of individual liberty in a society increasingly splintered along the lines of race, class, and often gender privilege? And finally, What is the status of religious beliefs in a secular society? The multifaceted nature of the abortion debate became the central argument of our analysis. Such a finding could not have emerged from research based on survey methods alone.

THE METHODOLOGICAL SIGNIFICANCE OF THE STUDY

Our research helps illuminate women's ambivalence about abortion in a way that survey questions alone do not. By combining a small survey with focus group discussions, we were able to demonstrate that women's opinions about abortion are far more complex than survey categories might indicate. Specifically, our study showed that women who answer questions similarly do not always hold very similar views; that women may answer a general survey question in one way but respond to a particular situation in another; and that, when given the opportunity, women often dispute the meaningfulness of categories on a survey. In sum, our study challenges us to rethink the meaning of current data about abortion opinions in the United States, almost all of which are premised on survey research.

We believe the focus group method could be applied to several issues of interest to feminists on which people's opinions are often complex and ambivalent. Affirmative action comes to mind, as do attitudes toward feminism and feminists. Public debate indicates that current attitudes on both subjects in the United States are exceedingly complicated and contradictory. Combining face-to-face surveys with focus group interviews could shed light on this ambivalence.

Future researchers might also analyze the types of interactions within focus groups more fully than we did. There is a mine of information in our transcripts alone about the dynamics of opinion formation within small groups. Doing our research led us to question the popular assumption that people form and hold their opinions about social and moral issues in isolation, not influenced by interactions with friends and family. This in turn raises the question whether such opinions are best sampled by anonymous interviewers surveying individuals one at a time. Even a preliminary analysis of our data shows that women base their opinions in part on the comments of their friends. Compared with other currently popular methods of opinion research, close analysis of group interviews or even an ethnographic approach might better sample individuals' opinions and explore how they are formed. More thorough analysis of the group dynamics recorded in our transcripts might further clarify this topic.

INTERVIEW PROTOCOL

1. Go around and introduce yourselves (to us).

2. How do you spend your time as a group? (Do you ever watch TV together as a group?)

3. What do you and your friends (e.g., this friend group) talk about? (Edging into moral issues. See if abortion comes up.)

4. I'm interested in studying morality. Do you think morality is an abstract thing, or does it come up in your everyday life as something you have to think about?

5. Are moral issues generally covered in the news that you read or hear? Have you heard or read much about abortion in the news recently? What sorts of things have you read or heard discussed? What do you think about recent developments regarding this issue?

6. One of the moral issues people are talking about today is the issue of abortion. Did you ever know anyone (a friend, family member, or one of you if you want to talk about this here), man or woman, who had to make a decision about whether to have or not have an abortion that you wouldn't mind telling us about here?

OPTION 1

7. What were the choices that were considered in this case? (Marriage and childbirth; adoption; abortion; single motherhood?)

8. How did you feel about the decision that was made in this case? How hard a decision was it, and what made it hard?

9. (Open to the group): What would you have advised this person to do in this case?

10. What would you have done if you were in her position (or if you were her boyfriend)?

11. Do you think current abortion laws are moral?

OPTION 2

7a. What would you do if you found out your close friend was pregnant; she was not married and not planning to be married; and she came to you for advice. What sort of advice would you give? Would this be difficult for you to decide?

8a. What options do you think she should consider?

9a. What would you do in her position? Would it be a hard decision?

10a. Do you think current abortion laws are moral?

APPENDIX B: CHARACTERISTICS OF THE GROUPS

In general, we chose group names to reflect some shared characteristic connecting all or most of the members. Descriptions here are intended to give readers a sense of the women's demographic characteristics. To preserve respondents' anonymity, we have not described individuals.

PRO-LIFE GROUPS

Group (Size)	Show	Description
Service Workers (3)	*Roe vs. Wade*	The woman who organized this group invited her neighbor and her young adult daughter. One of the respondents worked at a fast-food restaurant, another worked at a gas station, and the third was a homemaker. Two had high school diplomas, and the third had some college. The two older women were in their late thirties, married with children; their husbands had blue-collar jobs. Two of the women had three children, a third had one. All were White; two identified their religion as Protestant, and the third marked "other."
Catholics (4)	*Roe vs. Wade*	The organizer of this group invited her daughter, her neighbor, and a friend from church. The women ranged from young adult to late middle age. Two of the women had clerical jobs, one worked in a medical lab, and another was a hospital volunteer. Three women were White and identified their religion as Catholic, and the fourth, who was African American, was Apostolic. One woman was married to a man in military service, the rest were single. One woman had three children, another had one, and the others were not mothers.
Quakers (4)	*Roe vs. Wade*	This group was composed of White women who were members of a Quaker meeting. All were married. Three were in their middle to late twenties, the other was in her mid-forties. Their level of education ranged from high school to four years of college; two were secretaries, one was a housewife, and the fourth was a teacher. Their husbands had blue-collar jobs in construction and building maintenance. They had one or two children each.

Group (Size)	Show	Description
Pentecostals (4)	*Roe vs. Wade*	These women, all White, were members of a Pentecostal church. Two were in their mid-thirties, and two were in their mid-sixties. Three had high school diplomas, and the fourth had some college. One was a homemaker, two were secretaries, and the fourth had retired from her factory job. Two were married to men with blue-collar jobs, the others were single. Three of the women had two or three children, and the fourth was not a mother.
Neighbors (2)	*Dallas*	This group was organized by a woman who had taken part in a different interview and who offered to set up another group composed of her neighbors. One woman in this group was in her early twenties, the other in her forties. The older woman had only a grammar school education, the younger had completed high school. One was Catholic, the other Protestant. One worked as a sewing machine operator, the other pieced together part-time jobs. Both were White and married to men with blue-collar jobs.
Suburban Group (4)	*Roe vs. Wade*	The woman who organized this group held a graduate degree, worked in education, and was married to a minister. Her friends differed from her in social class: none had as much as a bachelor's degree, nor did any of them hold professional jobs. One owned a small business that she ran with her husband, the others were homemakers. All were married, two to men with blue-collar jobs. All White, they ranged in age from late twenties to mid-forties. Three of the women had two or three children each, and the fourth was not a mother.
Nursery School Group (3)	*Cagney and Lacey*	These women knew each other through their participation in a cooperative nursery school. All were White and in their thirties; two were Catholic, and the third was Protestant. Two had bachelor's degrees and the third had some college, but none were currently working outside the home. One was married to a minister and the second to a college professor; the husband of the third woman was a professional emergency rescue worker. Women in this group had from two to four children each.
Christian Community Group (3)	*Cagney and Lacey*	These women became friends through a Christian community group. All were White, Catholic, and in their forties, had at least some college education, and were married. All were homemakers, raising four or five children. One woman home schooled her children. Their husbands had managerial jobs in corporate settings.
Baby-Sitters (2)	*Cagney and Lacey*	These women became friends through baby-sitting with each other's children. Both were White, in their late thirties and married, with two or three children. One was Catholic and one Protestant. One had an advanced degree, and the other had begun college but had not finished. Both worked in the medical field. One was married to a physician, and the other's husband was in sales.

Group (Size)	Show	Description
Parents' Group (2)	*Dallas*	These women met though a support group for parents. One was Catholic, the other Protestant. Both were in their late thirties, married, and each had three or four children. Both were homemakers with at least some college. Their husbands worked in human services and in the automotive industry. Both were White.
Volunteers (4)	*Roe vs. Wade*	This group was organized by a woman who managed the volunteers at a pro-life pregnancy counseling center. She invited several of the volunteers to take part in the group. Three were about thirty, and the fourth was in her early forties. One had completed a community college degree, two had bachelor's degrees, and the fourth had a master's degree. All were White, and all were married. Their husbands had professional jobs in research, engineering, and medicine. Two had one or two children, and the others were not mothers.
Stay-at-Home Mothers (3)	*Cagney and Lacey*	The woman who organized this group invited a friend from church and a woman she had worked with as a volunteer at a pregnancy counseling center. All were in their mid-thirties, were married, and worked in the home raising children. One also did part-time temporary work. Their level of education ranged from high school to bachelor's degree. Their husbands had jobs in human services, engineering, and restaurant management. They all were White and described their religion as Protestant.
Pro-Life Student Activists (4)	*Cagney and Lacey*	Early in the project we interviewed some groups of students to gather pilot data for the study. These students, all single White women in their early twenties, were members of a pro-life student group. One respondent was the president of this organization. The four had met through their membership in an interdenominational Christian fellowship and were currently roommates. Three were Catholic, and one was Protestant.

WORKING-CLASS PRO-CHOICE GROUPS

Group (Size)	Show	Description
Chain Store Workers (4)	*Roe vs. Wade*	The woman who organized this group invited a longtime friend, a cousin, and a woman she worked with at a large discount chain store. One had worked in the auto industry, and the other was a homemaker with an infant son, currently contemplating divorce. The women, all White, ranged from late twenties to late thirties. One had completed a community college degree; three others had high school diplomas. Three were married and had one or two children. The fourth was single. Three were Catholic, and one was Protestant.

Group (Size)	Show	Description
Ambitious Mothers (2)	*Cagney and Lacey*	These women, in their early thirties, both were mothers with two or three children, and much of their friendship involved doing things with their kids. Both had a high school education, and both were currently homemakers. They both discussed wanting to return to school. One was recently divorced, the other married to a man in the construction trades. Both were White. One described herself as Protestant, the second gave her religion as "other."
Landlady and Tenant (3)	*Dallas*	The woman who organized this group invited her landlady and a friend. Two of the women were White, and one was African American. The women ranged widely in age: one was in her mid-sixties and retired, another was about fifty, and a third was in her early forties. The two younger women had low-level sales jobs. One woman was married to a man who worked in security and had six children. The other two women were single, one with one child. Two had attended community college, the third had a bachelor's degree. Two were Protestant, and the third gave her religion as "other."
Family Friends (3)	*Cagney and Lacey*	This group was organized by a woman who had taken part in a different interview and offered to set up another group composed of women from her neighborhood. She invited her mother, who was in her sixties, a family friend, who was in her late teens, and a neighbor, who was about forty. The youngest woman was not a mother; the older two had four and six children. Two of the women were in school, the other had a high school education and worked as a custodian. Two were single, and one was married to a man who worked as a truck driver. Two of the women were White, and one was African American. One woman was Protestant, another gave her religion as "other," and the third did not specify her religion.
Single Mothers (2)	*Cagney and Lacey*	These two longtime friends were both White and in their thirties. Both had high school educations, and both were single mothers. One woman, with three children, received Aid to Families with Dependent Children. The other supported her one child by working as a waitress. One gave her religion as Jewish, the other was Protestant.
Nontraditional Students (3)	*Roe vs. Wade*	These women met at a local state college where all were pursuing bachelor's degrees, two in a field related to human services, and one in the humanities. Two were White, and one was African American. All were in their early twenties to early thirties, and all were single. One had four children, another had three, and the third was not a mother. One was Catholic, one was Protestant, and the third gave her religious preference as "other."
Cousins (2)	*Cagney and Lacey*	These women, cousins, were both White and in their middle to late twenties. One had a completed some college work, the other had a high school diploma. One was working in a clerical job, the other did agricultural work. Both were single, and neither had children. One was Protestant, the other marked "other" as her religious preference.

Group (Size)	Show	Description
State College Group (2)	*Dallas*	The parents of these women were friends, and they had grown up virtually as sisters. Both were single, White, Jewish, and in their mid-twenties. Neither had children.
Greek Organization (2)	*Cagney and Lacey*	These women met when they lived in the same apartment complex. Both were students at the state college and were members of women's groups associated with a fraternity on their campus. The women were single, African American, and in their mid-twenties. One had a child and considered herself a homemaker as well as a student; the other was not a mother and worked at a convenience store. One was Catholic, the other was Protestant.
Chain Store Managers (4)	*Roe vs. Wade*	Three of these women worked in management at the same discount chain store; the fourth was a secretary. One had completed high school, two had community college degrees, and a third had a master's degree. All were White and in their forties. One was married, the rest were single. One woman had three children, another had two, and the remaining group members were not mothers. Three were Protestant, and the fourth gave her religious preference as "other."
Young Mothers (4)	*Roe vs. Wade/ Cagney and Lacey*	Two of these women were single teenage mothers with infant children. The third, a friend in her early twenties, was married, without children. The fourth, in her mid-thirties and also single, was the mother of one of the younger women. All were African American. The two youngest women were both high school students, and the oldest woman had completed some college. One of the women was a waitress, another was a dietary aide, and the other two were students and not currently working outside the home. Two were Protestant, one gave her religious preference as "other," and the third did not answer the question. This group was interviewed twice.

MIDDLE-CLASS PRO-CHOICE GROUPS

Group (Size)	Show	Description
Presbyterians (5)	*Roe vs. Wade/Cagney and Lacey*	These women were all members of a fairly liberal Presbyterian church. Three were in their forties, one was in her mid-fifties, and one was in her mid-twenties. All were White. Four had bachelor's degrees, and one had a master's degree. Two had professional jobs in health-related fields, a third had a staff job at a community college, another worked in library science, and the youngest was a graduate student. Two were married, and three were single. All except the youngest woman were mothers, each with two children. This group was interviewed twice.

Group (Size)	Show	Description
Bowlers (5)	*Cagney and Lacey*	This group of friends began as a bowling group but later took up other activities together. Three were in their mid-forties, one was in her mid-fifties, and another was in her early thirties. Four were White, one was African American. They all had clerical jobs, most with management responsibility. Two had community college degrees, two had bachelor's degrees, and the fourth had done some college work but had not completed a degree. Two were married, one to a physician. Two had two children each; the others were not mothers. Two were Protestant, two identified their religious preference as "other," and the fifth did not answer the question.
Entrepreneurs (4)	*Roe vs. Wade*	The woman who organized this group invited three women she and her husband had known in college and graduate school. All were White, in their mid-thirties, and married. Each had one or two children. At the time, three of them ran small businesses out of their homes. The fourth was not working because she had recently had a baby. Their husbands held professional jobs in the auto industry and as college faculty. Three were Catholic, and one gave her religion as "other."
Campus Family Housing (3)	*Dallas*	The woman who organized this group invited two of her neighbors from the university family housing complex. All were married to men with academic careers; one was herself pursuing a doctorate. Another was a professional in the health field, and the third was a homemaker. Two were in their mid-thirties, and one was in her mid-forties. All were White and married with two or three children. Two were Jewish, one was Protestant, and all three were immigrants to the United States.
Sisters (2)	*Cagney and Lacey*	These two sisters, in their thirties, were White, Catholic, and college educated. One was single and worked in research, the other was a homemaker with a new baby, married to a man with a professional job in the computer industry.
Classroom Assistants (4)	*Cagney and Lacey*	These women all worked as classroom assistants in a local elementary school: one member of the group supervised the others. They were friendly outside school as well. Unfortunately this group had to leave early to pick up their children but promised to mail the questionnaires to us. Only one woman did so. She was White, Catholic, in her early forties, and married with four children.
Sorority Sisters (5)	*Cagney and Lacey*	Early in the project we conducted several interviews with student groups to gather pilot data. This group was composed of five members of a sorority at an elite public university, all in their early twenties. All were White and reported affluent family incomes. Two were Catholic, one was Jewish, and two others reported no religious preference.

Group (Size)	Show	Description
Pro-Choice Activists (4)	*Roe vs. Wade*	These women were all active in a group that worked for women's reproductive freedom, including holding counterdemonstrations at abortion clinics where pro-life groups were protesting. Group members were all White and ranged in age from mid-thirties to mid-forties. Three group members were single and without children, working in management and semiprofessional positions; the fourth was a homemaker, married to an engineer, and the mother of one child. Three had bachelor's degrees, the fourth had a degree from a two-year program. They represented several religious backgrounds, including Catholic, Protestant, and Jewish.
Individual Interviews (3)	*Cagney and Lacey*	Early in the project we conducted a few individual interviews in order to compare this method of data collection with the focus group method. Three middle-class women, all White, were interviewed in this way. They ranged in age from late twenties to late thirties. Two were married with one or two children, and the third, who was single, was not a mother.

NOTES

Chapter One

1. There is a large and growing body of literature about the way the mass media structure collective frames as well as personal experience. On the former, see especially Gamson (1992), Delli Carpini and Williams (1994, 1996), and Iyengar and Kinder (1987). On the latter, see especially Press (1991b) and Brown (1994).

2. Delli Carpini and Williams (1996) have also mentioned this.

3. We refer to our variation on the traditional focus group interview as the ethnographic focus group. See appendix A for a full discussion of our methodology.

4. Both Ginsburg and Luker have noted that the social class constituencies of pro-life and pro-choice activist groups differ, with pro-life groups appearing more working class in character.

5. On this point, and particularly on the point of how recent changes have affected women's class positions, see especially Spalter-Roth et al. (1995), Spalter-Roth and Hartmann (1991), Rubin (1994), Sidel (1996), and Stacey (1996). Schwarz and Volgy (1992), Wilson (1996), and Wright (1994, 1997) discuss in particular the increasing mobility between what is sometimes referred to as the "underclass" and those more traditionally defined as working class.

6. In this way, scholars in the past would have spoken of class consciousness as being more or less accurate: for example, they would have invoked the idea of false consciousness and true consciousness. However, paradigms of class have become increasingly complex over the last decade. Wright (1997) explicitly rejects the dichotomy between false and true consciousness in favor of a more differentiated notion of different types of consciousness (e.g., hegemonic, reformist, and revolutionary).

7. There is a vast literature on social class membership. For relevant information, interested readers might consult Emmison and Western (1990), Gabennesch (1972), Grabb (1979), Heaton (1987), Lipset (1963), Marshall (1983), Mills (1959), Middendorp and Meloen (1990), Jones (1983), Steedman (1987), and Wright (1985, 1997).

8. See appendix A for a fuller discussion of how our methodology answers Ang's critique.

9. We are extremely indebted in this section to Ortner's (1992) lively discussion of the relation between discourses of gender and class in American high schools and popular fiction.

10. Ortner's discussion foreshadows the distinction between working-class-identified and middle-class-identified members of the working class, which we develop in chapter 4.

11. We take issue with his interpretation of the culture wars as moral controversies. This definition deflects attention from their power dimension, which is critical to an adequate explication of the conflicts and their dynamics. Even Hunter's list of controversies constituting the culture wars is selective. He focuses on those issues that involve "morality" by his definition (e.g., abortion, sexual harassment, euthanasia, sex education). This leads him to ignore equally fundamental domains on which culture wars are being waged, such as welfare reform, affirmative action, and the "Ebonics" debate, which more obviously involve clashes between the interests of groups with differential power in our society.

12. This is the full text of the question we used, adapted from the one used on the National Election Study:

TEXT OF SURVEY ITEM MEASURING RESPONDENTS' VIEWS ON ABORTION

Which of the following opinions best agrees with your views on abortion?

a. By law, abortion should never be permitted.
b. The law should permit abortion only in the case of rape, incest, or when the woman's life is in danger.
c. The law should permit abortion for reasons other than rape, incest, or danger to the woman's life, but only after the need for the abortion has been clearly established.
d. By law, a woman should be able to obtain an abortion early in her pregnancy. After some point, however, abortion should not be permitted.
e. By law, a woman should always be able to obtain an abortion as a matter of personal choice.
f. Don't know.

This item was adapted from the National Election Study (Miller, Kinder, and Rosenstone 1993). We added response option (d) to approximate the wording of the *Roe vs. Wade* decision.

13. See Fielding and Fielding (1986) for an in-depth discussion of using multiple types of measures (including both qualitative and quantitative data) to investigate a research question.

14. More detailed descriptions of all groups are available in appendix B, but

in the text we have given brief sketches of each group the first time it is mentioned. Titles in brackets after quotations refer to the focus groups, which in most cases were assigned names reflecting the connection between group members.

15. See also the broader literature on the subject of ethnography and postmodernism. Much of the writing on feminist anthropology and ethnography touches on these issues as well. In particular see Lutz and Abu-Lughod (1990), Behar and Gordon (1995), Clough (1992), Cole and Phillips (1995), Denzin (1997), Strathern (1987), and the exchange in *Signs* 22, no. 2 (1997) between Hekman, Hartsock, Collins, Harding, and Smith.

16. The Progressive Era is generally defined as referring approximately to the years between the 1880s and 1930s. See Hanson (1985) and Williams and Matheny (1995) for a broader discussion of the era and its implications.

17. For a fuller discussion of the nature of therapeutic authority, see Lasch (1979, 1984). We discuss this in more depth in chapter 5.

18. *Habits of the Heart,* by Robert N. Bellah et al. (1984), is one of the better-known works that helped popularize discussions of communitarianism and liberalism.

19. Earlier debates between critical theory and hermeneutic perspectives, such as that between Jürgen Habermas and Hans Gadamer, echoed the more current discussions explained here.

20. Studies such as Carol Gilligan's (1982) may have emphasized the private dimension of women's reasoning about abortion because women actually contemplating their own unplanned pregnancies were interviewed.

Chapter Two

1. Montgomery (1989) offers a more complete analysis of the events leading to and following broadcast of the *Maude* abortion episode.

2. Murphy's discovery of her pregnancy, and her decision to carry it, were depicted in a two-part episode titled "Uh-Oh" that first aired as the closing episode of the third year of the series (20 May 1991) and as the fourth year's opening episode (16 September 1991).

3. This episode, titled "Labors of Love" was first aired on 2 February 1994, during the show's fourth season. Andrea's choice did not in fact, impede her career: in later episodes, after the baby was born, Andrea transferred to Yale to pursue a premed degree while her husband worked as a law intern.

4. Other recent programs on abortion include an episode of *Law and Order* in which two male police officers are called on to solve a murder resulting from the actions of violent antiabortion protesters. The episode focuses on solving the crime rather than on exploring the police officers' opinions about the issue. Also, in an episode of *Party of Five,* one of the teenage sisters in the family becomes pregnant and seeks an abortion.

5. Ortner (1992, 172–75) illustrates this point well, citing Gans (1967, 38), Willis (1977, 14), Sennett and Cobb (1972, 82), Hannerz (1969, 34–35), and

Halle (1984). Each of these ethnographies illustrates a split in the American working class between groups perceived as more upwardly mobile, disciplined, or regulated and those seen as less so. This split was reproduced both in the representations of the working class on prime-time television that we analyze here and in our sample of working-class pro-choice women (pro-life women, though they were not particularly upwardly mobile, generally led lives falling on the more stable side of this dichotomy).

6. In running focus groups to discuss media coverage of presidential candidates and their campaigns, Just and her colleagues (1996) found three possible patterns of media use in the ensuing focus group discussions. What they called a "following" pattern occurred when the group discussion was dominated by the topic and perspective of the media the participants had viewed. A "transforming" pattern occurred when group discussion began with a topic taken from the media they had viewed but rejected the media's evaluative perspective. An "ignoring" pattern occurred when group discussion moved entirely away from the media to a different topic. These results are similar to other political studies of the media that identify its "priming" or "agenda setting" functions, but Just et al. rename these "following" and "transforming" to emphasize their greater attention to audience interpretation in their study.

Chapter Three

1. All names, here and throughout, are pseudonyms. Additionally, we have attributed all quotations to the groups that made them, either explicitly in the text or in square brackets following each quotation. Descriptions of all groups can be found in appendix B.

2. Dr. Jack Wilke runs the Life Issues Institute in Cincinnati, "serving all the educational needs of the pro-life movement." The Life Issues Institute publishes a newsletter that comes out three times a year, titled the *Life Issues Connector*. See two publications written with his wife, Barbara (Wilke and Wilke 1971, 1991; the latter is available only on the Internet).

3. We thank an anonymous reviewer for clarifying this point.

4. Much recent work has commented on the nature of science and the divergence between commonsense notions of science and the reality of scientific practice. On these points, see in particular Jacobus, Keller, and Shuttleworth (1990), Keller (1983), Keller and Longino (1995), Latour (1987, 1993), Latour and Woolgar (1979), and Serres with Latour (1995).

5. There has been much discussion and criticism of the use of "mainstream" as applied to the mass media (see, for example, Bagdikian 1990; Faludi 1991; Lichter and Rothman 1982, 1983; on the idea that television takes a mainstream position on abortion specifically, see Condit 1990). Although with the advent of cable television in particular its meaning with regard to television has been shifting, we use the term here to refer to network television, the national cable television stations, national and local television news, national and local newspapers,

and popular Hollywood films distributed nationally in movie theaters and video stores. We juxtapose these media organs to, for example, the privately produced videotapes pro-life women rent from specifically Christian video stores. When we apply the term to scientific literature, we mean it to differentiate literature considered legitimate by university-supported journals recognized by most university-educated and affiliated scientists. In using the term mainstream for doctors, we simply mean doctors who have not publicly and explicitly identified their stand on the abortion issue.

6. There is a large and growing body of work that discusses the opposition of various groups to dominant cultural values and practices in the critical literature about media and cultural audiences. Some of the best-known works in this tradition are the products of the Centre for Contemporary Cultural Studies in Birmingham, England (see especially Hebdige 1979, 1984; McRobbie 1990; Morley 1980, 1986; and Willis 1977, 1978). See also Bacon-Smith (1991), Brown (1994), Press (1991b), and Radway (1984). Much of this work describes groups that are explicitly organized as "subcultures" of resistance to dominant cultural positions and discourses. Other works in this tradition (see especially Morley 1980) identify specific types of "decodings" of media products as dominant or preferred, negotiated, or oppositional. Williams (1978) introduces the idea of "alternative" cultures that we draw on here in describing pro-life women's media culture.

7. For a fuller discussion of the relation between various theologies and pro-life beliefs, see Lawless (1993) and Sweet (1985). On this topic, see also Rudy (1996), and on fundamentalism, and evangelicalism in particular, see Marsden (1991).

8. See also Nelkin (1982) on the uses of scientific discourse in evangelical and fundamentalist thinking.

9. Because of heated debate over the naming of the two positions in the abortion debate, we choose to call the women we discuss here "pro-life," largely because this is how they describe themselves. We realize that many persons identifying themselves as pro-choice object to this label, and we agree that it unfairly implies that other perspectives are "against life." We do not mean to imply that other perspectives are antilife, but we feel that ignoring these women's self-definition would be extremely confusing for our discussion.

10. One of our groups consisted of women who called themselves "nontraditional Quakers." Their beliefs were close to what is commonly regarded as fundamentalist thought. See Ammerman (1987), Liebman and Wuthnow (1983), and Marsden (1991) on current controversies over definitions of fundamentalism and the fundamentalist movement in the United States.

11. Marsden goes on to explicate how our modern understanding of the break between science and evangelical religions exaggerates religious rejections of Darwinism occurring in the early twentieth century while underemphasizing the degree to which Darwinism and other scientific theories were thought to illustrate and glorify accounts of God's handiwork in creating nature as described

in the Bible. See also Nelkin (1982) on the uses of scientific discourse in evangelical and fundamentalist thinking.

12. It is interesting that most people we talked to did not make the same arguments about birth control, except in the Catholic groups.

13. See Ginsberg (1986, 1990).

14. Not surprisingly, pro-life women were less disturbed by the presentation of the issue in our third clip, an episode of *Dallas* showing a couple choosing not to abort a fetus known to have Down's syndrome.

15. See Liebes and Katz (1990) for a more extended discussion of the varied interpretations the viewing of a single episode of *Dallas* inspired among different cultural groups.

16. It is interesting to note here the different reactions of the two authors to this extended example about Andrea. While Andrea herself did not experience the remarks as hostile—in fact, she felt a great deal of personal warmth coming from the woman speaking—Liz was quite put off by the comments and felt they meant the speaker was identifying Andrea as pro-choice and thus as hostile to the speaker's own point of view.

17. In the real story from which the TV movie was adapted, the woman's father was considerably less sympathetic than was his character in the television movie. In fact, he offered his pregnant daughter little support. The character as depicted in the movie lent fuel to the pro-life women's arguments that the heroine failed to draw on the family support that appeared to be available to her.

18. This is consonant with the pro-life women's view of doctors who perform abortions generally, as described above.

19. Contrary to popular perceptions of pro-life women, the vast majority of the women we interviewed approved of and encouraged the use of birth control, particularly among married couples. This is in contrast to the pro-life activists interviewed by Luker (1984).

20. In fact, we found in the course of our interviews that it was not uncommon for even decidedly pro-life women to consider abortion, sometimes quite seriously, in response to physical, financial, or other circumstances making pregnancy difficult or inconvenient. This pointed to a difference between women's espoused moral views and their response to actual situations that social scientists have noted in a variety of contexts. In particular, regarding the split between theory and practice in the context of various American religious traditions, DeBerg (1990) stresses the commonly wide divergence between theological doctrine as reported by scholars (almost invariably the work of men), and the lived doctrine of everyday practitioners of various religions (particularly women).

21. Applying the term "mainstream" to radio—whose shows have long catered to a more segmented, limited audience than television—is difficult. Here we simply discuss shows targeted to a Christian, pro-life audience; many other radio programs also target specific audiences, though perhaps most are not defined quite so narrowly.

22. Feminist scholars have exposed how *The Silent Scream* fabricates its pictures about abortion to give a decidedly false image of the procedure and its allegedly painful effect on the fetus; see especially Petchesky (1987).

23. Others have noted the importance of their devotion to a particular idea of motherhood in pro-life women's worldview. See Luker (1984) and Ginsburg (1989) for more discussion.

24. In Latour's (1993) words, the "hybridity" of modern life.

Chapter Four

1. As we argued in chapter 3, class differences were much less salient among pro-life women. Their focus on "truth" in discussing abortion seemed to override any differences of interest and orientation that class might have provoked.

2. Ortner's (1991) discussion of divisions within the belief systems of working-class Americans foreshadows the distinction we make here.

3. Interestingly, working-class women's belief that doctors will take care of themselves first strikingly resembles pro-life women's attitudes, which in the case of this particular doctor were couched in the same terms, but working-class women are at times even more explicitly critical and cynical. These working-class attitudes toward the helping role of professionals contrast sharply with the therapeutic ideology infusing middle-class women's perspective (which we comment on more extensively in chapter 5), possibly because they share an oppositional reading of this character.

4. A complete explanation of the criteria we used to classify people according to class categories is given in appendix A.

5. Women in other groups occasionally made comments that were consistent with the middle-class-identified position; however, in these groups these remarks were balanced by the greater incidence of comments that could be understood as working-class-identified. Only the Chain Store Managers consistently expressed this position, and they did so to the exclusion of the working-class-identified position.

6. Both of these groups were conducted by Elizabeth Cole, who identifies as African American but, because of her mixed parentage, is often not correctly identified by others (see preface). She also differs from the members of these groups by social class status, particularly in terms of education. On the other hand, women in the group were willing to disclose personal information about their sexual relationships and their experiences with abortion and childbearing. Thus it is not clear whether these conversations may have included more explicit material about race if they had been conducted by someone more "inside" their group.

7. At the time of this interview Norplant, a drug that is implanted under the woman's skin and can prevent pregnancy for five years, was new to the market.

8. Of course, not all African Americans maintain their belief in the dream. Hochschild (1995) also describes the views of people who distort and reject the ethos of success through individual struggle.

9. Downward social comparison is a well-researched concept in social psychology originating with the work on social comparison by Leon Festinger (1954), and it is by no means practiced only by poor African Americans. Many studies have shown that people experiencing negative emotions are likely to make comparisons between themselves and people whose circumstances are even worse. Such downward comparisons serve to improve mood and increase self-esteem (Wills 1981) and to aid in managing emotions under stress (Taylor, Buunk, and Aspinwall 1990); they may also blunt political discontent among oppressed groups (Wolf 1990). Reis, Gerrard, and Gibbons (1993) examined the specific example of contraceptive behavior and found that young women who compared themselves with other women using less effective forms of contraception had increased self-esteem. Similar motivations may drive the downward comparisons made by the middle-class-identified White working-class women.

10. See Bellah et al. (1985) for a fuller description of middle-class worldviews in our culture. In particular they describe the "therapeutic" perspective and the origins of liberalism in middle-class outlooks generally.

11. See Sandel (1984), particularly the introduction, for a fuller definition of "communitarianism" and a description of the different incarnations this position can assume.

Chapter Five

1. There has been an enormous amount of writing on the rise of therapeutic authority in our culture and its influence on our nontherapeutic institutions and ways of thinking. On this topic, a good place to begin is with Rieff's *Triumph of the Therapeutic* (1966). More current works on the topic include Lasch (1979, 1984) Rice (1996), and Wilkinson (1988). For a discussion of the particular relationship of women to therapeutic culture, see Grodin (1991) and Simonds (1992).

2. Hunter (1991) interviewed middle-class men and women about abortion. He claims that his informants could discuss their views about abortion only based on their personal experience and could not express abstract justifications for their opinions. We found that women could speak on both levels and often alternated between them. Perhaps our research design, which used the device of the television shows, allowed women to use less personal language more effectively in our interviews.

3. A summary of various feminist perspectives critiquing Carol Gilligan's work can be found in Auerbach, Blum, and Smith (1985).

4. Donagan (1977) discusses other examples of acts that many see as moral only when carried out with a troubled conscience. See also Stocker (1990), who cites Aristotle to discuss the importance of having the proper emotions toward an act in order for that act to be judged as moral.

5. We are not making a moral judgment here about whether this abnormality should lead women to abort. In fact, many troubling issues about amniocentesis

and the aborting of fetuses with Down's syndrome are raised in Michael Berube's book *Life as We Know It* (1996). Here we are simply noting the disparity between the actions that most often mark real-life awareness of this abnormality and this television narrative about it.

6. Morley (1980) and Press (1991b) both cite similarly distanced responses to television in analyzing reception by middle-class respondents.

7. For a clear explanation of liberal feminist thought, see Tong (1989), Tuana and Tong (1995), Jaggar (1983), and the classic Eisenstein (1981).

8. See Wolfe (1996) for an additional discussion of middle-class discourse that highlights these features of it.

Chapter Six

1. In Press's earlier study (1991b), middle-class women did not expect television entertainment to be "realistic"; instead, they looked for qualities such as good acting, production values, and characters they felt they could relate to.

2. See Katznelson (1982) for a fuller discussion of the more general problem of the traditional lack of class consciousness in American politics.

3. Bill Mesce, manager of corporate affairs, HBO/Cinemax, personal communication, 7 March 1997.

Appendix A

1. This issue has been written about extensively in the anthropological literature; see, for example, Rabinow (1977); Geertz (1983, 1988); Clifford and Marcus (1986); Marcus and Fischer (1986).

2. For a more in-depth discussion, issue, see Blum and Press (n.d.).

3. See Harding (1991) and Tong (1989) for a good discussion and critique of essentialism. Also, see Scott's (1988) review of several then-current works in feminist theory that she criticizes for this tendency.

4. See Long (1989) for a detailed overview of the work currently being done in feminist cultural studies.

5. See Morgan (1988) and Gamson (1992) on this point.

6. See Morgan (1988) for more on the traditional qualities of focus groups.

7. All comparisons were significant at the $p \leq .001$ level.

8. Burawoy in turn was influenced by the "Manchester school" of social anthropology, which he argues (1997) includes Gluckman (1958, 1961a,b, 1964), Van Velsen (1960, 1964, 1967); Mitchell (1956), and Epstein (1958).

REFERENCES

Abramovitz, Mimi. 1988. *Regulating the Lives of Women: Social Welfare Policy from Colonial Times to the Present.* Boston: South End Press.

Agar, Michael H. 1980. *The Professional Stranger: An Information Introduction to Ethnography.* New York: Academic Press.

Albert, M. Elizabeth. 1988. "In the Interest of the Public Good? New Questions for Feminism." In *Community in America: The Challenge of "Habits of the Heart,"* edited by Charles H. Reynolds and Ralph V. Norman, 84–96. Berkeley: University of California Press.

Alvarez, R. Michael, and John Brehm. 1995. "American Ambivalence towards Abortion Policy: Development of a Heteroskedastic Probit Model of Competing Values." *American Journal of Political Science* 39:1055–82.

Ammerman, Nancy Tatom. 1987. *Bible Believers: Fundamentalists in the Modern World.* New Brunswick: Rutgers University Press.

Ang, Ien. 1985. *Watching "Dallas": Soap Opera and the Melodramatic Imagination.* London: Methuen.

———. 1991. *Desperately Seeking the Audience.* New York: Routledge.

———. 1996. *Living Room Wars: Rethinking Media Audiences for a Postmodern World.* New York: Routledge.

Ang, Ien, and Joke Hermes. 1996. "Gender and/in Media Consumption." In *Living Room Wars: Rethinking Media Audiences for a Postmodern World,* by Ien Ang, 109–32. London: Routledge.

Auerbach, Judy, Linda Blum, and Vicki Smith. 1985. "*In a Different Voice:* Psychological Theory and Women's Development." *Feminist Studies* 11 (1): 149–61.

Bacon-Smith, Camille. 1991. *Enterprising Women.* Philadelphia: University of Pennsylvania Press.

Bagdikian, Ben H. 1990. *The Media Monopoly.* 3d ed. Boston: Beacon Press.

Barber, Benjamin R. 1984. *Strong Democracy: Participatory Politics for a New Age.* Berkeley: University of California Press.

Baritz, Loren. 1989. *The Good Life: The Meaning of Success for the American Middle Class.* New York: Knopf.

Basch, Charles E. 1987. "Focus Group Interview: An Underutilized Research

Technique for Improving Theory and Practice in Health Education." *Health Education Quarterly* 14 (4): 411–48.

Baudrillard, Jean. 1988. *Jean Baudrillard: Selected Writings*. Stanford: Stanford University Press.

Baxter, Janeen. 1994. "Is Husband's Class Enough? Class Location and Class Identity in the United States, Sweden, Norway and Australia." *American Sociological Review* 59:220–35.

Behar, Ruth, and Deborah A. Gordon, eds. 1995. *Women Writing Culture*. Berkeley: University of California Press.

Beisel, Nicola Kay. 1997. *Imperiled Innocents: Anthony Comstock and Family Reproduction in Victorian America*. Princeton: Princeton University Press.

Bellah, Robert N., Richard Madsen, William M. Sullivan, Ann Swidler, and Steven M. Tipton. 1985. *Habits of the Heart: Individualism and Commitment in American Life*. Berkeley: University of California Press.

———. 1991. *The Good Society*. New York: Knopf.

Bernstein, Richard J. 1985a. *Beyond Objectivism and Relativism*. Philadelphia: University of Pennsylvania Press.

———, ed. 1985b. *Habermas and Modernity*. Cambridge: MIT Press.

———. 1992. *The New Constellation: The Ethical-Political Horizons of Modernity/Postmodernity*. Cambridge: MIT Press.

Berube, Michael. 1996. *Life as We Know It: A Father, a Family, and an Exceptional Child*. New York: Pantheon Books.

Billig, Michael. 1992. *Talking of the Royal Family*. New York: Routledge.

Blanchard, Fletcher A. 1989. *Affirmative Action in Perspective*. New York: Springer-Verlag.

Blum, Linda, and Andrea L. Press. n.d. "What Can We Hear after Postmodernism? The Growing Gulf between Cultural Studies and Feminist Research." In *Across Disciplines and beyond Boundaries: Tracking American Cultural Studies*, edited by Cat Warren, Mary Vavrus, and Eve Munson. Urbana: University of Illinois Press. In press.

Bobo, Jacqueline. 1995. *Black Women as Cultural Readers*. New York: Columbia University Press.

Brint, Steven. 1994. *In an Age of Experts*. Princeton: Princeton University Press.

Brown, Mary Ellen. 1994. *Soap Opera and Women's Talk: The Pleasures of Resistance*. Thousand Oaks, Calif.: Sage.

Brunsdon, Charlotte, and David Morley. 1978. *Everyday Television: "Nationwide."* London: British Film Institute.

Burawoy, Michael. 1991. *Ethnography Unbound: Power and Resistance in the Modern Metropolis*. Berkeley: University of California Press.

———. 1998. "The Extended Case Method." *Sociological Theory* 16 (1): 4–33.

Butler, Judith. 1990. *Gender Trouble: Feminism and the Subversion of Identity*. New York: Routledge.

———. 1993. *Bodies That Matter: On the Discursive Limits of "Sex."* New York: Routledge.

———. 1997. *Excitable Speech: A Politics of the Performative.* New York: Routledge.

Cannon, Lynn Weber, Elizabeth Higginbotham, and Marianne L. A. Leung. 1991. "Race and Class Bias in Qualitative Research on Women." *Gender and Society* 2 (4): 449–62.

———. 1991. "Race and Class Bias in Qualitative Research on Women." In *Beyond Methodology: Feminist Scholarship as Lived Research,* edited by Mary Margaret Fonow and Judith A. Cook, 107–18. Bloomington: Indiana University Press.

Chauncey, George Austin. 1994. *Gay New York: Urban Culture and the Making of a Gay Male World, 1890–1940.* New York: Basic Books.

Clark, Jon, and Marco Diani, eds. 1996. *Alain Touraine.* London: Falmer Press.

Clifford, James. 1988. *The Predicament of Culture: Twentieth-Century Ethnography.* Cambridge: Harvard University Press.

Clifford, James, and George Marcus, eds. 1986. *Writing Culture: The Poetics and Politics of Ethnography.* School of American Research Advanced Seminar. Berkeley: University of California Press.

Clough, Patricia Ticineto. 1992. *The End(s) of Ethnography: From Realism to Social Criticism.* Newbury Park, Calif.: Sage.

Cole, Sally, and Lynne Phillips, eds. 1995. *Ethnographic Feminisms: Essays in Anthropology.* Ottawa: Carleton University Press.

Collins, Patricia Hill. 1990. *Black Feminist Thought.* Boston: Unwin Hyman.

———. 1997. "Comment on Hekman's 'Truth and Method: Feminist Standpoint Theory Revisited': Where's the Power?" *Signs* 22 (2): 375–81.

Condit, Celeste. 1987. "TV Articulates Abortion in America: Competition and the Production of a Cultural Repertoire." *Journal of Communication Inquiry* 11 (2): 47–59.

———. 1990. *Decoding Abortion Rhetoric: Communicating Social Change.* Urbana: University of Illinois Press.

Coontz, Stephanie. 1992. *The Way We Never Were: American Families and the Nostalgia Trap.* New York: Basic Books.

———. 1997. *The Way We Really Are: Coming to Terms with America's Changing Families.* New York: Basic Books.

Correa, Sonia, and Rosalind Petchesky. 1994. "Exposing the Numbers Game." *Ms.* 5 (2): 10–13.

Crosby, Faye J., Ann Pufall, Rebecca Claire Snyder, Marion O'Connell, and Peg Whalen. 1989. "The Denial of Personal Disadvantage among You, Me, and All Other Ostriches." In *Gender and Thought,* edited by Mary Crawford and Margaret Gentry, 79–99. New York: Springer-Verlag.

Cruz, Jon, and Justin Lewis, eds. 1994. *Viewing, Reading, Listening: Audiences and Cultural Reception.* Boulder: Westview Press.

D'Acci, Julie. 1994. *Defining Women: The Case of Cagney and Lacey.* Chapel Hill: University of North Carolina Press.

DeBerg, Betty A. 1990. *Ungodly Women: Gender and the First Wave of American Fundamentalism.* Minneapolis: Fortress Press.

Delli Carpini, Michael X., and Bruce A. Williams. 1994. "The Method Is the Message: Focus Groups as a Method of Social, Psychological and Political Inquiry." In *Research in Micropolitics,* edited by Michael X. Delli Carpini and Robert Shapiro, 57–85. New York: JAI Press.

———. 1996. "The Construction of Political Meaning: The Uses of Television in Conversations about the Environment." In *Political Communication and Public Understanding,* edited by Ann N. Crigler, 149-76. Ann Arbor: University of Michigan Press.

Delmar, Rosalind. 1986. "What Is Feminism?" In *What Is Feminism?* edited by J. Mitchell and A. Oakley, 8–33. New York: Pantheon.

DeMott, Benjamin. 1990. *The Imperial Middle: Why Americans Can't Think Straight about Class.* New York: Morrow.

Denzin, Norman K. 1997. *Interpretive Ethnography: Ethnographic Practices for the Twenty-first Century.* Newbury Park, Calif.: Sage.

DeVault, Marjorie L. 1991. *Feeding the Family: The Social Organization of Caring as Gendered Work.* Chicago: University of Chicago Press.

Dillon, Michele. 1993. "Argumentative Complexity of Abortion Discourse." *Public Opinion Quarterly* 57 (3): 305–23.

———. 1995. "Institutional Legitimation and Abortion: Monitoring the Catholic Church's Discourse." *Journal for the Scientific Study of Religion* 34 (2): 141–53.

Doane, Mary Ann, Patricia Mellencamp, and Linda Williams, eds. 1983. *Re-vision: Essays, in Feminist Film Criticism.* Frederick, Md.: University Publications of America.

Donagan, Alan. 1977. *The Theory of Morality.* Chicago: University of Chicago Press.

Donovan, Josephine. 1985. *Feminist Theory: The Intellectual Traditions of American Feminism.* New York: Ungar.

Donzelot, Jacques. 1979. *The Policing of Families.* New York: Pantheon Books.

Dornbusch, Sanford M., and Myra H. Strober. 1988. *Feminism, Children and the New Families.* New York: Guilford Press.

Dow, Bonnie J. 1996. *Prime-Time Feminism: Television, Media Culture, and the Women's Movement since 1970.* Philadelphia: University of Pennsylvania Press.

Dworkin, Ronald. 1993. *Life's Dominion: An Argument about Abortion, Euthanasia, and Individual Freedom.* New York: Knopf.

Ehrenreich, Barbara. 1989. *Fear of Falling.* New York: Pantheon Books.

Ehrenreich, Barbara, and Deidre English. 1978. *For Her Own Good: 150 Years of the Experts' Advice to Women.* Garden City, N.Y.: Anchor Press.

Eisenstein, Zillah. 1981. *The Radical Future of Liberal Feminism.* New York: Longman.

Ellis, Carolyn, and Michael G. Flaherty, eds. 1992. *Investigating Subjectivity: Research on Lived Experience.* Newbury Park, Calif.: Sage.

Emmison, Michael, and Mark Western. 1990. Social Class and Social Identity: A Comment on Marshall, et al. *Sociology* 24 (20): 241–53.

Epstein, A. L. 1958. *Politics in an Urban African Community.* Manchester: Manchester University Press.

Epstein, Barbara Leslie. 1981 *The Politics of Domesticity: Women, Evangelism and Temperance in Nineteenth Century America.* Middletown, Conn.: Wesleyan University Press.

Faludi, Susan. 1991. *Backlash: The Undeclared War against American Women.* New York: Crown.

Farley, Reynolds, and Walter R. Allen. 1987. *The Color Line and the Quality of Life in America.* New York: Oxford University Press.

Faux, Marian. 1988. *Roe v. Wade.* New York: Macmillan.

Festinger, Leon. 1954. "A Theory of Social Comparison Processes." *Human Relations* 7:117–40.

Fielding, Nigel G., and Jane L. Fielding. 1986. *Linking Data.* Newbury Park, Calif.: Sage.

Fiske, John. 1987. *Television Culture.* London: Methuen.

———. 1989a. *Reading the Popular.* Boston: Unwin Hyman.

———. 1989b. *Understanding Popular Culture.* Boston: Unwin Hyman.

———. 1990. *Introduction to Communication Studies.* New York: Routledge.

———. 1994. *Media Matters: Everyday Culture and Political Change.* Minneapolis: University of Minnesota Press.

Flax, Jane. 1990. *Thinking Fragments: Psychoanalysis, Feminism, and Postmodernism in the Contemporary West.* Berkeley: University of California Press.

Foucault, Michel. 1965. *Madness and Civilization: A History of Insanity in the Age of Reason.* New York: Pantheon Books.

———. 1977. *Discipline and Punish: The Birth of the Prison.* New York: Pantheon Books.

———. 1985. *The History of Sexuality.* New York: Vintage.

Frankenberg, Ruth. 1993. *White Women, Race Matters: The Social Construction of Whiteness.* Minneapolis: University of Minnesota Press.

Fraser, Nancy. 1989. *Unruly Practices: Power, Discourse, and Gender in Contemporary Social Theory.* Minneapolis: University of Minnesota Press.

———. 1997. *Justice Interruptus.* New York: Routledge.

Fraser, Nancy, and Linda J. Nicholson. 1988. "Social Criticism without Philosophy: An Encounter between Feminism and Postmodernism." *Theory, Culture and Society* 5 (2–3): 373–94.

Fried, Marlene Gerber, ed. 1990. *From Abortion to Reproductive Freedom: Transforming a Movement.* Boston: South End Press.

Gabennesch, Howard. 1972. Authoritarianism as World View. *American Journal of Sociology* 77 (5): 857–75.

Gallop, Jane. 1997. *Feminist Accused of Sexual Harassment.* Chapel Hill: Duke University Press.

Gamson, William A. 1992. *Talking Politics.* Cambridge: Cambridge University Press.

Gans, Herbert J. 1967. *The Levittowners; Ways of Life and Politics in a New Suburban Community.* New York: Vintage Books.

————. 1988. *Middle American Individualism: The Future of Liberal Democracy*. New York: Free Press.

Geertz, Clifford. 1983. *Local Knowledge*. New York: Basic Books.

————. 1988. *Works and Lives: The Anthropologist as Author*. Stanford: Stanford University Press.

Giddens, Anthony. 1990. *The Consequences of Modernity*. Stanford: Stanford University Press.

————. 1991. *Modernity and Self-Identity: Self and Society in the Late Modern Age*. Cambridge: Polity Press.

Gilligan, Carol. 1982. *In a Different Voice*. Cambridge: Harvard University Press.

Ginsberg, Benjamin. 1986. *The Captive Public: How Mass Opinion Promotes State Power*. New York: Basic Books.

————. 1990. *Politics by Other Means: The Declining Importance of Elections in America*. New York: Basic Books.

Ginsberg, Benjamin, and Alan Stone, eds. 1986. *Do Elections Matter?* Armonk, N.Y.: M. E. Sharpe.

Ginsburg, Faye D. 1989. *Contested Lives: The Abortion Debate in an American Community*. Berkeley: University of California Press.

Ginsburg, Faye D., and Anna Lowenhaupt Tsing, eds. 1990. *Uncertain Terms: Negotiating Gender in American Culture*. Boston: Beacon Press.

Ginsburg, Faye D., and Rayna Rapp, eds. 1995. *Conceiving the New World Order: The Global Politics of Reproduction*. Berkeley: University of California Press.

Gitlin, Todd. 1980. *The Whole World Is Watching*. Berkeley: University of California Press.

————. 1983. *Inside Prime Time*. New York: Pantheon Books.

————, ed. 1986. *Watching Television: A Pantheon Guide to Popular Culture*. New York: Pantheon Books.

Glaser, Barney G., and Anselm L. Strauss. 1967. *The Discovery of Grounded Theory: Strategies for Qualitative Research*. New York: Aldine de Gruyter.

Glendon, Mary Ann. 1991. *Rights Talk: The Impoverishment of Political Discourse*. New York: Free Press.

Glik, Deborah C., Andrew Gordon, William Ward, Kale Kouame, and Mahbi Guessan. 1987–88. "Focus Group Methods for Formative Research in Child Survival: An Ivoirian Example." *International Quarterly of Community Health Education* 8 (4): 298–316.

Glik, Deborah C., Kathleen Parker, Gabriel Muligande, et al. 1986–87. "Integrating Qualitative and Quantitative Survey Techniques." *International Quarterly of Community Health Education* 7 (3): 181–200.

Gluckman, Max. 1958. *Analysis of a Social Situation in Modern Zululand*. Manchester: Manchester University Press for Rhodes-Livingstone Institute.

————. 1961a. "Anthropological Problems Arising from the African Industrial Revolution." In *Social Change in Modern Africa*, edited by Aidan Southall, 67–82. Oxford: Oxford University Press for International African Institute.

———. 1961b. "Ethnographic Data in British Social Anthropology." *Sociological Review* 9:5–17.

———. 1964. *Closed Systems and Open Minds: The Limits of Naivety in Social Anthropology.* Chicago: Aldine.

Gordon, Avery F., and Christopher Newfield, eds. 1996. *Mapping Multiculturalism.* Minneapolis: University of Minnesota Press.

Gordon, Linda. 1982. "Why Nineteenth-Century Feminists Did Not Support 'Birth Control' and Twentieth-Century Feminists Do: Feminism, Reproduction, and the Family." In *Rethinking the Family,* edited by Barrie Thorne and Marilyn Yalom, 40–53. New York: Longman.

Grabb, Edward G. 1979. "Working Class Authoritarianism and Tolerance of Outgroups: A Reassessment." *Public Opinion Quarterly* 43:36–47.

Grodin, Debra. 1991. "The Interpreting Audience: The Therapeutics of Self-Help Book Reading." *Critical Studies in Mass Communication* 8 (4): 404–20.

Grossberg, Lawrence. 1988. "Wandering Audiences, Nomadic Critics." *Cultural Studies* 2 (3): 377–91.

———. 1989. "On the Road with Three Ethnographers." *Journal of Communication Inquiry* 13 (2): 23–26.

Grossberg, Lawrence, Carey Nelson, and Paula Treichler, eds. 1992. *Cultural Studies.* London: Routledge.

Gurin, Patricia, Arthur H. Miller, and Gerald Gurin. 1980. Stratum Identification and Consciousness. *Social Psychology Quarterly* 43 (1): 30–47.

Habermas, Jürgen. 1973. *Theory and Practice.* Boston: Beacon Press.

———. 1987a. *Knowledge and Human Interests.* Cambridge: Polity Press.

———. 1987b. *The Philosophical Discourse of Modernity: Twelve Lectures.* Cambridge: MIT Press.

Hadden, Jeffrey K., and Anson Shupe. 1988. *Televangelism: Power and Politics on God's Frontier.* New York: Henry Holt.

Hall, Stuart. 1973. "Encoding and Decoding in the Television Discourse." University of Birmingham Stencilled Occasional Paper.

———. 1977a. "Culture, the Media and the 'Ideological Effect.'" In *Mass Communication and Society,* edited by James Curran, Michael Gurevitch, and Janet Woolacott, 315–48. Beverly Hills, Calif.: Sage.

———. 1977b. "Re-thinking the 'Base-and-Superstructure' Metaphor." In *Papers on Class, Hegemony and the Party,* ed. John Bloomfield, 43–72. London: Communist University.

———. 1978. "Debate: Psychology, Ideology and the Human Subject." *Ideology and Consciousness* 3:113–27.

———. 1980a. "Cultural Studies and the Centre: Some Problematics and Problems." In *Culture, Media, Language,* edited by Stuart Hall, Dorothy Hobson, Andrew Lowe, and Paul Willis, 15–47. London: Hutchinson.

———. 1980b. "Cultural Studies: Two Paradigms." *Media, Culture, and Society* 2: 57–72.

————. 1980c. "Popular Democratic vs. Authoritarian Populism: Two Ways of Taking Democracy Seriously." In *Marxism and Democracy*, edited by Alan Hunt, 157–85. London: Lawrence and Wishart.

————. 1980d. "Race, Articulation and Societies Structured in Dominance." In *Sociological Theories: Race and Colonization*, 305–45. Paris: UNESCO.

————. 1981. "Notes on Deconstructing 'the Popular.'" In *People's History and Socialist Theory*, edited by Raphael Samuel, 227–40. London: Routledge.

————. 1982. "The Rediscovery of 'Ideology': Return of the Repressed in Media Studies." In *Culture, Society, and the Media*, edited by Michael Gurevitch et al., 56–90. London: Methuen.

————. 1983. "The Problem of Ideology—Marxism without Guarantees." In *Marx: A Hundred Years On*, edited by Betty Matthews. London: Lawrence and Wishart.

Halle, David. 1984. *America's Working Man: Work, Home, and Politics among Blue-Collar Property Owners*. Chicago: University of Chicago Press.

Hannerz, Ulf. 1969. *Soulside: Inquiries into Ghetto Culture and Community*. New York: Columbia University Press.

Hanson, Russell L. 1985. *The Democratic Imagination in America*. Princeton: Princeton University Press.

Haralovich, Mary Beth. 1992. "Sit-Coms and Suburbs: Positioning the 1950s Homemaker." In *Private Screenings*, edited by Lynn Spigel and Denise Mann, 111–42. Minneapolis: University of Minnesota Press.

Harding, Sandra. 1986. *The Science Question in Feminism*. Ithaca: Cornell University Press.

————. 1991. *Whose Science? Whose Knowledge? Thinking from Women's Lives*. Ithaca: Cornell University Press.

————. 1997. "Comment on Hekman's 'Truth and Method: Feminist Standpoint Theory Revisited': Whose Standpoint Needs the Regimes of Truth and Reality?" *Signs* 22 (2): 382–91.

Harding, Sandra, ed. 1987. *Feminism and Methodology: Social Science Issues*. Bloomington: Indiana University Press and Open University Press.

Hartsock, Nancy C. M. 1997. "Comment on Hekman's 'Truth and Method: Feminist Standpoint Theory Revisited': Truth or Justice?" *Signs* 22 (2): 367–74.

Heaton, Tim B. 1987. Objective Status and Class Consciousness. *Social Science Quarterly* 68:611–20.

Hebdige, Dick. 1979. *Subculture: The Meaning of Style*. London: Methuen.

————. 1984. *Hiding in the Light*. London: Routledge.

Heide, Margaret J. 1995. *Television Culture and Women's Lives: Thirtysomething and the Contradictions of Gender*. Philadelphia: University of Pennsylvania Press.

Hekman, Susan. 1997. "Truth and Method: Feminist Standpoint Theory Revisited." *Signs* 22 (2): 341–65.

Herman, Ellen. 1995. *The Romance of American Psychology: Political Culture in the Age of Experts*. Berkeley: University of California Press.

Hildreth, Anne, and Ellen M. Dran. 1994. "Explaining Women's Differences in Abortion Opinion: The Role of Gender Consciousness." *Women and Politics* 14 (1): 35–52.

Hobson, Dorothy. 1982. *Crossroads: The Drama of a Soap Opera*. London: Methuen.

Hochschild, Arlie Russell. 1983. *The Managed Heart: Commercialization of Human Feeling*. Berkeley: University of California Press.

———. 1997. *The Time Bind: When Work Becomes Home and Home Becomes Work*. New York: Henry Holt.

Hochschild, Arlie Russell, with Anne Machung. 1989. *The Second Shift: Working Parents and the Revolution at Home*. New York: Viking Press.

Hochschild, Jennifer L. 1995. *Facing up to the American Dream: Race, Class, and the Soul of the Nation*. Princeton: Princeton University Press.

Hofstadter, Richard. 1955. *The Age of Reform*. New York: Knopf.

Hollingshead, August B., and F. C. Redlich. 1958. *Social Class and Mental Illness: A Community Study*. New York: Wiley.

hooks, bell. 1994. *Outlaw Culture: Resisting Representations*. New York: Routledge.

Hunter, James Davison. 1991. *Culture Wars: The Struggle to Define America*. New York: Basic Books.

———. 1994. *Before the Shooting Begins: Searching for Democracy in America's Culture War*. New York: Free Press.

Hurtado, Aida. 1989. "Relating to Privilege: Seduction and Rejection in the Subordination of White Women and Women of Color." *Signs* 14 (4): 833–55.

Iyengar, Shanto, and Donald R. Kinder. 1987. *News That Matters: Television and American Opinion*. Chicago: University of Chicago Press.

Jacobus, Mary, Evelyn Fox Keller, and Sally Shuttleworth, eds. 1990. *Body/Politics: Women and the Discourses of Science*. New York: Routledge.

Jaggar, Alison M. 1983. *Feminist Politics and Human Nature*. Sussex: Rowman and Allanheld.

Jagger, Alison M., and Paula S. Rothenberg, eds. 1993. *Feminist Frameworks: Alternative Theoretical Accounts of the Relations between Women and Men*. New York: McGraw-Hill.

Jamieson, Kathleen Hall. 1992. *Dirty Politics: Deception, Distraction, and Democracy*. New York: Oxford University Press.

Jhally, Sut, and Justin Lewis. 1992. *"Enlightened" Racism: The Cosby Show, Audiences, and the Myth of the American Dream*. Boulder: Westview Press.

Jones, Gareth Stedman. 1983. *Languages of Class: Studies in English Working Class History, 1832–1982*. New York: Cambridge University Press.

Jones, James H. 1981. *Bad Blood: The Tuskegee Syphilis Experiment*. New York: Free Press.

Joyrich, Lynne. 1996. *Re-viewing Reception: Television, Gender, and Postmodern Culture*. Bloomington: Indiana University Press.

Just, Marion R., Ann N. Crigler, Dean E. Alger, Timothy E. Cook, Montague Kern, and Darrell M. West. 1996. *Crosstalk: Citizens, Candidates, and the Media in a Presidential Campaign*. Chicago: University of Chicago Press.

Katznelson, Ira. 1982. *City Trenches: Urban Politics and the Patterning of Class in the United States*. Chicago: University of Chicago Press.

Keller, Evelyn Fox. 1983. *A Feeling for the Organism: The Life and Work of Barbara McClintock*. San Francisco: Freeman.

———. 1985. *Reflections on Gender and Science*. New Haven: Yale University Press.

Keller, Evelyn Fox, and Helen E. Longino, eds. 1995. *Feminism and Science*. London: Oxford University Press.

Kent, Raymond, ed. 1994. *Measuring Media Audiences*. London: Routledge.

Kinder, Donald R., and Lynn M. Sanders. 1996. *Divided by Color: Racial Politics and Democratic Ideals*. Chicago: University of Chicago Press.

Kirschner, Don S. 1986. *The Paradox of Professionalism: Reform and Public Service in Urban America, 1900–1940*. New York: Greenwood Press.

Kohlberg, Lawrence. 1969. "Stage and Sequence: The Cognitive-Development Approach to Socialization." In *Handbook of Socialization Theory and Research*, edited by D. A. Goslin, 347–480. Chicago: Rand McNally.

———. 1973. "Continuities in Childhood and Adult Moral Development Revisited." In *Life Span Developmental Psychology: Personality and Scoialization*, edited by Paul B. Baltes and K. Warner Schaie, 179–204. New York: Academic Press.

———. 1976. "Moral Stages and Moralization: The Cognitive-Developmental Approach." In *Moral Development and Behavior: Theory, Research and Social Issues*, edited by T. Lickona, 31–53. New York: Holt, Rinehart and Winston.

———. 1981. *The Philosophy of Moral Development*. San Francisco: Harper and Row.

Kolko, Gabriel. 1976. *Main Currents in Modern American History*. New York: Harper and Row.

Kourany, Janet A., James P. Sterba, and Rosemarie Tong, eds. 1992. *Feminist Philosophies: Problems, Theories, and Applications*. Englewood Cliffs, N.J.: Prentice Hall.

Krueger, Richard A. 1988. *Focus Groups: A Practical Guide for Applied Research*. Beverly Hills, Calif.: Sage.

Kuhn, Thomas S. 1996. *The Structure of Scientific Revolutions*. 3d ed. Chicago: University of Chicago Press.

Landrine, Hope, Elizabeth A. Klonoff, and Alice Brown-Collins. 1992. "Cultural Diversity and Methodology in Feminist Psychology: Critique, Proposal, Empirical Example." *Psychology of Women Quarterly* 16 (2): 145.

Lane, Robert E. 1962. *Political Ideology*. New York: Macmillan.

———. 1972. *Political Man*. New York: Free Press.

Lasch, Christopher. 1979. *The Culture of Narcissism*. New York: Warner.

———. 1984. *The Minimal Self: Psychic Survival in Troubled Times*. New York: Norton.

———. 1988. "The Communitarian Critique of Liberalism." In *Community in America: The Challenge of "Habits of the Heart,"* edited by Charles H. Reynolds and Ralph V. Norman, 173–84. Berkeley: University of California Press.

Latour, Bruno. 1987. *Science in Action: How to Follow Scientists and Engineers through Society*. Cambridge: Harvard University Press.

———. 1993. *We Have Never Been Modern*. Translated by Catherine Porter. Cambridge: Harvard University Press.

Latour, Bruno, and Steve Woolgar. 1979. *Laboratory Life: The Social Construction of Scientific Facts*. Beverly Hills, Calif.: Sage.

Lawless, Elaine J. 1988. *God's Peculiar People: Women's Voices and Folk Tradition in a Pentecostal Church*. Lexington: University of Kentucky Press.

———. 1993. *Holy Women, Wholly Women: Sharing Ministries of Wholeness through Life Stories and Reciprocal Ethnography*. Philadelphia: University of Pennsylvania Press.

Leibman, Nina C. 1995. *Living Room Lectures: The Fifties Family in Film and Television*. Austin: University of Texas Press.

Lewis, Justin. 1990. *Art, Culture and Enterprise: The Politics of Art and the Cultural Industries*. New York: Routledge.

———. 1991. *The Ideological Octopus: An Exploration of Television and Its Audience*. New York: Routledge.

Lichter, S. Robert, Linda S. Lichter, and Stanley Rothman. 1991. *Watching America*. New York: Prentice Hall.

Lichter, S. Robert, and Stanley Rothman. 1982. "Media and Business Elites: Two Classes in Conflict?" *Public Interest* 69 (fall): 117–25.

———. 1983. "Class Warfare—the Media Elite vs. the Business Elite." *Across the Board* 20 (February): 4–9.

Lichterman, Paul. 1992. "Self-Help Reading as a Thin Culture." *Media, Culture, and Society* 14:421–47.

Liebes, Tamar, and Elihu Katz. 1990. *The Export of Meaning: Cross-Cultural Readings of "Dallas."* New York: Oxford University Press.

Liebman, Robert C., and Robert Wuthnow, eds. 1983. *The New Christian Right: Mobilization and Legitimation*. New York: Aldine.

Lindlof, Thomas. 1987. *Natural Audiences: Qualitative Research of Media Uses and Effects*. Norwood, N.J.: Ablex.

Lipset, Seymour Martin. 1963. *Political Man: The Social Bases of Politics*. Garden City, N.Y.: Anchor Books.

Livingstone, Sonia M., and Peter Lunt. 1994. *Talk in Television: Audience Participation and Public Debate*. New York: Routledge.

Lockwood, David. 1966. "Sources of Variation in Working Class Images of Society." *Sociological Review* 14:249–63.

Long, Elizabeth. 1985. *The American Dream and the Popular Novel*. Boston: Routledge and Kegan Paul.

———. 1986. "Women, Reading, and Cultural Authority: Some Implications of the Audience Perspective in Cultural Studies." *American Quarterly* 38 (4): 591–612.

———. 1988. "Reading at the Grassroots: Local Book Discussion Groups, Social

Interaction, and Cultural Change." Paper presented at American Sociological Association meeting, Atlanta, Georgia, August.

———. 1989. "Feminism and Cultural Studies: Britain and America." *Critical Studies in Mass Communication* 6 (4): 427–35.

———. 1994. "Textual Interpretation as Collective Action." In *Viewing, Reading, Listening: Audiences and Cultural Reception,* edited by Jon Cruz and Justin Lewis, 181–211. Boulder: Westview Press.

Longino, Helen E. 1990. *Science as Social Knowledge: Values and Objectivity in Scientific Inquiry.* Princeton: Princeton University Press.

Luke, Carmen, ed. 1996. *Feminisms and Pedagogies of Everyday Life.* Albany: State University of New York Press.

Luker, Kristin. 1984. *Abortion and the Politics of Motherhood.* Berkeley: University of California Press.

———. 1996. *Dubious Conceptions: The Politics of Teenage Pregnancy.* Cambridge: Harvard University Press.

Lull, James. 1990. *Inside Family Viewing: Ethnographic Research on Television's Audience.* New York: Routledge.

Lutz, Catherine A., and Lila Abu-Lughod, eds. 1990. *Language and the Politics of Emotion.* Cambridge: Cambridge University Press.

Lyotard, Jean François. 1984. *The Postmodern Condition: A Report on Knowledge.* Minneapolis: University of Minnesota Press.

MacIntyre, Alasdair C. 1984. *After Virtue: A Study in Moral Theory.* Notre Dame: University of Notre Dame Press.

Malinowski, Bronislaw. 1948. *"Magic, Science and Religion," and Other Essays.* Boston: Beacon Press.

Marcus, George E., and Michael M. J. Fischer. 1986. *Anthropology as Cultural Critique.* Chicago: University of Chicago Press.

Marsden, George M. 1991. *Understanding Fundamentalism and Evangelicalism.* Grand Rapids, Mich.: Eerdman's.

Marshall, Gordon. 1983. "Some Remarks on the Study of Working Class Consciousness." *Politics and Society* 12 (3): 263–301.

Martin, Emily. 1989. *The Woman in the Body.* Boston: Beacon Press.

Mays, Vickie M., in collaboration with Nancy Felipe Russo, Pamela Trotman Reid, and the Committee on Women in Psychology, American Psychological Association. 1984. *Black Women in Psychology: A Resource Directory.* Washington, D.C.: The Committee.

McCombs, Maxwell E., and Donald L. Shaw. 1972. "The Agenda Setting Function of the Mass Media." *Public Opinion Quarterly* 36:176–87.

McLaughlin, Lisa. 1993. "Chastity Criminals in the Age of Electronic Reproduction: Re-viewing Talk Talk Television and the Public Sphere." *Journal of Communicaton Inquiry* 8 (3): 141–55.

McRobbie, Angela. 1978. "Working Class Girls and the Culture of Femininity." In *Women Take Issue,* edited by Women's Studies Group, 96–108. London: Hutchinson.

————. 1981. "Just Like a *Jackie* Story." In *Feminism for Girls,* edited by Angela McRobbie and Trisha McCabe, 113–28. London: Routledge.

————. 1984. "Dance and Social Fantasy." In *Gender and Generation,* edited by Angela McRobbie and Mica Nava, 130-62. New York: Macmillan.

————. 1990. *Feminism and Youth Culture.* London: Routledge.

Mellencamp, Patricia. 1990. *Indiscretions: Avant-Garde Film, Video and Feminism.* Bloomington: Indiana University Press.

Merton, Robert. 1987. "The Focused Interview and Focus Groups: Continuities and Discontinuities." *Public Opinion Quarterly* 51:550–56.

Merton, Robert, K. Fiske, and P. Kendall. 1956. *The Focused Interview.* Giencoe, Ill.: Free Press.

Mickelsen, Alvera, ed. 1986. *Women, Authority and the Bible.* Downers Grove, Ill.: Inter-Varsity Press.

Middendorp, C. P., and J. D. Meloen. 1990. The Authoritarianism of the Working Class Revisited. *European Journal of Political Research* 18:257–67.

Miller, Nancy. 1997. *Bequest and Betrayal: Memoirs of a Parent's Death.* Oxford: Oxford University Press.

Miller, W. E., Donald R. Kinder, Steven J. Rosenstone, and National Election Studies. 1993. American National Election Study: Pooled Senate Election Study, 1988, 1990, 1992. 2d release [computer file]. Ann Arbor: University of Michigan, Center for Political Studies [producer]; Inter-university Consortium for Political and Social Research [distributor].

Mills, C. Wright. 1959. *The Sociological Imagination.* New York: Oxford University Press.

Mitchell, Clyde. 1956. *The Kaela Dance.* Manchester: Manchester University Press for Rhodes-Livingstone Institute.

Mollenkott, Virginia Ramey, ed. 1987. *Women of Faith in Dialogue.* New York: Crossroad.

Montgomery, Kathryn. 1989. *Target, Prime-Time: Advocacy Groups and the Struggle over Entertainment Television.* New York: Oxford University Press.

Morgan, David. L. 1988. *Focus Groups as Qualitative Research.* Newbury Park, Calif.: Sage.

Morley, David. 1980. *The "Nationwide" Audience: Structure and Decoding.* Television Monograph 11. London: British Film Institute.

————. 1981. "'The 'Nationwide" Audience'—a Critical Postscript." *Screen Education* 39:3–14.

————. 1986. *Family Television.* London: Comedia.

————. 1992. *Television, Audiences and Cultural Studies.* London: Routledge.

Nelkin, Dorothy. 1982. *The Creation Controversy.* New York: Norton.

Nicholson, Linda. 1986. *Gender and History: The Limits of Social Theory in the Age of the Family.* New York: Columbia University Press.

Nicolson, Linda, and Steven Seidman, eds. 1995. *Social Postmodernism: Beyond Identity Politics.* Cambridge: Cambridge University Press.

Neitz, Mary Jo. 1987. *Charisma and Community: A Study of Religious Commitment within the Charismatic Renewal.* New Brunswick, N.J.: Transaction.

Ortner, Sherry. 1991. "*Reading America:* Preliminary Notes on Class and Culture." In *Recapturing Anthropology,* edited by Richard G. Fox, 163–89. Santa Fe, N.Mex.: School of American Research Press.

Parkin, Frank. 1971. *Class Inequality and Political Order: Social Stratification in Capitalist and Communist Societies.* New York: Praeger.

Petchesky, Rosalind Pollack. 1987. "Fetal Images: The Power of Visual Culture in the Politics of Reproduction." *Feminist Studies* 13:263–92.

———. 1990. *Abortion and Woman's Choice: The State, Sexuality, and Reproductive Freedom.* Boston: Northeastern University Press.

Potter, Jonathan, and Margaret Wetherell. 1987. *Discourse and Social Psychology.* London: Sage.

Press, Andrea L. 1990. "Class, Gender, and the Female Viewer: Women's Responses to *Dynasty.*" In *Television and Women's Culture,* edited by Mary Ellen Brown, 158–82. Newbury Park, Calif.: Sage.

———. 1991a. "Working Class Women in a Middle-Class World: The Impact of Television on Modes of Reasoning about Abortion." *Critical Studies in Mass Communication* 8 (4): 421–41.

———. 1991b. *Women Watching Television: Gender, Class and Generation in the American Television Experience.* Philadelphia: University of Pennsylvania Press.

Press, Andrea L., and Elizabeth R. Cole. 1992. "Pro-Choice Voices: Discourses of Abortion among Pro-Choice Women." *Perspectives on Social Problems* 4 (spring): 73–92.

———. 1994. "Women Like Us: Working-Class Women Respond to Television Representations of Abortion." In *Reading, Viewing, Listening: Audiences and Cultural Reception,* edited by Jon Cruz and Justin Lewis, 55–80. Boulder: Westview Press.

———. 1995. "Reconciling Faith and Fact: Pro-Life Women Discuss Media, Science and the Abortion Debate." *Critical Studies in Mass Communication* 12 (4): 380–402.

Rabinow, Paul. 1977. *Reflections on Fieldwork in Morocco.* Berkeley: University of California Press.

Radway, Janice A. 1984. *Reading the Romance.* Chapel Hill: University of North Carolina Press.

———. 1988. "Reception Study: Ethnography and the Problems of Dispersed Subjects." *Cultural Studies* 2 (3): 359–76.

Rapping, Elayne. 1996. *The Culture of Recovery: Making Sense of the Recovery Movement in Women's Lives.* Boston: Beacon Press.

Rawls, John. 1971. *A Theory of Justice.* Cambridge: Belknap Press of Harvard University Press.

Reid, Pamela Trotman. 1993. "Poor Women in Psychological Research: Shut Up and Shut Out." *Psychology of Women Quarterly* 17 (2): 133–50.

Reis, Theresa J., Meg Gerrard, and Frederick X. Gibbons. 1993. "Social Comparison and the Pill: Reactions to Upward and Downward Comparison of Contraceptive Behavior." *Personality and Social Psychology Bulletin* 19:13–20.

Reynolds, Charles H., and Ralph V. Norman, eds. 1988. *Community in America.* Berkeley: University of California Press.

Rice, John Steadman. 1996. *A Disease of One's Own: Psychotherapy, Addiction, and the Emergence of Co-dependency.* New Brunswick, N.J.: Transaction.

Rieff, Philip. 1966. *The Triumph of the Therapeutic: The Uses of Faith after Freud.* New York: Harper and Row.

Rorty, Richard. 1991. *Objectivity, Relativism, and Truth.* Cambridge: Cambridge University Press.

Rosenblum, Nancy L., ed. 1989. *Liberalism and the Moral Life.* Cambridge: Harvard University Press.

Rubin, Lillian. 1976. *Worlds of Pain.* New York: Basic Books.

———. 1979. *Women of a Certain Age: The Midlife Search for Self.* New York: Harper and Row.

———. 1994. *Families on the Fault Line: America's Working Class Speaks about the Family, the Economy, Race, and Ethnicity.* New York: HarperCollins.

Rudy, Kathy. 1996. *Beyond Pro-Life and Pro-Choice.* Boston: Beacon Press.

Sandel, Michael J. 1982. *Liberalism and the Limits of Justice.* Cambridge: Cambridge University Press.

———, ed. 1984. *Liberalism and Its Critics.* New York: New York University Press.

———. 1996. *Democracy's Discontent: America in Search of a Public Philosophy.* Cambridge: Belknap Press of Harvard University Press.

Schuman, Howard, and Jacqueline Scott. 1987. "Problems in the Use of Survey Questions to Measure Public Opinion." *Science* 236:957–59.

Schwarz, John E., and Thomas J. Volgy, eds. 1992. *The Forgotten Americans.* New York: Norton.

Scott, Jacqueline. 1989. "Conflicting Beliefs about Abortion: Legal Approval and Moral Doubts." *Social Psychology Quarterly* 52 (4): 319–26.

Scott, Jacqueline, and Howard Schuman. 1988 "Attitude Strength and Social Action in the Abortion Debate." *American Sociological Review* 53 (5): 785–93.

Scott, Joan Wallach. 1988. *Gender and the Politics of History.* New York: Columbia University Press.

———, ed. 1996. *Feminism and History.* New York: Oxford University Press.

Seiter, Ellen. 1993. *Sold Separately: Children and Parents in Consumer Culture.* New Brunswick, N.J.: Rutgers University Press.

———. n.d. *Television and New Media Audiences.* Oxford: Oxford University Press. In press.

Seiter, Ellen, H. Borchers, G. Kreutzner, and E. M. Warth. 1989. *Remote Control: Television Audiences and Cultural Power.* London: Routledge.

Sennett, Richard, and Jonathan Cobb. 1972. *The Hidden Injuries of Class.* New York: Vintage.

Serres, Michel, with Bruno Latour. 1995. *Conversations on Science, Culture, and Time*. Translated by Roxanne Lapidus. Ann Arbor: University of Michigan Press.

Sidel, Ruth. 1986. *Women and Children Last: The Plight of Poor Women in Affluent America*. New York: Viking.

———. 1990. *On Her Own: Growing Up in the Shadow of the American Dream*. New York: Viking.

———. 1996. *Keeping Women and Children Last: America's War on the Poor*. New York: Penguin.

Simonds, Wendy. 1992. *Women and Self-Help Culture: Reading between the Lines*. New Brunswick: Rutgers University Press.

———. 1996. *Abortion at Work: Ideology and Practice in a Feminist Clinic*. New Brunswick: Rutgers University Press.

Smith, Dorothy E. 1997. "Comment on Hekman's 'Truth and Method: Feminist Standpoint Theory Revisited.'" *Signs* 22 (2): 392–98.

Smith, John M. 1992. *Women and Doctors*. New York: Dell.

Spalter-Roth, Roberta, Beverly Burr, Heidi Hartmann, and Lois Shaw. 1995. *Welfare That Works: The Working Lives of AFDC Recipients, a Report to the Ford Foundation*. Washington, D.C.: Institute for Women's Policy Research.

Spalter-Roth, Roberta, and Heidi Hartmann. 1991. *Increasing Working Mothers' Earnings*. Washington, D.C.: Institute for Women's Policy Research.

Spigel, Lynn. 1992. *Make Room for TV: Television and the Family Ideal in Postwar America*. Chicago: University of Chicago Press.

Spigel, Lynn, and Denise Mann, eds. 1992. *Private Screenings: Television and the Female Consumer*. Minneapolis: University of Minnesota Press.

Stacey, Judith. 1990. *Brave New Families*. New York: Basic Books.

———. 1996. *In the Name of the Family: Rethinking Family Values in the Postmodern Age*. Boston: Beacon Press.

Steedman, Carolyn Kay. 1986. *Landscape for a Good Woman: A Story of Two Lives*. New Brunswick: Rutgers University Press.

Steinem, Gloria. 1992. *Revolution from Within: A Book of Self-Esteem*. Boston: Little, Brown.

Stocker, Michael. 1990. *Plural and Conflicting Values*. Oxford: Clarendon Press.

Strathern, Marilyn. 1987. "An Awkward Relationship: The Case of Feminism and Anthropology." *Signs* 12 (2): 276–92.

Sweet, Gail Grenier. 1985. *Pro-Life Feminism: Different Voices*. Toronto: Life Cycle Books.

Taylor, Charles. 1991. *The Malaise of Modernity*. Concord, Ont.: Anansi.

———. 1992a. *The Ethics of Authenticity*. Cambridge: Harvard University Press.

———. 1992b. *Multiculturalism and "The Politics of Recognition": An Essay*. Princeton: Princeton University Press.

———. 1995. *Philosophical Arguments*. Cambridge: Harvard University Press.

Taylor, Ella. 1989. *Prime-Time Families: Television Culture in Postwar America*. Berkeley: University of California Press.

Taylor, Shelley E., Bram P. Buunk, and Lisa G. Aspinwall. 1990. "Social Comparison, Stress and Coping." *Personality and Social Psychology Bulletin* 16:74–89.

Tedesco, Nancy S. 1974. "Patterns in Prime Time." *Journal of Communication* 24 (2): 119–24.

Tompkins, Jane. 1997. *A Life in School: What the Teacher Learned.* Reading, Mass.: Addison-Wesley.

Tong, Rosemarie. 1989. *Feminist Thought: A Comprehensive Introduction.* Boulder: Westview Press.

Touraine, Alain. 1995. *Critique of Modernity.* Cambridge: Blackwell.

Traube, Elizabeth. 1992. "Disturbing Differences: Hollywood and the New Conservatism." Paper delivered at the Comparative Study of Social Transformations Seminar, University of Michigan, Ann Arbor.

Tribe, Laurence H. 1990. *Abortion: The Clash of Absolutes.* New York: Norton.

Tuana, Nancy, and Rosemarie Tong, eds. 1995. *Feminism and Philosophy: Essential Readings in Theory, Reinterpretation, and Application.* Boulder: Westview Press.

Unger, Roberto Mangabeira. 1975. *Knowledge and Politics.* New York: Free Press.

Valdivia, Angharad N., ed. 1995. *Feminism, Mulitculturalism, and the Media: Global Diversities.* Thousand Oaks, Calif.: Sage.

Van Velsen, Jaap. 1960. "Labour Migration as a Positive Factor in the Continuity of Tonga Tribal Society." *Economic Development and Cultural Change* 8:265–78.

———. 1964. *The Politics of Kinship.* Manchester: Manchester University Press for Rhodes-Livingstone Institute.

———. 1967. "The Extended Case Method and Situational Analysis." In *The Craft of Urban Anthropology,* edited by A. L. Epstein, 29–53. London: Tavistock.

Veroff, Joseph. 1981. *Mental Health in America, 1957 to 1976.* New York: Basic Books.

Veroff, Joseph, Elizabeth Douvan, and Richard A. Kulka. 1981. *The Inner American: A Self-Portrait from 1957 to 1976.* New York: Basic Books.

Warde, Alan. 1994. "Consumption, Identity-Formation and Uncertainty." *Sociology* 28:877–98.

Warhol, Robyn R., and Diane Price Herndl, eds. 1991. *Feminisms: An Anthropology of Literary Theory and Criticism.* New Brunswick: Rutgers University Press.

Warner, R. Stephen. 1988. *New Wine in Old Wineskins: Evangelicals and Liberals in a Small-Town Church.* Berkeley: University of California Press.

Watts, Mike, and Dave Ebbutt. 1987. "More Than the Sum of the Parts: Research Methods in Group Interviewing." *British Educational Research Journal* 13 (1): 25–34.

Weber, Max. 1946. "Science as a Vocation." In *From Max Weber,* edited by H. H. Gerth and C. Wright Mills, 129–58. New York: Oxford University Press.

Weeks, Jeffrey. 1985. *Sexuality and Its Discontents: Meanings, Myths, and Modern Sexualities.* London: Routledge.

———. 1989. *Sex, Politics and Society: The Regulation of Sexuality since 1800.* London: Longman.

———. 1995. *Invented Moralities: Sexual Values in an Age of Uncertainty.* New York: Columbia University Press.

Weibel, Kathryn. 1977. *Mirror, Mirror: Images of Women Reflected in Popular Culture.* Garden City, N.Y.: Anchor Books.

Weinstein, James. 1968. *The Corporate Ideal in the Liberal State, 1900–1918.* Boston: Beacon Press.

Wilke, Jack, and Barbara Wilke. 1971. *Handbook on Abortion.* Cincinnati: Hayes.

———. 1991. *Abortion: Questions and Answers.* Rev. 1991. Http://www.ohiolife.org/qa/qatoc.htm. Accessed 1/8/1998.

Wilkinson, Rupert. 1972. *The Broken Rebel.* New York: Harper and Row.

———. 1988. *The Pursuit of American Character.* New York: Harper and Row.

Wilkinson, Sue, and Celcia Kitzinger. 1995. *Feminism and Discourse: Psychological Perspectives.* Thousand Oaks, Calif.: Sage.

Williams, Bruce A., and Albert Matheny. 1995. *Democracy, Dialogue, and Social Regulation: The Contested Languages of Environmental Disputes.* New Haven: Yale University Press.

Williams, Raymond. 1978. "Base and Superstructure in Marxist Cultural Theory." *New Left Review,* no. 82:3–16.

Willis, Paul. 1977. *Learning to Labour: How Working-Class Kids Get Working-Class Jobs.* New York: Columbia University.

———. 1978. *Profane Culture.* London: Routledge.

Wills, Gary. 1990. *Under God: Religion and American Politics.* New York: Simon and Schuster.

Wills, Thomas Ashby. 1981. "Downward Comparison Principles in Social Psychology." *Psychological Bulletin* 90:245–71.

Wilson, William J. 1996. *When Work Disappears: The World of the New Urban Poor.* New York: Knopf.

Wolf, Charlotte. 1990. "Relative Disadvantage." *Symbolic Interaction* 13 (1): 37–61.

Wolf, Naomi. 1997. *Promiscuities: The Secret Struggle toward Womanhood.* New York: Random House.

Wolfe, Alan. 1996. *Marginalized in the Middle.* Chicago: University of Chicago Press.

Wright, Erik Olin. 1985. *Classes.* London: Verso.

———. 1994. *Interrogating Inequality: Essays on Class Analysis, Socialism, and Marxism.* London: Verso.

———. 1997. *Class Counts: Comparative Studies in Class Analysis.* New Brunswick: Rutgers University Press.

Wright, Erik Olin, Andrew Levine, and Elliott Sober. 1992. *Reconstructing Marxism: Essays on Explanation and the Theory of History.* London: Verso.

Wuthnow, Robert. 1989. *The Struggle for America's Soul: Evangelicals, Liberals, and Secularism.* Grand Rapids, Mich.: Eerdman's.

Wyche, Karen Fraser, and Faye J. Crosby, eds. 1996. *Women's Ethnicities: Journeys through Psychology.* Boulder: Westview Press.

Yack, Bernard. 1988. "Liberalism and Its Communitarian Critics: Does Liberal Practice 'Live Down' to Liberal Theory?" In *Community in America: The Challenge of "Habits of the Heart,"* edited by Charles H. Reynolds and Ralph V. Norman, 147–72. Berkeley: University of California Press.

Zoonen, Liesbet van. 1994. *Feminist Media Studies.* Thousand Oaks, Calif.: Sage.

INDEX

abnormalities: Down's syndrome in *Dallas* episode, 30, 38, 55, 57; pro-choice argument in cases of, 16–17; thalidomide in Finkbine case, 141

abortion: as birth control, 83; deleterious consequences of, 46–47, 49–50; economic reasons for, 34–35; emotional consequences of, 47; illegal abortions, 31, 36, 55; legality as of only secondary concern, 2; as murder, 62, 108; as necessary evil, 32; opinion poll results on, 67; other medical procedures sharply distinguished from, 18; on prime-time television, 25–28, 104; as profitable, 52; pro-life women considering having, 60–61, 169n. 20; repeated, 39, 83–84; safety of, 46–47, 55; three types of authority coming into play in, 20. *See also* abortion debate

Abortion and the Politics of Motherhood (Luker), 9

abortion clinics, 52

abortion debate: authority as element of, 19, 125, 142, 154; broader questions as involved in, 18–19; as clash of absolutes, 1–2; and class, xii, 6–9, 142, 164n. 4; class in prime-time television discourse of abortion, 6, 25–40, 71–72, 126–31; as "culture war" issue for Hunter, 12; existing research on, 9; feminism's influence in, 9–10; future of, 140–42; the "generally acceptable abortion," 32, 141; Ginsburg on, 11; in liberal/communitarian terms, 24; the

liberal position in, 106; Luker on, 10; medical and scientific authority in, 21; moral ideas expressed in, 23; in the political landscape, 125–42; political language in, 23; power as element of, 19, 125, 142; public opinion research on, 147–54; and race, xii; rights as theme in, 69–70; state's authority in, 21; surveys as measures of opinion in, 13–18; as symbol for myriad contested values, 2; women as having to take a stand in, 115–16. *See also* pro-choice perspective; pro-life perspective

Absolute Strangers (television movie), 141

abstract empiricism, 146

academy, the, and liberal/communitarian debate, 123, 134

activists: existing research as focusing on, 9, 149; Ginsburg on, 10; Luker on, 10; as not typical of American women, 11; pro-choice and pro-life labels as developed by, 12; in this study, 151. *See also* pro-life activists; pro-choice activists

African American women: on authority, 88, 95; class consciousness in, 76–77, 88, 91; on the medical establishment, 88–90; on the pro-life movement, 90–91; recruiting for research, 87; in this study, 151; on upward mobility, 94, 100, 170n. 8; on welfare, 88, 91–93, 94; working-class women, 87–95, 99–100

alternative cultures, 168n. 6

Ambitious Mothers (focus group), 160